Acts and apparitions

MANCHESTER
1824

Manchester University Press

Acts and apparitions
Discourses on the real in performance practice and theory, 1990–2010

Liz Tomlin

Manchester University Press

The right of Liz Tomlin to be identified as the author of this work has been asserted
by her in accordance with the Copyright, Designs and Patents Act 1988.

Published by Manchester University Press
Altrincham Street, Manchester M1 7JA, UK
www.manchesteruniversitypress.co.uk

British Library Cataloguing-in-Publication Data is available

Library of Congress Cataloging-in-Publication Data is available

ISBN 978 1 7849 9376 4 *paperback*

First published by Manchester University Press in hardback 2013

This edition first published 2016

The publisher has no responsibility for the persistence or accuracy of URLs for any external or third-party internet websites referred to in this book, and does not guarantee that any content on such websites is, or will remain, accurate or appropriate.

Printed by Lightning Source

In memory of my grandparents
Dorothy and Edward Emery
&
James and Isabella Tomlin

Dedicated, in their names,
to all those who dare to dream of alternative realities
for future generations to inherit

Contents

List of figures

Acknowledgements

Thanks to all the publishers who have supported my work throughout this period of study and given permissions for the inclusion of previously published material here. An extended analysis of Martin Crimp's *The City*, which I touch on in Chapter 3, was previously published in the essay, 'And their stories fell apart even as I was telling them: poststructuralist performance and the no-longer-dramatic play-text' in *Performance Research*, 14:1, 2009 (www.informaworld.com). A section of Chapter 3 was previously published by Oberon Books in my essay entitled, 'A "new tremendous aristocracy": tragedy and the meta-tragic in Barker's Theatre of Catastrophe', in *Theatre of Catastrophe: New Essays on Howard Barker* edited by David Ian Rabey and Karoline Gritzner (2006). An extended analysis of *Nights in this City* which I draw on in Chapter 5 was previously published in my essay entitled, 'Transgressing boundaries: postmodern performance and the tourist trap', in *The Drama Review* 43:2 (T162), Summer 1999 (copyright 1999, New York University and the Massachusetts Institute of Technology.) The analysis of *After Dubrovka* in the same chapter was published in extended form as the essay 'Beyond representation: re-membering the "ghosts" of recent history in contemporary performance' in *Critical Stages* vol. 2 (2010) (www.criticalstages.org/criticalstages2/18).

The ideas behind this book have taken shape over many years, through performances as well as publications, student seminars, conference panels and countless late-night conversations. Thanks must go to all of those friends, students, colleagues, artists and scholars who have inspired me and who are too numerous to name. I would like to extend special thanks all my former colleagues at Manchester Metropolitan

University where this project was first conceived, and to my colleagues at the University of Birmingham where this project reached completion, with particular thanks to Kara Reilly who looked at early drafts of key chapters, and Caroline Radcliffe who read the finished manuscript prior to submission. I would also like to thank Graham Ley for his belief in the book in its early stages, the AHRC for the research fellowship that enabled me to complete the manuscript away from the distractions of university life, and the team at Manchester University Press for seeing the project through to completion. Thanks are also due to everyone I worked with during my time at Point Blank Theatre, where the real conditions of making work have never ceased to inform my analysis of contemporary performance and helped to ensure that I never forget how much harder it is to make the work than it is to write about it.

My sincerest thanks must also go to John Bull for his inspirational mentorship of my work from the earliest stages of my academic career, and for his support and careful readership of this study throughout its many drafts. Any remaining mistakes or weaknesses are, of course, entirely my own. Particular thanks and appreciation must also go to Linda Taylor and Steve Jackson who have been my collaborators in thought throughout this period of research, and to whom much of the thinking within this book is indebted (which is not, of course, to hold either of them to any of its conclusions!) To my parents, Ted and Dorothy, and to my partner Joseph, who have been my collaborators in life, I can only say this book is your achievement too; my heartfelt thanks for your constant love and support.

Arts & Humanities
Research Council

Introduction

If we're not quite at the end of the real – bereft in an imaged world, with its superfetation of signs, no referentials, no metaphysics, only the vanity of a redundancy without any substance at all, not even the imaginary substance once thought of as illusion – the undeniable truth is that we're not quite sure where we are. (Blau, 2006: 232)

We all live our lives as if they were real and believe in the reality of the world we see around us. We rely on the perceptions of our own senses to guide our decisions both in everyday situations and extraordinary ones. Those of us who have a shared understanding of a more or less consensual reality are designated sane, whilst those of us who at times may not, are designated otherwise. Yet, despite this sometimes pragmatic and always ideological confirmation of the value of a shared notion of what 'reality' might mean, no concept has come under as much sustained interrogation in recent intellectual history. From Jacques Derrida's metaphysical scepticism to Jean Baudrillard's integral reality, philosophical, sociological and psychoanalytical theory throughout the late twentieth century has been driven by questions of the real, and the ensuing political implications of the concept's rapidly disintegrating authority.

Into the second decade of the twenty-first century, some fifty years after these discourses began to take shape, concerns surrounding the authority or otherwise of 'the real' are far from being merely academic. Technology and mass media are now able to create and disseminate versions of the real that are entirely fabricated, yet indistinguishable from any other 'reality', and these simulacra can be employed in the service of sustaining vested interests and immense economic power on a global scale. Furthermore, our increased awareness of technology's capacity for such fabrication has contributed to a predominantly cynical culture where everything that is shown as real is now read as strategic. From the images of warfare atrocities, filmed by one side or the other, to the tearful politician using emotional performance to gain empathy and political currency, the notion that a mediated image might be 'authentic' is, as I explore in Chapter 5, no longer widely held as credible. In addition, for better and worse, a broad acceptance of postmodern relativism, certainly in the liberal Western democracies, now underpins a mainstream consensus that one person's or culture's 'truth' may be different from another's, and that there is not always an objective perspective that can be called upon to determine between them.

Narratives of poststructuralism

The strands of thinking that have contributed to the discourses on the real explored in this study are diverse and complex. In Chapter 1, I offer an overview of how certain theoretical perspectives, that were to underpin the philosophical and political characteristics that define the historical period of this study, began to develop and inform each other in the latter part of the twentieth century. Whilst, throughout the subsequent chapters, I draw on a wide range of theoretical influences in relation to particular trends in performance practice in the 1990s and 2000s, a re-examination of the discourse of Derridean poststructuralism is most central to the book's concerns. Discussed in detail in Chapters 2 and 3, Derrida's project set out to deconstruct the metaphysical myths of the Enlightenment through a destabilising of the notion of originary meaning on which the discourses of theology, reason, science and the law had hitherto based their entire systems of validation. No longer could meaning, truth or morality be assured by any reference to an authority that had itself, Derrida argued, been constructed by the very same discourse for precisely this purpose. Once the notion of originary truth or meaning had been exposed as a strategic myth, calculated to support whatever version of 'reality' it benefitted those in power to propagate, all claims to meaning, truth or morality were rendered relative. They could now only refer, for their validity, to 'foundational truths' that had likewise been revealed to be constructed and relative, and so on, in an endless deferral of meaning.

In one sense, as I discuss in Chapter 1, there were meeting points between Derridean poststructuralism and the Marxist discourse that had inspired twentieth-century avant-garde thinkers from Bertolt Brecht to Guy Debord, in the shared recognition that what had appeared to be the 'reality' of people's lives was now exposed as ideological illusion, constructed to maintain the bourgeois capitalist status quo. However, the critical distinction between the two strands of thought lies in the divergent responses to this revelation. For the Marxists, the bourgeois ideological illusion of the real was conspiring to conceal the 'true reality' of the oppression of the working class, and therefore the aim of exposure was to awaken people's consciousness to this 'truth' in order to inspire a revolution that could overthrow the current order. For poststructuralists, the Marxist notion of a 'true reality' concealed by the ideological illusion of bourgeois capitalism was, in itself, another ideological attempt to claim a 'truth' on which a particular political system could be validated.

The poststructuralist reduction that revealed Marxism to be no less an ideology than the capitalist ideology it aimed to demystify inevitably began to complicate the very notion and definition of ideology in the postmodern era that followed the 1960s and 1970s. Slavoj Žižek outlines the broadening scope of the term as follows:

> 'Ideology' can designate anything from a contemplative attitude that mis-recognizes its dependence on social reality to an action-orientated set of beliefs, from the indispensable medium in which individuals live out their relations to a social structure to false ideas which legitimate a dominant political power. (Žižek, 1994: 3–4)

For the purpose of this study I will draw, in particular, on two of the uses Žižek indicates. Firstly, I will use the notion of ideology to designate a particular set of beliefs or, as Žižek further expands, 'a complex of ideas (theories, convictions, beliefs, argumentative procedures)' (1994: 9), so that in using terms such as 'ideological analysis' or 'ideological critique' I mean to imply that the analysis or critique in question is directed at uncovering or demystifying certain belief systems that can be seen to be underpinning the work. Secondly, I will draw on Žižek's notion of ideology as the propagation of 'false ideas which legitimate a dominant political power'. This latter sense of ideology underpinned the Marxist-driven discourse of avant-garde artists such as Brecht, but, as Žižek goes on to explain, the notion of 'ideological mystification' becomes an infinitely more complex concept in a postmodern era. Firstly, the question of whether an act or idea can be described as ideological, in this latter sense, should not necessarily rest on its truth or falsehood but on the degree to which it conceals the truth of its own agenda that lies behind the narrative it proposes. As Žižek argues, '[w]e are within ideological space proper the moment this content – "true" or "false" … – is functional with regard to some relation of social domination … in an inherently non-transparent way' (1994: 8). However, such a definition, Žižek then contends, opposes an ideological act or statement to a non-ideological act or statement that does not hold, or at the very least does not hide, its own agenda. This latter notion of a language that is beyond ideology due to either its neutrality or its transparency is a highly dubious one within the poststructuralist discourse. Drawing on Oswald Ducrot's theory of argumentation, Žižek explains that

> one cannot draw a clear line of separation between descriptive and argumentative levels of language: there is no neutral descriptive content; every description (designation) is already a moment of some argumentative scheme; descriptive predicates themselves are ultimately reified-naturalized argumentative gestures. (1994: 11)

Consequently, Žižek concludes, there is nothing more ideological than statements that claim to be non-ideological; in their very claim to neutrality, transparency or truth, they are concealing the inevitability that there is an unspoken and unacknowledged agenda that has constructed the position of illusory transparency in order to claim superior ground (to that which they charge with being ideological). Ultimately, the question Žižek poses is key to the subject of this study: '[i]s our final outcome, therefore, the inherent impossibility of isolating a reality whose consistency is not maintained by ideological mechanisms, a reality that does not disintegrate the moment we subtract from it its ideological component?' (1994: 15–16)

Once every reality is understood as ideological, what happens to the 'extra-ideological ground supposed to provide the standard by means of which one can measure ideological distortion' (1994: 16)? This question, inherent to the narrative of radical resistance within the postmodern era, is addressed fully in Chapter 1 and is key to understanding the distinction between historical Marxism and the poststructuralist discourse which is at the heart of this study. For once the ideological imperative behind Marxism was exposed and defined as such, Derrida's deconstruction of all originary authority was seen by many as the new radical thesis with the capacity to discredit claims of any 'true reality', including the Marxist narrative which could likewise now be revealed as strategically constructed and so open to challenge.

Yet there were also those who remained highly cynical of the radical narrative that was being proposed for poststructuralist thinking and opposed it on material grounds. Marxist and post-Marxist theorists argued that the destabilising of an objective reality might actually be a gift in disguise to the global capitalist enterprise as oppositional discourses would never have the cultural or economic resources to compete on equal terms with the narratives of the dominant political order. Moreover, once all narratives are treated as equivalent ideological fictions with only a subjectively constituted authority, the potential for a marginal narrative to overpower a dominant narrative through recourse to now discredited notions such as 'truth' or 'originary authority' also becomes effectively disabled. Whilst this is not a recent debate, neither is it a redundant one, and this study will doubtless not be the last to address its implications. The global events following 11 September 2001 that trapped us between the rock of pre-modernist fundamentalism and the hard place of advanced neo-liberalism, and the global economic meltdown which began in 2008 and seems set to dominate the second decade, would seem to call urgently for a renewed consideration of what might now constitute a radical performance practice in the less than auspicious dawn of the twenty-first century.

My use of the term 'radical' throughout this study attempts to combine both the etymological origins of the term and its most common political application in relation to the history of avant-garde performance. Stemming from the Latin word *radix* (roots), the term implies the imperative to dig down to the roots or the origins of the subject under examination (Bennett *et al.*, 2005: 296–7). In the political context of the historical Marxism that informed the oppositional radicalism of the socialist avant-garde and neo-avant-garde movements, the aim of such an imperative was to excavate the ideological myths of bourgeois capitalism in order to expose the 'reality' that such myths attempted to conceal. In the context of the radical narrative of Derrida's poststructuralist project, this 'digging down' can be seen to correspond to the deconstructive movement which aims to 'to shake the totality' in order to show, as Alan Bass explains, that '[e]very totality ... can be *totally shaken*, that is, can be shown to be founded on that which it excludes' (Bass, 2001: xviii).

That this notion of 'digging down', in order to reveal the contradictions, falsehoods or hidden agendas at the heart of ideological illusions of the real, is central to both the Marxist and the poststructuralist projects has permitted the mantle of 'radical' to have a fairly smooth passage from its earlier applications to avant-garde and neo-avant-garde Marxist-orientated theatre to the subsequent wave of experimental performance practice in the 1980s and 1990s where the influence of Derrida's poststructuralism dominated. However, despite the continued application of the radical narrative to new performance throughout the 1990s, when I was first beginning to make and write about theatre, I became increasingly convinced, not that deconstruction did not hold radical potential for oppositional political efficacy, but that such a promise was failing to be upheld by much of the work that was promoted as 'political' or 'radical' under the auspices of Derrida's poststructuralist project.

What I began to observe was that the self-reflexive imperative of Derrida's deconstructive project, the 'radical' urge to dig down to the roots of anything which appeared to offer a conclusive narrative, was becoming less and less central to the work in question. What I was rather witnessing was the repetition of a series of conventions which had grown out of the first tentative conclusions to the emergence of Derridean deconstruction on the performance scene in the 1970s and 1980s. The self-reflexive questions posed by Derrida, it seemed, were no longer being asked, and the initial answers were now accepted as conclusive, reified and in danger of consolidating into a new totalising narrative of their own. Such a narrative, this study proposes, was predominantly constructed on the basis of a growing scepticism of the real, one of the most significant early conclusions to be drawn from Derrida's deconstructive imperative. Yet, such scepticism may well turn out to be, as Žižek describes it, 'the last trap that makes us slide into ideology under the guise of stepping out of it' (1994: 17):

> That is to say, when we denounce as ideological the very attempt to draw a clear line of demarcation between ideology and actual reality, this inevitably seems to impose the conclusion that the only non-ideological position is to renounce the very notion of extra-ideological reality and accept that all we are dealing with are symbolic fictions, the plurality of discursive universes, never 'reality'. (17)

This postmodern conclusion, as Žižek confirms, is in itself 'ideology par excellence' (17) as it places all ideological myth making beyond challenge. As this narrative has become conclusive, new binaries have inevitably begun to emerge that are now, in turn, in need of deconstruction. Throughout this study, therefore, I intend to be guided by Žižek's exhortations to persist 'in this impossible position: although no clear line of demarcation separates ideology from reality, although ideology is already at work in everything we experience as "reality", we must none the less maintain the tension that keeps the *critique* of ideology alive' (17, original emphasis). Accepting that every narrative is implicitly ideological does not equate to the acceptance that any given narrative is thus beyond ideological analysis or distinction. The artist or critic's choice to propagate one narrative over another will still result in a 'real' impact on the artists, the audiences and, to some degree at least, the ideological shape of the historical period in which the work is situated. It is these choices, which operate at both conscious and subconscious levels and are at play in the reception, analysis and production of new work, that will be the focus of this study.

The anti-theatrical prejudice

The relationship between theatre and the real has always been a vexed one. Not only do the representational strategies of theatre position the notion of 'the real' at the heart of its own discourse, but the apparatus of theatre is also called into question through the appropriation of terms of reference such as performativity, theatricality and spectacle to describe social and political representations designed to offer the appearance of a reality that is now open to question. In *The Anti-theatrical Prejudice*, Jonas Barish traces the suspicion of theatre's representational apparatus back to Plato, who condemned all artists on the grounds that they were imitators who merely replicated objects and actions as they existed in the 'real' world, which were themselves merely copies of the 'eternal Idea' of that thing or act in the 'kingdom of the forms' (Barish, 1981: 6). Theatre, with its superior representational resources for imitations of the real was, Barish noted, particularly vulnerable to Plato's attack.

Shannon Jackson persuasively argues that the anti-theatrical prejudice 'is not a singular thought-structure but itself, multiple, opportunistic, and a constantly moving target' (2004: 38). And it is indeed the case that Plato's original objections, due to both the specificity of their historical context and, as Barish argues, the obvious flaws in his logic, are not specifically upheld beyond his time. However, the underlying suspicion of an art form that is able to offer an illusion of the real through representation remains a remarkably consistent factor in subsequent anti-theatrical moments. In *Against Theatre*, Alan Ackerman and Martin Puchner distinguish between the anti-theatricalism that comes from disciplines outside the theatre and that which arises from within the theatre itself, noting that 'in no period before modernism has the theatre been more ready to take to heart the arguments and obsessions of its detractors' (2006: 8). This was, to some degree, the result of a shift in the modernists' perception of the social real that was configured no longer as an independent, objective world, against which the illusions of theatre could be straightforwardly opposed, but as a constructed artifice that was itself guilty of theatricality and illusion. In this sense, rather than being the accused, theatre could use its representational apparatus to instigate its own critique of theatricality in the 'real' world. It was this notion of theatricality that the movement of Naturalism addressed, '[f]ocusing on material detail … to expose hypocrisy and idealism for what they were and, within the drama, to reject metaphor' (Ackerman and Puchner, 2006: 5). However, as Kirk Williams observes, 'the theatre is never more theatrical, more metaphorical, than when it attempts to transcend its own conditions of representation'(2006: 101), and before long it was the illusory representations of reality that characterised Naturalism which were to come under attack in subsequent movements of the avant-garde.

In Chapter 1, I pick up the narrative at this historical moment to examine how the work of Bertolt Brecht and Antonin Artaud prepared the foundations for the sustained twentieth century interrogations of theatrical representations of the real that were to continue to dominate performance practice and theory up to and throughout the 1990s and 2000s. In an overview of avant-garde, neo-avant-garde and early postmodernist practice this examination proposes that the twentieth-century critique of theatrical representation has been bolstered firstly by Marxist theories of the spectacle and more recently by the poststructuralist scepticism of the real. In my overview, I draw on Jon McKenzie's notion of 'the liminal norm' (2001: 49) to identify the consistent ideological alignment of a narrative of radicalism with the aesthetic imperatives of performance that looks to reroute the anti-theatrical critique of representational practice, previously seen as inherent to all theatre, towards the conventions of specifically dramatic theatre. Through this misalignment, I argue, a long-standing binary has been consolidated, which this study seeks to deconstruct.

As Chapter 1 outlines, this binary opposition is played out in various calibrations, the most familiar of which include performance against theatre (when theatre is understood as dramatic theatre), performance theatre against dramatic theatre, devised theatre against text-based theatre, and postdramatic theatre against dramatic theatre. In each opposition the first term is commonly aligned with a radical, oppositional narrative of deconstruction, the second term with a reactionary, traditional narrative of logocentrism, whilst the binary itself is underpinned by a poststructuralist scepticism of representations of the real. Whilst the premise of the binary, as outlined above, is surprisingly consistent throughout the twentieth century, the definition of what constitutes 'dramatic' shifts strategically along the way, as I examine in detail in Chapter 2. Brecht's epic theatre, for example, one of the first avant-garde models to oppose the representations of the 'dramatic' form of naturalism, itself becomes reframed as predominantly dramatic in Hans-Thies Lehmann's

1999 study, *Postdramatisches Theater* (Postdramatic Theatre), in respect of its representation of fictional worlds and its upholding of the textual authority of the playwright. The fluidity of the 'dramatic' label across time does suggest that this particular anti-theatricality might well constitute, to borrow Ackerman and Puchner's term, a 'strategic opposition, one that uses the rhetoric of anti-theatricalism in order to differentiate itself from contemporary rivals' (2006: 13). This is a possibility that I will return to in Chapter 2, when I re-examine the theoretical premises of the post-structuralist and postdramatic critiques of theatrical representation and interrogate their strategic application to an exclusively dramatic theatre practice.

A discursive act

The construction of an ideological opposition between a dramatic theatre practice on the one hand and, to adopt the most recent term, a postdramatic theatre practice on the other, is a discursive act that has consequences reaching well beyond the academy. I undertook my initial commitment, in the late 1990s, to what would become a sustained interrogation of poststructuralist discourse not only as an emerging scholar but as a writer/director with Point Blank Theatre, the company I co-founded in 1999. Whilst explicit reference to poststructuralist discourse was rare to hear in professional contexts, those who were working in the programming, funding and promotion of new performance work in the early 2000s were, in the main, theatre graduates from the 1980s and 1990s. As I detail in Chapter 1, their pedagogical legacy from theatre and performance studies departments in the United Kingdom would inevitably include the inheritance of an increasingly polarised binary, heard most commonly at that time in the opposition that pitted a 'radical' devising or non-text-based practice against a 'traditional' text-based practice assumed to operate in a more or less dramatic framework. Perhaps, partly for this reason, there were few leading artists in Britain who were engaged in radical deconstructions of classic texts, a practice which was predominant in the work of North American artists such as Charles Mee, or North American ensembles like the Wooster Group and Elevator Repair Service. This mode of experimentation resulted in performances that were more or less 'text-driven', whilst remaining clearly postdramatic, thus offering a perspective that seemed to be lacking in the British context at this time.

The text-based/non-text-based binary revealed itself in the UK theatre industry in the choice that emerging theatre-makers were constrained to make between the development opportunities offered by the 'traditional' new-writing flagship theatres such as the Traverse, the Bush Theatre and the Royal Court and those offered by the growing proliferation of art centres such as Bristol's Arnolfini, London's Battersea Arts Centre and Manchester's Green Room. The latter most often explicitly defined the practice they wished to support as devised practice that was characterised by its rejection of text-based processes, thus offering essential alternatives to artists whose work was not text- or writer-driven. However, a less positive impact was the strengthening of the binary division for which both sides were culpable, requiring young theatre-makers, as I have argued elsewhere, 'to categorize themselves, for strategic development purposes, as either playwrights or non-text-based artists, reducing the potential for productive cross-pollination and dissolution of the two binary positions' (Tomlin, 2009: 58). In addition, the binary, on both sides, left theatre-makers like myself, who were writer-directors wishing to work outside of the realist tradition and through theatrical as well as literary strategies, falling between two narrow remits which were constraining the potential for new forms of work to develop. The new-writing venues were rarely willing to offer dramaturgical support to work that went too far beyond familiar dramatic models and had little capacity to develop dramaturgical or ensemble processes that went beyond script development. On the other hand, the new-work venues instantly categorised work that appeared to be driven by text as falling outside of their remit. This binary system undoubtedly bolstered the ideological alignment of text-based work as 'reactionary' and non-text-based work as 'radical'. The authority of 'the text' was seen to be upheld by the well-established, predominantly London-based new-writing venues, and challenged by the emerging, multi-disciplinary art venues which were scattered throughout the country. Furthermore, the latter were often attached to those university departments where the emphasis on non-text-based work as the radical and contemporary alternative to the literary tradition of 'drama' was most strongly advocated.

This binary was at its most acute in the late 1990s and early 2000s, and there have been significant moves from art centres and independent producers, if less so from new-writing houses, to widen their remits towards the end of this period of study, reflecting a renewed and welcome interest in text-based performance across a range of models at the time of writing. Nevertheless, I would argue that, in this expanding field of contemporary performance that still tends to deal with new 'work' rather than new 'plays', the ideological implications of the binary that are the subject of this book's interrogation remain embedded in the subconscious of the global industry network that selects and markets all new work on an international basis, and in the minds of the newspaper critics of new performance who are instrumental in highlighting work for the industry's attention. It is my contention that, despite a renewed interest in text-based work, this market continues to be too often informed by mythologised and misapplied approximations of an ideological critique of dramatic representation that is now far adrift from its rigorous philosophical origins. The influence that this global network wields over the funding, selection and profiling of new work, and thus implicitly over what will come to be seen as significant trends in twenty-first century theatre practice, necessitates the urgent interrogation which this book aspires to initiate, both of the original premises of the poststructuralist critique of representation and of the legitimacy of the terms of its varied and ongoing applications.

The technical fallacy

To question the validity of the radical narrative of poststructuralism is scarcely a new venture. Whether defined as poststructuralist or postmodernist, the late twentieth-century scepticism of 'the real' has long come under sustained attack from Marxist critics, such as Christopher Norris, for its 'wholesale collapse of moral and intellectual nerve' (2000: 19). Likewise, in the field of performance, the early opposition of socialist artists and scholars to the discrediting of Marxist ideology and dramatic representation that was central to the poststructuralist narrative of radicalism has not altogether been silenced, as I discuss further in Chapter 1. In the United Kingdom in particular, the continuing dominance of realist drama in mainstream theatres and new-writing venues demonstrates a resolute refusal, on the part of many established and emerging playwrights and directors, to accept the theoretical framework that the varied applications of the poststructuralist critique of dramatic theatre, now established in the theatre departments of most academic institutions, would seek to impose on their practice. Unlike the ideological battlefield of literary theory, however, theatre scholars and artists who still adhere to a predominantly Marxist understanding of the political have tended to dismiss or simply ignore the radical claims of the poststructuralists, rather than engaging with the work defined as such or the discourse that underpins it. As I will discuss in Chapter 2, this mirrors the wholesale dismissal of 'the dramatic' by those advocating the radical narrative of poststructuralism, with a few notable exceptions (for exceptions see Fuchs, 1996, 2001; Power, 2008; Bottoms, 2009, 2011). This reluctance to break down the ideological binary from either side has ensured that the radical narrative of poststructuralism is too often unquestioningly embraced or steadfastly rejected, but rarely put under rigorous interrogation.

This study aims neither to offer its unequivocal support for the existing poststructuralist narrative of radicalism (which is based on the conclusions of a particular reading of Derrida's project) nor to reverse the ideological terms of the binary to advocate a resurgence of historical Marxism and political drama, but rather to argue that the basis of the binary, whichever way it swings, is fundamentally misconceived. It is my contention that the conclusive alignment of ideological characteristics on the basis of form alone is ultimately self-defeating, and destructive to the future development of new strategies and contexts in which radical models of performance, and their relationship with ever-changing notions of 'the real', can be conceived. Radical practice should be based, not on its simplistic opposition or otherwise to dramatic form, or on the reification of its own totalising conclusions, but on a self-reflexivity which can serve to always and already destabilise its own particular claims to authority, wherever these might lie. Thus, in my analysis of the radical claims made on behalf of practice that departs from the dramatic conventions of theatre, I will be guided by Mike Sell's caution against the 'technical fallacy' that arises from 'the belief that formal innovation is political innovation' and that disguises those instances whereby 'effective tools' are 'carried beyond the contexts and situations for which they were devised' (2006: 29–30). I will seek instead to propose that for every notable strategic departure from traditional dramatic methods of representing the real, there are many possible and divergent ideological readings. In this sense, I will apply the deconstructive 'movement' of Derrida's project to the conclusions that have been arrived at in its name.

I have tried to draw predominantly on examples of work that have a relatively strong international presence, in order to directly engage the widest possible readership and evidence the influential reach of the discourses under discussion. The artists and companies that I reference are drawn from across the United Kingdom, Western Europe, Australia and North America, and the strategies discussed should be familiar enough for readers to adapt and apply my analytical frameworks to a significantly broader spectrum of work than it has been possible to cover in this one book. I will examine significant trends in performance practice through an analysis of specific aspects of individual productions in the context in which they were witnessed, in order to offer substantiation for the theoretical claims I am making, and to enable readers to understand how the theory can inform readings of the practice, and vice versa. For this reason, my references to specific productions will sometimes be too partial and strategic to constitute case studies, although I have never knowingly misrepresented the whole through a decontextualisation of its parts. Neither, in any sense, is my analysis of practice throughout the book intended to suggest any conscious political agenda on the part of the artists, unless their direct contribution to the theoretical discourses surrounding their practice indicates otherwise. Far from asserting that my own particular analysis is in any sense more authoritative, or less ideological, than any other, my aim is merely to suggest that there is a much greater diversity of ideological readings of certain performance strategies than those that currently dominate this field of research. In this sense, I seek to throw a spoke in the wheel that is fast approaching consensus, and offer some alternative perspectives to provoke a more rigorous and genuinely pluralistic debate on the future of what might constitute radical performance practice in the twenty-first century.

Acts of discourse and apparitions of the real

In part one of this study, 'The Discursive Act', I will address the existing poststructuralist narrative of radicalism that currently dominates con-temporary performance theory, and seek to deconstruct its conclusions. In Chapter 1, which acts as an extended introduction to this study, I will trace the artistic and philosophical developments that laid the ground for the sustained twentieth-century interrogations of theatrical representa-tions of the real, and examine the emergence of the discursive act which aligned the narrative of radicalism exclusively with such interrogations. In Chapter 2, I will focus on the most recent manifestation of this nar-rative, the postdramatic, and examine how key strands of Derrida's post-structuralist critique, such as the deconstruction of authorship, mimetic representation and presence, have been applied to performance practice in order to strengthen the ideological binary opposition between 'dra-matic' representations of the real and 'postdramatic' deconstructions of representational practice. Through my own deconstruction of this binary I seek to establish that dramatic theatre can also deconstruct representa-tional practice, that no model of theatre is immune from Derrida's chal-lenge to representation, and that all would-be radical models of theatre must acknowledge and interrogate their own inevitably ideological nar-ratives of authority.

In part two of this study, 'Apparitions of the Real', I will embark on an ideological examination of a wide spectrum of performance models that share an engagement with the problematics of representation and the real, but undertake their own distinct interrogations through a diversity of methodologies and forms. Chapter 3 engages in an analysis of representational strategies of characterisation employed in various performance models, including work by Forced Entertainment, the Wooster Group, Katie Mitchell, Roland Schimmelpfennig and Howard Barker. Identifying the common citational aesthetic that underpins contemporary notions of performer and character, this chapter argues that formalistic distinctions between characters in play texts, and performance personae who address the audience 'as themselves', conceal an underlying similarity of post-Stanislavskian and post-Freudian engagement with the notion of poststructuralist subjectivity that no longer recognises an 'authentic' or 'essential' self. Nevertheless, there is, as I will argue, a diversity of ideological implications that can arise from the widespread use of the citational aesthetic, on account of the distinctive ways in which the 'citations' of character or performer are variously conceived and represented.

Chapter 4 directs this investigation specifically towards an analysis of the representations of 'real' people in performances which adopt verbatim methodologies drawn from the documentary theatre tradition. Looking at performances that include Recorded Delivery's *The Girlfriend Experience,* National Theatre of Scotland's *Aalst* and Paper Birds' *Others,* I analyse the frameworks created by diverse strategies of representation, and examine the ideological implications of the aesthetic constructions of 'the real' people who are the source material of the work. From this perspective, the chapter explores the seemingly paradoxical rise of a documentary theatre practice amidst the culturally dominant scepticism of the real, and interrogates the inevitable tensions that arise from the conflicting needs of verbatim practice, in this period, to demonstrate an ethical and political commitment to an external reality, whilst simultaneously throwing that very reality into sceptical doubt.

In Chapter 5, I begin my examination of performance models that have explicitly rejected the staged representation of narrative and the actor/audience configuration that has historically characterised the theatre event. Instead, the artists discussed here locate their audience as participants in an environment from which they must actively reconfigure, re-imagine, or re-member a 'new', subjectively constructed version of reality. Analysis of *En Route, Nights in this City* and *After Dubrovka* will draw on a range of theoretical insights, including the perspectives of Jacques Lacan and Michel de Certeau, but this chapter will particularly foreground the thinking of Jean Baudrillard. Revisiting Baudrillard's well-known concept of the simulacrum, I will argue that his work does offer the potential for distinctions between orders of the real and can be used as the basis for determining the diverse ideological implications of a range of work that appears to deny the notion of objective reality and advocate the conflation of fact with fiction.

Chapter 6 will continue to explore performance environments that break down the dichotomy of performer/spectator and seek to replace mediated representations with experiential realities. With reference to the avant-garde practice that still underpins the recent resurgence of interactive and immersive theatre, and drawing on Nicolas Bourriaud's work on relational aesthetics, I will interrogate the notion that experiential participation (as opposed to 'passive' spectatorship) necessarily constitutes a more radical practice. I will argue that the 'critically active' spectator has become problematically conflated with the 'physically active' spectator and the radicalism that was aligned to critical thought has now been harnessed unquestioningly to physical action. Through a detailed analysis of a wide range of work, including the one-to-one confessionals of Adrian Howells, Melanie Wilson's *Iris Brunette,* Uninvited Guests' *Love Letters Straight from Your Heart* and Ontroerend Goed's *Internal,* I will examine the claims of empowerment and democracy that continue to underpin discussions of the radical potential of audience participation.

Whilst this study offers an argument that builds and develops from chapter to chapter, I have tried to ensure that each chapter can also be read independently of the others, although there is inevitably much cross-referencing throughout. I would like to acknowledge with genuine gratitude all the artists and scholars whose work is represented in this book for their contributions to the ideas and debate within it; without the sometimes extraordinary work I have seen and read throughout the course of my research this book simply couldn't exist. I suspect that there will be some among these who will object to certain conclusions I have arrived at, and I can only hope that the book will stimulate further deconstructive responses from them, in the way that the conclusions of others have provoked my own passion and commitment to 'dig down' more deeply into the existing discourses on the real and make, what will hopefully prove to be, a productive contribution to a necessarily ongoing debate.

Part I

The discursive act

1

Discourses of resistance: representation and the real in the twentieth-century avant-gardes

Before embarking on an investigation of performance practice and theory from the 1990s onwards, it is necessary to take a look back over the twentieth century at the practices and theories that laid the ground for such work and that are still visibly influential in the later period that is the focus of this study. This chapter will argue that the new performance practices that emerged in the 1990s and 2000s are predominantly categorised by artists and scholars as drawing implicitly, or explicitly, on the avant-gardes of the twentieth century in relation to their experimentation with form and their desire to position themselves as radical practice. My particular historical overview of the avant-gardes will focus on their common and recurring tendency to develop a narrative of radical opposition through challenges to received notions of the real as reflected in the representational strategies of dramatic theatre. I will trace this antagonism from the historical avant-garde, through the post-war, or neo, avant-gardes, and into early postmodernist performance to examine how the tension between representational practice and work that seeks to challenge or undermine such practice prevails as a defining feature of new performance practices into the twenty-first century. By interrogating the ideological ambiguities that still underpin studies of both the historical and the neo-avant-gardes this chapter seeks to provide a particular historical lens through which to investigate the ensuing theories and practices that will form the basis of this study.

Quest for the 'real'

Whilst the early modernist movement of Naturalism attempted to develop precise and mimetic theatrical representations of the real world

beyond the theatre, the avant-garde movements that followed can be usefully characterised by their suspicion of mimetic representation and their attempts to establish non-representational, or anti-representational, practices as politically radical alternatives. Central to the development of such movements were the figures of Bertolt Brecht and Antonin Artaud, whose influences are still discernible in the recurring trends of twenty-first century practice, as I will demonstrate throughout this study. Despite the clear distinctions between the visions of Brecht and Artaud, both were responding to an ontological suspicion of the political landscape that constituted their historical reality. The 'real' that mimetic practices of representation were aspiring to imitate seemed, to them, to be an ideological illusion that, in Brecht's view, was constructed by bourgeois powers to maintain the myth of an inevitable and unchangeable capitalist reality. Artaud's vision was never articulated through such clear ideological imperatives but was conceived as the necessity to reject the superficial illusion of bourgeois reality in order to obtain a mystical, or spiritual, experience that was more real and authentic than the constructed social reality of the time. As their interpretations of the real differed, so did their responses. For Brecht, the answer lay in exposing the frame of representational practice to illuminate the illusion of both the theatrical representation and the reality to which it referred. For Artaud, the theatre must reject any attempt to imitate the illusory reality of the world to enable a psychic encounter with a more authentic real.

What both responses share, however, is an ideological and critical analysis of theatrical practice that maintains a commitment to mimetic representation. If the reality beyond the theatre is a constructed illusion, then mimetic representational practice that seeks to replicate reality and confirm the latter's ontological status as the real can only serve to uphold the deception. Consequently, Brecht and Artaud would both hold that representational practice is guilty of collusion with the cultural powers who have constructed such an illusion for their own ideological ends. The ontological and ideological reading of the real that underpins such theory finds its clearest and most influential exposition in Guy Debord's *The Society of the Spectacle,* first published in 1967, which opens with the following statement: '[t]he whole life of those societies in which modern conditions of production prevail presents itself as an immense accumulation of *spectacles*. All that was once directly lived has become mere representation.' (1995: 12) As Martin Puchner makes clear,

> The term 'spectacle' denotes not simply the mediatization of post-war Western capitalism but its entire ideology: television, advertising, com-

modity fetish, superstructure, the whole deceptive appearance of advanced capitalism. Debord anticipated what Althusser would soon call the ideological state apparatuses. (2006: 221)

Debord's reading of the real was, like Brecht's, explicitly Marxist in its condemnation of bourgeois society, arguing that '[t]he unreal unity the spectacle proclaims masks the class division on which the real unity of the capitalist mode of production is based' (1995: 46). His claim that the spectacle repressed 'all directly lived truth beneath the *real presence* of the falsehood maintained by the organization of appearances' also supported the Artaudian vision of a more authentic reality that only a theatre that resisted representational practice would be able to access (1995: 153, original emphasis). Mike Sell describes the widespread impact of Artaud's vision on neo-avant-garde artists in post-war North America, writing that 'the theatrical "cruelty" advocated by Artaud enjoyed a sudden rise in fortune during the 1950s as he and his work were rediscovered by a younger generation of artists and intellectuals eager to renew the intransigence of the prewar avant-garde' (2006: 60). Artaud's vision was of a theatre that refused repetition, calling for artists to recognise

> that what has already been said no longer needs saying; that an expression twice used is of no value since it does not have two lives. Once spoken, all speech is dead and is only active as it is spoken. Once a form is used it has no more use. (Artaud, 1970a: 56)

Artaud's resistance to the Western theatre's tradition of text-based mimetic representation, which he condemned as the slavish repetition of a written text that was itself no more than a copy of a superficial and illusory social reality, has proved one of the most durable critiques of dramatic practice, as will be further discussed in Chapter 2. However, in one key sense, as Martin Puchner observes, Artaud's vision was implicitly contradictory, calling for a theatre that was paradoxically against everything that could be defined as theatre. Artaud was rather seeking a 'lifeness' that pointed beyond the theatre, for, '[i]f all repetition were eliminated, nothing would remain to which we could point and which we could identify as a theatrical event' (Puchner, 2006: 202). However, such contradictions did nothing to deter neo-avant-garde artists, such as the Living Theatre, from their attempts to evade representational practice. To this end the neo-avant-garde created performances that were built on the imperatives of each performance taking place in the present time and space of the event. Strategies included performers eschewing representations of characters to speak directly to the gathered audiences, improvisational practice that could not and was not designed to be repeated, and extensive audience involvement that rejected the concept of rehearsal and enabled the audience members to be present and directly experience the event that unfolded in real time. In their search for a practice that could evade the representational fallacies of traditional Western theatre, key movements of the neo-avant-garde, sharing Artaud's distrust of the dramatic framework that prohibited direct and unmediated experience, were drawn more and more into practices that sought to eliminate the theatrical frame altogether. Martin Puchner explains how '[i]n conceiving of situations as a form of participatory theater that becomes life, the situationists attacked the representational quality of theater as such' (2006: 232). Whilst the core of the Situationist movement, including Guy Debord, ultimately came to reject anything that could be identified as art, due to its potential for capitalist commodification (McDonough, 2002: 147; Sell, 2006: 202), other seminal figures from the neo-avant-garde, such as Allan Kaprow and John Cage, contributed to the development of the new art forms that came to be known as 'Happenings'. Here, performative acts were placed in the midst of everyday activity and were only viewed by chance, often without the spectators even realising that a performance was taking place. True to the lineage of Artaud as they understood it, such artists were seeking a direct and unmediated 'lifelike' experience for their audiences that would enable access to a more authentic 'presence' than the dramatic representations of theatre or the capitalist and commodified spectacles of daily life could offer.

The influence of these innovations can be seen to underpin the resurgence of interactive and immersive theatre experimentation in the first decade of the twenty-first century, as will be discussed in Chapter 6, but even at this earlier point in history the belief in an autonomous and more authentic reality that could somehow circumvent the capitalist structures it was attempting to evade was already being placed under interrogation. The conflicting ideological discourses that have always surrounded the attempts of the historical and neo-avant-gardes to make art which was radical and oppositional can offer us vital insight into the subsequent ideological ambiguities that underpin the practices and discourses at the turn of the twenty-first century, and so will now be explored in some detail.

Transgression or complicity?

In his 1960s study of the historical avant-garde, Renato Poggioli argues that early uses of the term pre-dating the French Revolution, 'demonstrate how the avant-garde image originally remained subordinate, even within the sphere of art, to the ideals of a radicalism which was not cultural but political' (1968: 9). Poggioli argues that an alliance of political and artistic radicalism survived in France until the late nineteenth century up to the point when the term was adopted by 'the international market of ideas' (1968: 12). At this point, Poggioli suggests, the term 'avant-garde' became 'without qualification, another synonym for the artistic avant-garde', as it has since remained (1968: 12). These revolutionary roots of the artistic avant-garde, however, were explicitly adopted and drawn on by the neo-avant-gardes making work in the 1950s and 1960s. Their shared ideological basis was consequently Marxist in derivation, and was founded upon the belief that the experimental strategies that they were exploring could build positions of opposition to the commodifying imperative of the capitalist economy that had hitherto controlled, financially and ideologically, the processes of bourgeois art production. This conviction was prevalent in the fields of both visual art and theatre, which, in their different but ultimately convergent ways, sought to remove the art object or performance event from the cultural frameworks that positioned them as commodities within the capitalist economy.

However, it very soon became clear, as Paul Mann persuasively argues in his seminal study, *The Theory-Death of the Avant-Garde*, that

> There is no outside-the-frame in art. The artist's desire to be free of the frame is a function of the frame's need to expand [...] [F]ar from bringing us to a nihilistic state in which nothing can any longer be art, Duchamp's careful reframings help set the frame loose to become a more flexible, expansive, comprehensive tool for cultural absorption, a net thrown out into cultural space for greater and greater catch. (1991: 103)

Mann further explains how 'the attack on the institution of art made the attack itself a work of art susceptible to commodification, circulation, exchange; the attack on the institution of art became an institutional mode' (1991: 62). The neo-avant-garde may have rejected the authored creation of a unique and aesthetically significant 'work of art' that, however ideologically transgressive in intent, could too easily be transformed into a commodity fetish by the workings of capital. But they had not, it seems, always fully calculated capitalism's enthusiasm for the 'new', and its capacity to absorb the anti-art projects into its own systems of economic exchange by happily extending its borders and frames ever further. Mann continues, 'art against the institution of art ends by advancing the institution's interests, revitalizing its moribund agencies, providing it with alternatives that constitute its next stage of development' (1991: 82). In the same way Mike Sell notes that, '[b]y dematrixing objects, actions, and signifiers from their customary social significance, Happenings and Fluxus events engaged the cultural logic of American capitalism, a logic that is more concerned with discovering new sources of value than sustaining old ones' (2006: 194). In both cases, all attempts by artists of the historical and the neo-avant-gardes to perform a resistance to the traditional and institutional rules on what was or wasn't art seemed destined to merely advance such rules into new territory, without any detriment to the underlying economic structures. In fact, as is now commonly acknowledged, the avant-garde movements could, in one sense, be seen as 'research-and-development labs for a hipper, gentler, more interesting capitalism' (Sell, 2006: 190). As Poggioli concludes, the 'fevered experimentation which is one of the most characteristic manifestations of the avant-garde' is 'condemned to conquer, through the influence of fashion, that very popularity it once disdained – and this is the beginning of its end' (1968: 82).

Mann observes how the conflation, which is certainly not incidental, of the 'growing power of the idea of novelty' within the histories of the avant-gardes, and the way in which the same idea of novelty has been 'conscripted by and deployed in a certain economy, in the culture of capitalism' (1991: 68) leave the idea of radical opposition, that is fundamental to avant-garde thinking, endlessly yoked to the capitalist exchange that it seeks to escape. He concludes that 'the avant-garde is bound to both commodity aesthetics and its supercession, and the very means by which it attempts this supercession only drives it deeper into the logic of the commodity' (1991: 70).

If this was, indeed, the case, then how could the traditional function of radical opposition be maintained by this or any future avant-garde movement in the face of the increasingly voracious appetite and endless capacity for absorption of potential transgression that were the hallmarks of late capitalism? Indeed there are many who have located the death of the artistic avant-garde precisely around this point in history, predominantly for the reasons outlined above, and the obvious potential of the events of 1968 to provide a point of closure. For others, it lingers a little longer. In an article published in 2005 David Savran defines such a death as a 'long decline' that stretches from the late 1970s and early 1980s as identified by Richard Schechner, to the 1990s that were designated as the avant-garde's final resting place by Arnold Aronson (Savran, 2005: 11–12). Yet, despite such repeated obituaries, the term prevailed, in North American scholarship at least, as a common reference for the new wave of experimental work which emerged in the 1980s, 1990s and beyond. Richard Schechner himself, in 2006, refers to a continuing avant-garde as a current strand of practice that is central to the Performance Studies discipline (Schechner, 2006 : 1), and Marvin Carlson includes Robert Wilson, Richard Foreman and the Wooster Group in his examples of recent avant-garde theatre in *Performance* (Carlson, 1996: 99). Although David Savran notes that the Wooster Group's work from the 1980s through to the 2000s has been continually referenced as avant-garde practice, he ultimately finds the counter-evidence too hard to overcome. He cites Amin's conclusion that 'because it is "impotent to contest capitalist globalization," deconstruction – along with what passes for the avantgarde – has arguably for almost 30 years "been co-opted through the main strategies of the globalized neoliberal project"' (Amin, 1998: 66, in Savran, 2005: 34). Savran further suggests that the continuing application of the term avant-garde to companies like the Wooster Group in the late 1980s and 1990s was part of a process which he describes as

> a *branding* of the avantgarde, the production of the label 'avantgarde' as a kind of registered trademark [...] Ironically enough, the production of the avantgarde as brand, collective hallucination, endlessly alluring and prestigious commodity, signals less a modification than a complete reversal of its original meaning. If the first avantgarde (as exemplified by Max Ernst) represented a protest against the commodification of art, its now-consecrated remains represent a kind of hommage to mediatized culture, an attempt both to scorn and embrace the commercial sphere. (2005: 36, original emphasis)

Yet despite the numerous obituaries for the avant-garde, to which Savran adds his own, it is clear that the term itself, along with alternative terms which are understood to replicate the avant-garde's core characteristics, has persisted in holding onto its radical currency up to and into the twenty-first century. As Paul Mann observes, the much-proclaimed death of the avant-garde has prevented neither a flourishing field of discourse, nor an ever expanding field of new performance practices that could be characterised as 'avant-garde' under the terms of the most authoritative definitions (1991: 31–2). Any analysis of the ensuing work that emerged in the wake of the 1960s and 1970s necessitates traversing a multiplicity of diverse and overlapping terminologies that replaced the more singular definition of the avant-garde, or neo-avant-garde, up to that point. This fact, in itself, is a logical development given the diffusion of many different avant-garde legacies across a whole spectrum of ideologically and contextually diverse practice. In roughly chronological terms, the new performance practices following in the wake of the neo-avant-garde period are variously identified as the next wave of the avant-garde, performance art, performance art theatre, performance, performance theatre, alternative theatre, postmodern performance, contemporary performance, live art or postdramatic theatre. It is beyond the scope of this chapter to attempt to map the distinctions between the different terminologies precisely; a task, in any case, made more difficult by the absence of definitive definitions to which all scholars and artists adhere. But, whilst these terms are certainly not synonymous, their boundaries are permeable, and one of the grounds on which they converge can be identified as the radical heritage of resistance left by the earlier avant-gardes; a resistance that continues to be characterised by its opposition to the representational premises and predicates of dramatic theatre.

But how can the notion, if not always the label, of the avant-garde have seemingly survived its absorption by the economic and ideological structures of late capitalism, in an era when the forces of global capitalism have become ever more hegemonic and all-consuming? How can artists working in the shadow of the long death of the avant-garde be under any illusion that their work can escape appropriation, or hope to transgress the endlessly elastic boundaries of the capitalist enterprise? In the following section I will explore how an alternative discourse of opposition was consequently constructed to underpin the continuing possibility of radical practice in the post-avant-garde, postmodern landscape of the final decades of the twentieth century.

From transgression to resistance

In his 'fractionally alternative history of the avant-garde' (1991: 64), Paul Mann maps five periods, the last three of which he defines as 'not fixed spans of time but simultaneous, overlapping features of the post-1945 period' (66). Despite such overlapping, they are, as Mann concedes, 'localizable to some extent' and, I would argue, can offer an almost chronological journey through the remainder of the twentieth century (66). The third of Mann's periods can be seen to correspond to the historical period of the neo-avant-garde as discussed above. Mann describes this period as one of 'consolidation and recuperation of the mode of anti-art' (65). This period, in his chronicle, is followed by 'the supersaturation and therefore the crisis of recuperation [...] one manifestation of the death of the avant-garde' (65). This is then followed by the fifth and final period which is characterised by

[a]tomization, decentering, and hence both a reorganization effort and a few strange disappearances. In the face of the inevitability of recuperation the avant-garde abandons its traditional dialectic and rhetoric and seeks other modes ... proliferation of undergrounds, of margins, of microdiscourses ... The visible surface ... of this stage is called postmodernism and defined as pluralist, decentered, eclectic, deconstructive [*sic*], self-consciously ideological, non-or hypersubjective (the same thing), and largely indifferent to charges that it has abandoned the tasks historically assigned to the avant-garde. Around this postmodernism: an economy frantically struggling to retool discursive technology in order to recuperate it. (65–6)

Mann's conflation of the postmodern condition with an advanced capitalist agenda of recuperation mirrors Fredric Jameson's seminal analysis of postmodernism as the cultural logic of late capitalism, published in book form in the same year (Jameson, 1991). Jameson, like Mann, fears that what becomes inconceivable within the terms of postmodernism is the very possibility of critical or radical opposition:

No theory of cultural politics current on the Left today has been able to do without one notion or another of a certain minimal aesthetic distance, of the possibility of the positioning of the cultural act outside the massive Being of capital, from which to assault this last ... [H]owever ... distance in general (including "critical distance" in particular) has very precisely been abolished in the new space of postmodernism (1991: 48)

The cultural act of potential opposition, Jameson argues, is now co-opted into a simulacrum of images without referents, or 'an immense and historically original acculturation of the Real' (1991: x). As the 'Real' has become aestheticised, so 'aesthetic production ... has become integrated into commodity production generally' (4) and feeds the consumer's appetite for 'a world transformed into sheer images of itself' (18). In such a simulacrum there is no 'outside' position from which to mount a critique as the oppositional act is always already commodified as a consumable image of itself.

The concept of the simulacrum is foregrounded in the work of Jean Baudrillard and can be traced conceptually back to Guy Debord's notion of the spectacular society (Debord, 1995). Unlike the simulacrum, however, Debord's spectacle was understood as something that was used by those in power to obscure the real. Accordingly, the real still remained to be uncovered or fought for as there were still conceptual positions from which the spectacle on offer could be either accepted or denied. The role of resistance in this context was clear; it was to disrupt or destroy the spectacular in order to gain access to the real or the truth. Baudrillard's theory of the simulacrum, however, argues that our culture is now at the point whereby the real itself is constructed by the simulated which, in turn, is a copy of the real, resulting in a mobius strip of simulations that make up the totality of our contemporary reality. As all conceptual positions are thereby also within the simulacrum, there appears to be no position from which it can either be accepted or denied. Revisiting his original thesis twenty-one years after *The Society of the Spectacle* was first published, Debord's understanding of the advancement of the spectacle begins to align itself somewhat with Baudrillard's conclusions:

> the final sense of the integrated spectacle is this – that it has integrated itself into reality to the same extent as it was describing it, and that it was reconstructing it as it was describing it. As a result, this reality no longer confronts the integrated spectacle as something alien. (Debord, 1990: 9)

In other words, there is no longer an accessible real, existing beyond and independent of the 'integrated spectacle', or simulacrum, to uncover or to fight for. The critical distinction between Debord's initial conception of the spectacle and Baudrillard's simulacrum is that the latter, as Baudrillard explains, 'conceals not the truth, but the fact that there isn't any' (Baudrillard, 2008: 102). In *The Intelligence of Evil or the Lucidity Pact*, Baudrillard defines the ultimate consequence of the technological advancement of simulacra as an 'Integral Reality' whereby 'the whole system of information' has become 'an immense machine for producing the event as sign, as an exchangeable value on the universal market of ideology, of spectacle, of catastrophe, etc.' (2005: 121), and argues that the simulated nature of what we now perceive as reality does not obscure or annihilate the true real but, perversely, the fact that there is no true real:

> We have exchanged one illusion for another, and it turns out that the material, objective illusion, the illusion of reality, is as fragile as the illusion of God and no longer protects us, once the euphoria of science and the Enlightenment is past, from the fundamental illusion of the world and its absence of truth. (2005: 43–4)

Throughout his work, Baudrillard draws attention to this double-implosion of the real that has sometimes been oversimplified by those drawing on his ideas. The first implosion is that of a perceived political or social reality, the simulacrum arising from the spectacle that Debord first identified as the construction of an ideological illusion of the real, and that Brecht sought to demystify through his work. The second is the implosion of epistemological or metaphysical certainty, an implosion which the simulacrum attempts to cover over by providing its own illusion of the real. This distinction between the two orders of the real that feature in Baudrillard's writing is addressed in more detail in Chapter 5. Here it is sufficient to note that it is Baudrillard's influential theory of the simulacrum that has been significant in underpinning contemporary thinking that if there is no 'real' beyond the simulacrum, then there is no 'real' for any cultural referent to refer to, or validate itself upon. As a consequence, any representation that purports to model itself on a corresponding reality is called into question, and the concept of authoritative meaning or truth claim finds itself without any ultimate origin or transcendental basis on which it can unequivocally validate its account.

The emergence of the simulacrum as the new paradigm of the real marks the end of any confidence in a metaphysical certainty that might offer recourse to a reality lying beyond the ideological constructs of the spectacle, and with it comes an end to the old distinctions between truth and falsehood, the real and the fictional. In a previously published article I noted how the politics of English theatre in the 1990s, across diverse forms of practice, 'became obsessed with the failure of 'reality' to provide any stable counterpoint to the 'simulated' where the self's identity might be found' (Tomlin, 2004: 500). From Blast Theory's performance of *Something American* (1996) to Mark Ravenhill's dramatic playtext, *Faust: Faust is Dead* (1997) theatre was repositioning 'the real' as a subjective and self-constructed fiction.

The scepticism of the real that was prevalent up to and throughout the period of this study does hold real problems for the question of legitimation. Compounding the implications of Baudrillard's theories for new work in the 1980s, 1990s and beyond was the steadily rising influence of the poststructuralist theories of Jacques Derrida, as will be discussed in depth in Chapters 2 and 3. Derrida's project was to deconstruct Modernity's grand narratives of theology, reason, science and law and demonstrate how they were merely contingent upon other narratives that themselves were contingent upon other narratives and so on, and thus could not provide the foundational truths on which further hypotheses or meanings could be securely constructed. Postmodern theorist Jean-François Lyotard also categorises the postmodern condition as one of 'incredulity toward metanarratives' (1984: xxiv) such as the speculative narrative of Enlightenment science and the emancipatory narrative of Marxism, which had both previously acted as legitimising bases of knowledge. He argues that as neither of these narratives can secure their authority beyond their own self-constructed premises, their ability to act as legitimation for claims to knowledge, truth or justice is fatally flawed. In their place, he argues, we are left with micro-narratives or, in Wittgenstein's terminology, language games, which 'do not carry within themselves their own legitimation, but are the object of a contract, explicit or not, between players' (1984: 10). So rules become constructed rather than given, and progress is redefined as the players' capacity to uncover a new move that can lead to a destabilisation of the accepted conditions. In terms of artistic practice, Lyotard compares the postmodern artist with the philosopher whose text is not 'in principle governed by preestablished rules, and … cannot be judged according to a determining judgement, by applying familiar categories to the text or to the work. Those rules and categories are what the work of art itself is looking for' (1984: 81).

The deconstruction of the rules of dramatic convention and the explicit construction of new rules for a new kind of performance have become a key aesthetic in work undertaken in the postmodern period. The exposure of the mechanics of dramatic representation can, of course, be traced back to the avant-garde practice of Bertolt Brecht, as has been well chronicled (see Wright, 1989; Diamond, 1997). In Brecht's work, the highlighting of the theatrical frame was intended to gesture to the comparable frame of the spectacular society which offered its ideological constructions as objective reality. By demystifying the rules of theatrical construction, Brecht hoped that his audience would, in turn, be more competent at demystifying the illusions of the spectacle in order to understand the 'truth' of the capitalist system as substantiated by the Marxist narrative of emancipation. However, as outlined above, in the postmodern period there is no longer unproblematic recourse to such a narrative, which, in turn, makes the revelation of any kind of 'truth' that might be obscured by the spectacle difficult to conceive. What is revealed by the exposure of theatrical construction at the turn of the twentieth century is not a greater truth but the absence of truth, and the conclusion that all reality is subjectively constructed in accordance with rules of our own making. Seen through the lens of theorists such as Baudrillard, Derrida and Lyotard, everything, in this historical period, becomes an equivalent fictional text, a representation without referent, a copy without origin. So how, within this simulacrum where every real is ideological, where no micro-narrative can be conclusively legitimised or authorised over any other, and where no recourse to scientific truth or the emancipatory narrative of Marxism is available, can a radical political opposition be sustained?

Jameson's response to the 'increasingly closed and terrifying machine'

(1991: 5) that threatens to paralyse the capacity for critical distance and radical action is to call for a new kind of cognitive mapping of this 'historically original' and unchartered spatiality (1991: x). Jameson confronts the impossibility of critical distance within this new paradigm by locating the potential for radical opposition within the predicates of the postmodern condition itself, rather than as an ideal of Utopia that can be found beyond it. He argues that '[t]his model of the presence of the future within the present is then clearly quite different from the attempt to "step outside" actually existing reality into some other space' (1991: 206).

This shift from the transgressive and revolutionary politics that sought to overturn the structures of the capitalist spectacle from a position of critical and cultural distance, to a resistant politics that is implicated within such structures and thus seeks, in the main, to expose the workings of the spectacle from within, has been instrumental in shaping the ideological analysis of theatre and performance in the late twentieth and early twenty-first century. Hal Foster's account of this shift, in particular, has proved highly influential, through its dissemination in Philip Auslander's seminal article, 'Toward a concept of the political in postmodern theatre' (1997). Foster argues that 'more than any avant garde, capital is the agent of transgression and shock – which is one reason why such strategies in art now seem as redundant as resistance seems futile' (1985: 147). Foster's conclusion, as Auslander summarises, is that 'a resistant political/ aesthetic practice might work to reveal the counterhegemonic tendencies within the dominant discourse ... along with a deconstruction of the processes of cultural control' (Auslander, 1997: 60–1).

However, Paul Mann questions the precarious nature of this resistance, defining it as the latest 'desiccated, spectral, marketable semblance of the critical' (1991: 122), and paraphrases the position as one in which 'critical distance might be abolished but a new sort of difference opens up, this one even truer because it is lodged in the belly of the beast. What looked like absorption is rewritten as a romance of subversive infiltration' (129). He goes on to parody the claims of resistance to the inevitable commodification of the would-be oppositional, stating that '[a]ll one needs is to remain alert, as if consciousness of recuperation were enough to produce a counterrecuperation. The latest refuge from recuperation is recuperation itself. Postdialectical criticism becomes a maze of reflections of mutual recuperation' (129). Whereas Brecht and other avant-garde artists sought to demystify the spectacle's illusions in order to point to the greater truth of a Marxist utopian alternative, all postmodern deconstruction can do, it seems, is to expose and self-reference the strategies of containment, commodification and recuperation to which the artist, the work, and the critic are all subjected, without offering any way out of the bind. Mann lucidly and persuasively argues that

> The notorious fragmentation of modern knowledge [...] masks the systemic and material accord of all discourses. High and low [...] bourgeois and revolutionary, critical and affirmative, engaged and autonomous – the overarching economy that sustains and is sustained by such distinctions asserts itself more and more. In the end there is only one discourse and its law is economic. (1991: 27)

Throughout *The Theory-Death of the Avant-Garde,* Mann argues that all artistic acts, however oppositional in intention, are already implicated by the white discourse of economy in which they necessarily circulate. Moreover, all theoretical or critical positions of resistance inevitably feed that same economy which relies on counter-arguments to move it forward and to sustain its development and control. Where critics like Foster, Mann argues, may use their academic currency to establish a radical analysis for work that, through its exposure of the practices of representation, seeks to self-consciously recognise its own recuperation by the establishment, those same critics rarely acknowledge their own 'entanglement in discourse' (Foster, 1985: 108, in Mann, 1991: 132). Much like his argument that the anti-institutional art practice of the neo-avant-garde merely served to extend the reach and influence of the art institutions, so Mann argues that any attempt to present theoretical critiques of the economic structures of global capitalism paradoxically sustains its control by ever-extending the terms of its discourse:

> In the naming of the avant-garde we can already see the prototype of a cultural system that could gear every mode of alterity into the machinery of progress, that could yoke radical change to the very institutions and ideals it sought to supercede: a system for instrumentalizing contradiction that has taken more than a century to make itself plain. (1991: 46)

The danger, of course, that Mann himself identifies, is that such a position leaves us in the depths of nihilism where all ideological positions and intentions merely feed the machinery of the economy that relies on the oppositional and contradictory to sustain its advancement. Evil now triumphs, it seems, when good men or women do anything at all. Short of merely waiting for Jameson's 'new international proletariat (taking forms we cannot yet imagine)' to 'reemerge from this convulsive upheaval' and destroy the white discourse of capitalism in utopian revolutionary style (Jameson, 1991: 417), the most radical thing an artist or theorist can do, it seems, is to remain silent.

In order to evade the consequences of, what Mann terms, postdialectical criticism, Jameson urges that we return to the Marxist notion of the dialectic and transform it for our own time. He cites how Marx urges us, in the *Manifesto,* to think historical development 'positively *and* negatively all at once ... [w]e are somehow to lift our minds to a point at which it is possible to understand that capitalism is at one and the same time the best thing that has ever happened to the human race, and the worst' (1991: 47). Jameson concludes that 'if postmodernism is a historical phenomenon, then the attempt to conceptualize it in terms of moral or moralizing judgements must finally be identified as a category mistake' (1991: 46). To do as Jameson suggests is to abandon the binary consisting of, on the one hand, the wholly immoral system that wishes only to disable all opposition and, on the other, the wholly moral opposition that wishes only to destroy or overthrow the system. Instead, the system is repositioned as potentially both progressive and regressive and subsequently can be moderated, amended or fundamentally changed by counter-narratives which may well be recuperated but may also be transformative at the same time. Hal Foster likewise suggests that we need to conceptualise postmodernism not as 'a "total system"' but as 'a conjuncture of practices, many adversarial, where the cultural is an arena in which active contestation is possible' (1985: 149). The same strategy is also echoed in Lyotard's call for an agonistics of language which understands that 'to speak is to fight, in the sense of playing' (1984: 10) and accepts that '[m]ost people have lost the nostalgia for the lost narrative ... [L]egitimation can only spring from their own linguistic practice and communicational interaction' (41). In this way, the artist can attempt to shape the ideological contours of postmodern spatiality by continuing to make distinctions, however relative, between one narrative claim and the next, and by assuming responsibility, 'not only for the statements they propose, but also for the rules to which they submit those statements in order to render them acceptable' (Lyotard, 1984: 62). Accepting that everything is subject to recuperation, which Lyotard concedes (15), and that no statement can be legitimated with reference to some foundational narrative, is not the same as accepting that the micro-narratives themselves are thus beyond ideological analysis or distinction. As noted in the Introduction, the artist or critic's choice to propagate one narrative over another, or, with a new move, to change the rules entirely, will still result in a 'real' impact on the ideological shape of the historical period in which the work is situated. What is of interest here is not so much whether would-be radical work is, to whatever degree, recuperated into the system. This now seems an almost inevitable given for any practice framed as artistic or cultural, as distinct from performative modes of direct action which follow the anti-art agenda of the late Situationists and lie beyond the remit of this book. What is of more interest here is how an insistence on ideological distinctions between one narrative and the next in the wake of the poststructuralist collapse of the 'real', might lead to a re-examination of what constitutes radical performance practice in the wake of the transgressive politics of the avant-garde.

The postmodern discourse of resistance outlined by Jameson, Foster and Lyotard, among others, continues to serve the vast majority of scholars and artists who seek to underline the radical nature of new performance practices produced at the turn of the century. This study, in its turn, will draw on, as well as challenge, such a discourse throughout the subsequent chapters, but there are limitations to the continued applications of this discourse that need to be highlighted, however briefly, at this stage.

Firstly, the work under analysis in the remainder of this book has been produced some twenty to thirty years after the postmodern and poststructuralist discourses began to emerge in the 1970s, and, given the accelerating speed of 'the new', it is not inconceivable that the spatial co-ordinates of twenty first century culture may have become almost unrecognisable from those chartered by theorists such as Lyotard, Jameson and Foster during the 1980s. I will argue at various points throughout the book that certain philosophical discourses of the real and corresponding narratives of radical resistance that artists and scholars are still bringing forth as evidence, may need to be re-interrogated in the light of the developments in global capitalism since their original conception.

Secondly, I will argue that there is too little account taken of the uneven global playing field on which Lyotard's language games are played out. Lyotard does recognise the possibility that 'moves' or narratives can be ignored or repressed when they too abruptly destabilise accepted conditions. He defines this as moving into the rule of terror, or 'the efficiency gained by eliminating, or threatening to eliminate, a player from the language game one shares with him' (1984: 63). He does not, however, sufficiently highlight the myriad and more subtle uses of power that are at work to ensure that the contestation of narratives that lies at the heart of the concept of postmodern resistance takes place in a landscape that is already designed to make winning much easier for some players than others, particularly once recourse to truth becomes invalidated. The critical importance of the wider ideological context of this historical period, defined, according to Lyotard, by the performativity criterion which seeks to maximise efficiency for the ends of power, must not be obscured by a too-narrow focus on the multiple and contesting narratives which the performance criterion itself enables to thrive. To this end, it would be wise to follow Fredric Jameson's attempts to maintain some sense of a field always and already mapped by unequal privilege, even if his recourse to an essentially Marxist dialectic as a tool to dissect postmodernism is questioned by many theorists for its potential contradictions (see for example Radhakrishnan, 1989: 214–15).

Finally, the very dominance of the narrative of radical resistance in theatre and performance studies over the last few decades, as I will demonstrate, threatens to entirely overwhelm any would-be counter-narratives, raising the possibility that the potential radicalism of resistance becomes the new master narrative with its own set of emerging binaries and imperative to totalising all opposition. Whilst individual articulations may be placed in conflict with each other in order to prevent the formation of a totalising meaning in the old sense, the legitimacy of resistance as the only viable means of opposition is not sufficiently challenged, I will argue, by much of the work or analysis that employs its philosophical predicates. In this way, the multiple and contesting micro-narratives may well be open to interpretation, but the *über*-discourse of the spatial mapping itself is not.

The 'liminal norm'

The shift in strategy from the transgressive politics of the avant-garde to the resistance adopted by the successive performance practices of the postmodern era did nothing to dislodge the binary opposition that has been sustained throughout the twentieth century between, on the one hand, dramatic theatre and, on the other, performance that sets out to deconstruct representational practice. The opposition remains familiar, but the particular arguments have necessarily shifted to keep pace with the changing theoretical terrain. The conviction that we are, to some degree or other, now living in a simulacrum, conjoined with the widespread discrediting of grand narratives, has brought about an ultimate collapse of the boundaries between the fictional and the real that once formed the basis of dramatic theatre's mimetic representational apparatus. Hal Foster's hugely influential argument that 'the political artist today might be urged not to represent given representations and generic forms but to investigate the processes and apparatuses which control them' (1985: 153), has underpinned the positioning of the radical within postmodern performance discourse in the hands of those who set out to deconstruct dramatic representation. Despite the cautionary 'perhaps' which precedes the above citation (Foster, 1985: 152), but is omitted from Auslander's rendering of it (Auslander, 1997: 60), and Foster's important rider earlier in his chapter that '[t]o re-think the political … is not to rule out any representational mode but rather to question specific uses and material effects' (1985: 143), his political imperative has consistently been used to deny the potential of radicalism to artists who continue to rely on predominantly dramatic representational practices, even if such practices are intended to communicate political opposition. The discourse of postmodern resistance has thus resulted in potentially evoking an ideological binary whereby dramatic theatre is pitted against the work that challenges its representational predicates. I will evidence the existence of this binary and fully interrogate its philosophical premises in Chapter 2, but would now like to chart, in conclusion to this historical overview, how the emergence of such a binary has been strengthened and consolidated by a number of converging influences in the 1980s and 1990s.

In 'Radicalism and the theatre of genealogies of live art', Beth Hoffmann recounts the recurrence in post-war British theatre of the 'cycle of self-perpetuating attacks' between the emerging performance/live art movement and the dramatic literary tradition: 'the boundary between them becoming more and more rhetorically overdetermined even as it becomes less obvious to locate in actual performance practice' (2009: 97). Hoffmann argues that the concept of live art has grown out of the history of the neo-avant-garde and shares with that history 'a reserved site of interdisciplinarity, a kind of rhetorical and curatorial space that operates at the margins, culturally and aesthetically, and that eschews institutionalized recognizability' (101). As a consequence, Hoffmann contends, 'live art emerges not from a model of positive affinity and formal resemblance among works but from a principle of non-identity, the lack of a definition outside the negation, subversion or transgression of a received practice or set of practices' (101–2), namely those of dramatic theatre. Hoffmann observes that the same binary relationship is being drawn in 2007, at the first SPILL Festival of Experimental Performance and Live Art, as was drawn at the Edinburgh Festival International Drama Conference in 1963, with Forced Entertainment director Tim Etchells' 2007 key note speech uniting the diversity of work represented at the festival primarily by its shared investment in 'breaking' theatre (Hoffmann, 2009: 98). Hoffmann recognises Etchells' intentions to 'break a conservative model of cultural value that exasperatingly tends to privilege one particular model of performance-making' (98), but she contends that 'in spite of this nuance, "theatre" operated successfully as a seamless placeholder for that conservative cultural model in the imagination of the artists, funders, promoters, scholars and critics in the audience, many of whom continually referenced Etchells's accidental rallying cry throughout the remainder of the symposium' (98). In analysing the rhetoric of Tim Etchells, Hoffmann discusses how 'the language of continuity and expansion of "theatre" might also apply [to his company's practice], and yet the language of rupture and break remains more common, familiar and persuasive'(98). Hoffmann acknowledges the dual culpability of both those advocating experimental practice and those who might be perceived as dramatic traditionalists in ensuring that, on the British stage, 'this "new" work ... and the dramatic canon remain engaged in a zero-sum struggle for survival' (99). Ultimately, however, her greatest concern is that the emphasis placed by advocates of the 'new' work on the counter model of drama is in danger of leading 'to a troubling fetishizing of tradition-as-form rather than a critique of the kind of cultural authority that validates and authenticates what counts as "traditional"' (104).

In the United States a similar pattern can be seen to emerge. Marvin Carlson's emphasis on 'performance' as a radical form distinguished by its opposition to the implicitly reactionary 'culture-bound structures of the conventional theatre' (1996: 24) is pervasive throughout *Performance*, and he concludes that 'theatre was probably the most common "other" against which the new art could be defined' (104). This common 'other', distinguished, in the main, by its reliance on a pre-written playtext, is correspondingly relegated to a demonised, marginal, or occluded form within the discipline of Performance Studies, despite it being a significant aspect of the performance arts spectrum that falls under the Performance Studies remit. In 'The decline and fall of the (American) avant-garde', Richard Schechner aligns experimental (or avant-garde) practice explicitly with non-text-based work, and positions text-based work as a product of tradition which renders it incapable of radical intent or impact within the theatrical landscape (1981: 56). As Stephen Bottoms has convincingly argued, Schechner's dismissal of 'the staging of written dramas' as 'the string quartet of the 21st century: a beloved but extremely limited genre, a subdivision of performance', has become an influential position within Performance and Theatre Studies fields, despite the contradictions inherent in such a position which Bottoms goes on to highlight in some detail (Schechner, 1992: 8, in Bottoms, 2011: 23). Nevertheless, despite his reservations about the dramatic form that is only reluctantly acknowledged as a subdivision of performance, Schechner ultimately couches the entire discipline of Performance Studies within a radical narrative, proposing that 'if performance studies were an art, it would be avant-garde' (2006: 4). In *Professing Performance,* Shannon Jackson acknowledges how Performance Studies has been consistently aligned with 'the canon-busters', despite the fact that, as she points out, the 'canons' in question of dramatic literature and oral performance were themselves already on the margins of literary history (2004: 23). Jon McKenzie's *Perform or Else* rigorously interrogates the radical narrative of the Performance Studies paradigm and identifies how it has tended to focus predominantly on performance as a counter-cultural force, rather than acknowledging that 'performance will be to the twentieth and twenty-first centuries what discipline was to the eighteenth and nineteenth: an onto-historical formation of power and knowledge' (2001: 176). McKenzie argues that the recurring definition of performance, advanced by leading Performance Studies scholars as a radical and liminal force, refuses to acknowledge that 'the performance stratum cannot be thought outside of postmodern, information-based capitalism' (182). McKenzie argues that the proposed radical liminality of performance studies has become a liminal norm that occurs 'where the valorisation of liminal transgression or resistance itself becomes normative' and concludes that this normalisation has impacted on the potential radicalism of the discourse itself (50). McKenzie convincingly argues that theorists such as Marcuse and Lyotard explicitly propose that 'performance operates throughout certain societies as a distinct mode of power and knowledge' (164). Yet both Marcuse's performance principle and Lyotard's performativity criterion have been largely bypassed by cultural performance theorists, despite the influence on the discourse of other aspects of their work. Such particular and partial readings, McKenzie argues, precisely reveal 'the workings of performative power within the Performance Studies paradigm' (164).

Marvin Carlson, in fairness, does acknowledge the potential of performance both to 'reinforce the assumptions of that culture' and 'to provide a possible site of alternative assumptions' (1996: 15), and Richard Schechner does include fleeting references to the other performance paradigms of corporate management and technology that McKenzie has accused Performance Studies of strategically occluding. In *Performance Studies,* Schechner concedes that although '[m]any who practice performance studies resist or oppose the global forces of capital ... [f]ewer will concede that these forces know very well – perhaps even better than we do – how to perform, in all the meanings of that word' (2006: 23). Yet despite his acknowledgement of McKenzie's work, and his admission that there are other paradigms of performance that might utilise performance strategies to maintain hegemonic power rather than to resist it, Schechner maintains an absolute commitment to the radical nature of performance art. This he continues to locate on the other side of the ideological binary in opposition to the paradigms highlighted by McKenzie, insisting that today's poststructuralists and postmodernists continue the work of previous avant-gardes by 'subverting the established order of things' (141). However, he continues:

> the ideas of poststructuralism and the techniques of performativity ... – have been eagerly taken up by business, science, and the military, eager to enhance their control over knowledge; anxious to acquire more power. How the contradiction between the performance studies ... intellectuals and artists and the power brokers will be resolved is not certain. (141)

Schechner thus responds to McKenzie's charges by drawing an impermeable dividing line between the artists and intellectuals of performance who are unarguably on the side of the subversive, and the 'power brokers' of other performance paradigms who have appropriated the strategies of the artists and intellectuals to maintain their own hegemonic dominance. Rather than utilising the insights of the alternative performance paradigms to investigate how performance within the artistic movements and the academy might also be utilised as a form of power and control, as suggested by the work of McKenzie, Schechner maintains a clear ideological distinction between the two. He applies Lyotard's concept of the performativity criterion to an 'optimization of performance (in the business and technical senses)', whilst allocating Linda Hutcheon's more radical definition of postmodern performance, one which focuses 'not on business, government, or technology but on postmodern art' as a continuation of 'the subversive project of the historical avant-garde' (Schechner, 2006: 129). McKenzie's study rather seeks to explore where strands of each performance paradigm can be seen to be infiltrating the other, such as the increasing importance of play within performance management models, an aspect of performance which Schechner, on the contrary, describes as of 'the kind ... associated with the arts, with creativity, with childhood' and explicitly not 'a claim that stands up well to the technical or business applications of performance' (2006: 89). In this way Schechner admits McKenzie's alternative paradigms reluctantly under the Performance Studies umbrella, but only, it seems, to further strengthen the radical nature of avant-garde performance in opposition to the devious appropriation strategies of the newcomers which McKenzie has introduced to the discourse. As McKenzie, Roms and Wee rightly caution, Performance Studies cannot be reduced to Schechner's work alone (2010: 6), but his influential upholding of the liminal norm identified by McKenzie remained unarguably central to the spread of Performance Studies departments and discourse across the Atlantic in the 1990s. Heike Roms offers a detailed and insightful analysis of the ways in which Performance Studies has productively influenced the study of performance and theatre in the British context, arguing that it has reinvigorated theatre studies 'through widening its objects and approaches of study, and thereby ultimately re-establishing "theatre" as a theoretical, aesthetic, and political concern' (2010: 55). Nevertheless, I would still contend that Performance Studies also served, less productively, to consolidate the growing binary in the United Kingdom between text-based dramatic theatre practice and performance that sought to challenge its representational predicates. Most significantly, it was influential in firmly yoking the radical avant-garde legacy to the latter in a way that, as I will now demonstrate, reversed the preferred ideological binary that had existed until the 1980s in the British context.

In Britain, unlike in the United States, the specific term 'avant-garde' was rarely used to reference work which occurred from the 1970s onwards. Throughout the 1970s and early 1980s non-text-based devised practice, such as Welfare State and the People Show, had tended to be gathered, along with a wide range of ensemble and radically orientated practice, under the umbrella 'alternative theatre' (see Craig, 1980, Freeman, 2006, and Kritzer, 2008: 5). What was at the vanguard of British theatre at this time was not the avant-garde emphasis on formal innovation, but the avant-garde inheritance of Marxist politics accompanied by an artistic process and context which reflected those aims. Catherine Itzin explains that

> All theatre is political. But the significant British theatre of 1968–1978 was primarily theatre of political change. In the words of John McGrath it was theatre 'that exists somewhere within the shadow, or at least the penumbra, of the ideas of Marx and Marxists'... [i]n short – socialist theatre (McGrath, 1978, in Itzin, 1980: x)

However, by the beginning of the 1990s, as Heddon and Milling observe, 'the targeted focus and agendas of the political companies that all but disappeared throughout the 1980s have, to some extent, been redirected into community theatre' (2006: 122). It is significant, though beyond the parameters of this study to pursue, that the politics of much community-orientated or applied theatre practice, as Heddon and Milling note, preferred to 'effect personal change in participants, principally that they might become more successful within existing structures and institutions', rather than seeking, in the tradition of the avant-garde, to challenge those structures and institutions themselves (155). By the first decade of the twenty-first century, radical performance that challenged the status quo had, in the main, relocated to the sphere of direct action, with collectives such as Radical Jesters and My Dads Strip Club following the Situationist strand of the avant-garde to abandon artistic frameworks altogether and harness the power of theatrical spectacle to explicitly radical ends. By the late 1980s it was text-driven theatre, within the institutional theatre context, that was most often acknowledged as upholding the radical Marxist politics of the avant-garde within a broadly dramatic tradition that drew, predominantly, on the epic structures of Brecht. 'Political theatre', which was neither applied practice nor actively interventionist, was thus commonly identified, in late 1980s Britain, as the theatre of political drama (see Bull, 1984). The strong literary heritage of the United Kingdom that had ensured that the playwright had remained central to cultural and political developments for much longer than had been the case in continental Europe or the United States sustained the radical mantle for representational, epic dramas well into the 1980s. Yet, as Sara Freeman observes, the return of the term 'avant-garde' when it began to be briefly applied to British work in the late 1980s, was not used to define the new writing. Instead it referred to the emerging work of devising companies like Forced Entertainment, that demonstrated 'form-orientated innovation', as distinct from the 'content-orientated innovation' which had been the hallmark of alternative or 'political' theatre, scripted or devised, up to that point (2006: 370). Although I would argue that the term avant-garde was quickly superseded by the much more frequently used 'postmodern' performance (Kaye, 1994) or 'contemporary' performance (Etchells, 1999), Freeman's distinction between the Marxist 'content-orientated' theatre practice of the 1960s and 1970s and the postmodernist or avant-garde 'form-orientated' theatre practice of the 1980s and early 1990s is significant to this study as it was the politics of the emergent postmodern work which was greeted with suspicion at that time. Elaine Aston is only one commentator among many who argued that the ideologically driven arts cuts led by the Thatcher government in the 1980s was 'in part responsible for the displacement of issue-based, political theatre and the rise of a theatre which prioritised style over (political) content' (Aston, 1999: 14), and Amelia Howe Kritzer, looking back on the 1980s, concurred that 'new theatre companies tended to direct their energy towards aesthetic experimentation rather than social or political goals' (2008: 6)

The spread and influence of Performance Studies across the United Kingdom in the 1990s was one possible factor in the shift that was to see the radical mantle switched from the text-based dramatic theatre over to the 'form-orientated' new work that was beginning to challenge dramatic representational predicates, but there were other complementary forces at work. If the United Kingdom was slow to adopt the radical narrative of the new avant-garde, it led the vanguard of scholarly practice throughout the 1990s in the development of Practice-as-Research. Pursued by academic researchers in the visual arts, music, and performance in particular, this agenda called for acts of artistic or performative research to be recognised as research in their own right, without the necessity for accompanying written scholarly analysis. Like Performance Studies, Practice-as-Research is commonly seen as interdisciplinary, or anti-disciplinary, and deeply transgressive of the disciplinary codes and con-ventions of academic research, succinctly characterised by Baz Kershaw as a 'radical creativity upsetting the traditional cautions of scholarship' (2009: 2). Heike Roms situates the development of Practice-as-Research in the particularly British context that, she argues, has a long history of 'persistent anxiety' in relation to the 'position of performance practice within the academy' (2010: 59). Her analysis focuses on the more recent developments at doctoral and postdoctoral level that have seen a shift from an emphasis of 'disciplinary mastery' to a re-articulation of practice within the academy 'according to scholarly parameters such as knowledge-making and knowledge-distribution' (59). Whilst the many progressive consequences of an increased emphasis on research through practice which Roms outlines are not ones I would wish to question, the predominant discourse surrounding Practice-as-Research can nevertheless be seen to mirror the discourse of Performance Studies in its insistence on a radical and liminal narrative that, once again, consolidates the text/performance binary, only now in an academic, rather than an artistic context.

Recalling the ideological aims of the avant-garde, those who advocate

Practice-as-Research in its purest form (that is, artistic practice which stands independently of any theorised written discourse) tend to stress that this form of knowledge, which is embodied and ephemeral rather than textual and reproducible, can consequently escape from the commodification of knowledge that is part and parcel of advanced global capitalism. Baz Kershaw describes how Simon Jones, among others, is explicit in positioning such research in opposition to 'an essential product of writing – producing scripts – about practice, which automatically delivers up all practices to judgement, in the process transforming them into commodities and placing them in the service of capital' (Kershaw, 2009: 5). Jones himself asserts that

> In the current economy of rampant commoditization, performance as a research object always runs the risk of remaining proper to writing, playing support to the production and handling of texts of one sort or another. This making will always emerge from an established matrix of textual practices with their own evolutionary logic; and serve the purpose of exploring, refreshing and eventually embedding a *tradition* of textual enterprise. (Jones, 2009: 29–30)

Jones stresses the familiar poststructuralist shift in emphasis from the object of knowledge to the process of knowing, and from the static matter which is known to the more fluid event of the knowing, as the evidence that underpins the radical potential of Practice-as-Research to evade the recuperative strategies of commodification that now constrain traditional forms of written research (Jones, 2009: 19). However, it is worth recalling, at this point, that Jon McKenzie's analysis of the same poststructuralist shift to performance and the event concludes that such a shift is far from being liminal or oppositional, but has actually become all-pervasive:

> And yet what if this explosion in knowledge was itself 'performative'? What if the diversification and proliferation of researchers, projects, and fields over the past fifty years signal not only a quantitative leap in research initiatives, but also a qualitative mutation in what we call knowledge, the becoming-performative of knowledge itself? (McKenzie, 2001: 13–14)

Such an analysis would position the emergence of Practice-as-Research not as a move that came about in resistance to the dominant cultural landscape but as a movement that could only have been possible within 'the age of global performance' and capitalism in which, as McKenzie argues:

> performatives and performances are in the midst of becoming the onto-historical conditions for saying and seeing anything at all. 'Everything is

performative,' 'everything is performance' – what is most striking about
these sweeping generalizations is that their ontological exaggeration carries a historical precision. (2001: 176)

The metaphor of performance has not been deviously appropriated
by performance management, as Jones, in common with Schechner,
would suggest. Rather, as McKenzie clearly argues, some advocates
of Performance Studies, and in this case, Practice-as-Research, are
choosing to ignore how Lyotard's performativity criterion is embedded
at the heart of global capitalism, and how performance can as easily
serve self-legitimising discourses of knowledge and power as it can serve
radical opposition. In the case of both discourses, the self-legitimation of
their own practices as radical has been a discursive performance which
precisely exemplifies McKenzie's point.

The postdramatic

In conclusion, we can see that, despite the much proclaimed death of
the avant-garde, it has somehow succeeded in withstanding the crisis of
recuperation to re-emerge – in concept if not always in name – with its
radical credentials intact. The de-legitimisation of the grand narrative,
the simulacrum, and the resulting scepticism of the real all conspired,
in conjunction with the developments outlined above, to resurrect
an avant-garde narrative in the late 1980s and 1990s that continued to
position itself as radical in opposition to the dramatic text-based form
that was again characterised as an ideologically regressive model in need
of radical deconstruction. This emerging binary was finally consolidated
with the publication of Hans-Thies Lehmann's *Postdramatisches Theater*
in 1999. This was published in English as *Postdramatic Theatre* in 2006,
but the influence of Lehmann's theory was already strongly felt across
the continent and the United Kingdom by this time. Lehmann defines
the various movements of the historical avant-garde as prehistories to
the postdramatic, and thus implicitly locates the postdramatic in the
ongoing avant-garde narrative outlined in this chapter. He later makes
this connection explicit, writing that postdramatic theatre is a term that
can be read 'als repulsiver, diskutierender Bezug des neuen Theaters zur
dramatischen Tradition, als eine Fülle von »konkreten Negationen« des
Dramatischen, die in den historischen Avantgarden und in der Neo-
Avantgarde der 50er und 60er Jahre begonnen hat' (Lehmann, 2002:
16) ('as the new theatre's challenging, combative reference to dramatic
tradition; as a number of "concrete negations" of the dramatic which
began with the avant-garde and the neo-avant-garde of the 50s and 60s')[1]

Where Lehmann's theory significantly diverges from all previous terminologiesisinhisreclaimingoftheterm'theatre'fromtheperformance/ theatre binary, where the term theatre was always implicitly understood, as Karen Jürs-Munby clarifies in her introduction, as the *'theatre of dramas'* (Jürs-Munby, 2006: 21). Lehmann seeks to refine this notion of theatre more explicitly as 'dramatic theatre', which now encompasses Brecht's epic theatre also, leaving space under the wider theatre rubric to position the various models of practice, previously defined as performance, as 'postdramatic theatre'. I interrogate the grounds and applications of Lehmann's definitions in detail in the following chapter, but for now it is most important to note how the postdramatic appears to follow the same ideological positioning and discursive performance of radicalism as the terms of reference it has partially displaced. In her introduction to *Postdramatic Theatre,* Jürs-Munby identifies the 'connection between the historical dominance of drama and a teleological philosophy of history' (Jürs-Munby, 2006: 13) as evidence of the ideological bind which ties the form of dramatic theatre to the Western history of logocentric authority. Consequently, the postdramatic, which interrogates, critiques or deconstructs the dramatic form, simultaneously acts ideologically in its implicit subversion of the logocentric Western history to which drama is bound. Central to this analysis is an understanding of the dramatic theatre form as a representational practice that strives to replicate an external reality. Postdramatic theatre, on the other hand, is described by Lehmann as 'an attempt to conceptualize art in the sense that it offers not a representation but an intentionally unmediated experience of the real' (2006: 134). Consequently, '[i]t is not through the direct thematization of the political that theatre becomes political but through the implicit substance and critical value of its *mode of representation*' (2006: 178, original emphasis). Whilst Lehmann is not entirely convinced by the shift described by Hal Foster between the transgressive political potential of the avant-garde and the resistant political potential of the postmodern, his own theories echo Foster's description of a postmodern political that can only seek to expose the representations that now make up the whole of lived 'reality', and that encompass even the practice that seeks to deconstruct them. Beyond this 'politics of perception', Lehmann concludes, '[a]ll else, even the most perfected political demonstration, would not escape Baudrillard's diagnosis that we are dealing only with circulating simulacra' (2006: 185–6).

The majority of European scholars who have adopted Lehmann's terminology of the postdramatic have also taken up his ideological narrative of radicalism, which is performed in opposition to a dramatic framework that can no longer constitute radical practice in light of its adherence to representational strategies. Nikolaus Müller-Schöll, for example, distinguishes a dramatic tradition of political theatre that accepts the frame of representation, from theatre that is done 'in a political way' by questioning the very frame of the representational form of dramatic theatre (Müller-Schöll, 2004: 42). Müller-Schöll explicitly positions the dramatic model of 'political theatre' as an affirmation of dominant ideology against which postdramatic theatre can be radically opposed:

> Political theatre illustrates or doubles the assumed political reality – be it in order to protest against or to affirm it – and also stabilizes one of the most powerful ideologies of the twentieth century, the so called realism of cinematic narration. It mixes up referential potential and reality and thereby hides the performativity of its performance. Thus it reduces theatre to its plot, forgets the difference between the plot and what is being presented in it and replaces the presented – the 'real' in its continuing 'retreat' – by its concept. (42–3)

The failure of representation

The legacies of the avant-garde, the rise of performance studies, and the emergence of the postdramatic have combined to produce a discursive act which positions representational strategies and dramatic realism as politically moribund in order to assert the radical efficacy of new performance practices in the postmodern era. In his essay on the seminal European company Forced Entertainment, Florian Malzacher dismisses the political efficacy of the Brechtian model which, he claims, 'has become a mere affirmation or mirror of reality and as such, fails as a valid political argument in the same way the bourgeois theatre failed before Brecht began to revolutionize it' (2004: 132). Instead, he holds Forced Entertainment's sceptical deconstructive practice as the new model for a political theatre of our time:

> The art work resists and at the same time points to the world that it can no longer represent: Since this theatre does not work primarily on the level of content, the pressure for attitude that it produces cannot be acted out; the form prevents identification and thus the work becomes political. (134–5)

Sara Jane Bailes likewise identifies the 'failure of representation' in the 'performance theatre' of Forced Entertainment, Goat Island and the Elevator Repair Service as an 'engaged mode of practical resistance' which can be traced through postmodernism back to Marxist theory (2011:

xix). Although Bailes does not support the particular binary opposition between performance and dramatic theatre practice identified by Hoffman, rather insisting that performance expands, rather than breaks, the potential of theatre (Bailes, 2011: 2), the radical nature of the political project that she describes is, like Lehmann's postdramatic, ultimately based on the distinction between a theatre that 'merely reflects or imitates the world' and one that has 'moved us beyond representation' (27).

The radical potential of failure, in Bailes's work, can be traced through a number of different, but related, arguments. Principally, that it counters 'the very ideas of progress and victory that simultaneously dominate historical narratives' and 'undermines the perceived stability of mainstream capitalist ideology's preferred aspiration to achieve, succeed, or win' (2). Correspondingly, failure also mitigates against the commodification of the 'successful' artwork, and 'challenges the cultural dominance of instrumental rationality and the fictions of continuity that bind the way we imagine and manufacture the world' (2). Most significantly, however, the radical nature of Bailes's project ultimately rests on her argument that the highlighting of the failure of representation in performance theatre continues the avant-garde trajectory of Brecht and Artaud in its refusal to replicate the dominant ideological fictions of the real. Rather it seeks to expose them as prescriptive and contingent, and to offer the sense of alternatives through the multiplicity of possibilities that failure shows up. This echoes Tim Etchells's conviction that the 'deeply and always political' theatre of Forced Entertainment 'had to forgo the suspect certainties of what other people called political theatre, that it had to work the territory between the real and the phantasmic' (1999: 19). By rejecting the established or successful forms of theatre that offer convincing representations of the existing real, Bailes argues, performance that seeks out a poetics of failure is theoretically capable of destabilizing the very strategies by which capitalism ensures its own continued hegemony. Drawing on Marx, Bailes argues that

> the effective continuation of the bourgeoisie as the dominant ideology and class comes about through its ability to continually reproduce the (next and imminent) 'world after its own image'; this is instigated through its control over the 'instruments of production'. Thus, the dominant class not only oppresses its people; more critically it prevents the possibility – the imagination and realization – of all other images of the world, and the potential worlds and relationalities those images index. (36)

Such claims arise from Bailes's readings of Adorno, who was one of the first to identify the radical potential of aesthetic form that refused to lend itself to replication of world representations, arguing that '[i]t is not the office of art to spotlight alternatives, but to resist by its form alone the course of the world, which permanently puts a pistol to men's heads' (Adorno, 1977: 180). Adorno's advocation of an autonomous art that could be suspended in isolation from the political world may have become increasingly untenable in the light of the recuperative capacity of late global capitalism, but his argument that aesthetic form can offer radical political transgression, regardless of the specific content or context of the work, remains at the heart of similar claims at the turn of the twenty-first century.

Bailes's argument is persuasive, not least due to her rejection of over-simplistic binary oppositions, and her understanding that the act of failure is just as authored, constructed and skill-based as any other aesthetic. But there is a logical conclusion to the 'success' of such a poetics within the performance during this period, that lies beyond Bailes's own field of concern; namely, the potential of the aesthetic act of failure, through repeated use of the convention, to become the new mark of artistic sophistication and success. This danger echoes the recuperation of the avant-garde whereby an initial challenge to the orthodoxy inevitably becomes, in time, its own orthodoxy, or liminal norm. Whilst a poetics of failure as revealed through 'unconvincing acting, coping (or not), awkwardness, and inability' (Bailes, 2011: 22) might, at one time, or in one context, be read against the values of bourgeois or commercial reproduction, in a different context the same poetics of failure might be read simply as the approved way to achieve a particular aesthetic that has now become well-established with its own rules and prescriptions.

Indeed, artists themselves are beginning to recognise and reference such strategies as conventions that, through overuse and familiarity, have been emptied of their original efficacy. Vincent Dance Theatre's *If We Go On* (2009)[2] begins with two performers coming hesitantly forwards from the back of the stage, nervously huddling together by the microphone, each pressing the other to begin. This is a recognised convention of the aesthetic of failure, offering the illusion that the piece is unrehearsed, and that the performers are inadequately constructing the show in the space and time of the performance. Finally, one performer thrusts a piece of text she is holding into the other's hands, and the second performer reluctantly begins to read from it. What follows is a list of conventions that the piece has pledged to move beyond, including: 'no more dancing, no more classical music, especially Bach, no more partner work'.[3] However, it also acknowledges the accepted vocabularies of its own time, the list continuing: 'no more cliches, including this one, and nothing stolen or borrowed or quoted ... and no more lists after this one'. After four decades in which poststructuralist discourse has added its own motifs to the classical conventions of both theatre and dance, the piece appears to be asking, what is there left that can be done? If not only the classical conventions of dance and theatre but also the strategies of their deconstruction are now little more than comparable representational motifs, what can dance or theatre offer beyond countless reconfigurations of familiar historical vocabularies. As one of the performers uncomfortably realises, 'If we start like this ... it doesn't really leave us anywhere to go, does it?'

The Marxist understanding, on which Bailes draws, of the capacity of radical form to subvert the capability of the bourgeois world 'to continually reproduce the (next and imminent) "world after its own image"' (Marx and Engels, 1988: 213, in Bailes, 2011: 36), takes insufficient account of the capacity for late capitalism to recuperate the radical forms that were originally devised to combat its hegemony and employ them, instead, as highly marketable 'alternatives' for its own economic and ideological ends. As James Frieze astutely comments, '[f]ailure may not exactly be the new success, but ... in some respects it is the new power' (2009: 20), an observation which the artistic longevity of the aesthetic amongst leading international companies and emerging new work bears out.

In the following chapter, the postdramatic challenge to dramatic representation will be analysed in detail, but what I hope this chapter has highlighted is the sustained discursive performance of radicalism that has supported the legacy of the avant-garde narrative up to and into the twenty-first century. However this legacy is labelled, and however diverse its manifestations, its recurring characteristics are pinned to the same ideological imperative that seeks to undermine, critique, expose or deconstruct the representational practices, or mimetic repetitions of the real, which are, in turn, bound to the text-based, dramatic and, arguably, logocentric tradition of Western theatre. What the following chapter aims to achieve is not a reversal of this discursive performance but a rigorous analysis of its arguments and deconstruction of its imperatives, to investigate where its own logos, or centre of authority, might lie. What I hope will become clear throughout the remainder of this study is that the plurality of new performance practices at this point in history can no longer be categorised as an ideologically coherent movement purely on the basis of their shared opposition to a particular, and strategically defined, model of dramatic theatre.

Notes

1   All quotations from Lehmann, 2002 are translated by Leila Mukhida for the purposes of this study.

2   This analysis is based on the performance of *If We Go On* at Carriageworks Theatre, Leeds, on 8 October 2009.

3   This and all following quotations are taken from the unpublished performance text of *If We Go On*, written by Charlotte Vincent and Wendy Houstoun, made available to me courtesy of Vincent Dance Theatre.

2

Deconstructing the postdramatic: questions of mimesis, authorship and representation

Lehmann's categorisation of postdramatic theatre has offered scholars, students and artists useful and much needed vocabularies that can be employed in the analysis of performance practice (2006). However, in common with any groundbreaking study, there remains much to be debated and challenged concerning the initial premises that have been laid down. While it may have been far from Lehmann's intention, the enthusiastic uptake of his definition of the postdramatic, and his own focus on the 'dramatic' as the postdramatic's 'other', too often encourage the division of theatre practice into an either/or binary configuration. Yet, as Jerzy Limon observes in his historical overview of theatrical precedents to the postdramatic from the medieval theatre to the court masque, 'what Lehmann understands as the dramatic theater is in fact just one of many theatrical trends, which did not predominate in all periods' (Limon, 2011: 261). Moreover, whilst Lehmann does specifically detach performance art from the theatre umbrella altogether, there is little said about other new performance practices that do not take the dramatic tradition as their reference point. I would argue that contemporary manifestations of physical theatre, such as the UK's Company F/Z and North American company Pig Iron, whilst clearly not working within a dramatic rubric, are equally difficult to categorise as postdramatic, as their wide range of performance vocabularies are not devised in primary relation to the conventions of the dramatic but are rather drawn from traditions such as dance, music, cabaret and circus in order to tell stories in ways that move beyond the verbal.

As I argued in Chapter 1, Lehmann's analysis has also consolidated an existing ideological binary through his configuration of the postdramatic as radical and its dramatic 'other' as logocentric. Key to this binary has been the postdramatic's rejection of the theocratic authority held by the playwright in the dramatic tradition, as I will detail in this chapter. Yet, the ideological binary has remained firmly in place even as the definitions of the postdramatic have expanded to accommodate text-driven work and may, moreover, have been the very trigger for such expansion. As the dramatic became characterised as a form that was incapable of radical impact, it is easy to see how it might become a strategic act for artists and theorists to protect all new work they wished to develop or support from its pejorative implications. So when work emerges, such as that of Sarah Kane, which is arguably both broadly dramatic in form and radical in its poststructuralist rupturing of the governing principles of the dramatic, then the coherence of Lehmann's initial conflation of ideology and form is threatened. Rather than a return, on the part of theorists, to reconsider and re-evaluate the conflation, what has occurred, I would suggest, is an ever-widening of the postdramatic boundaries to ensure that all potentially radical work can be encompassed within its ever-broadening remit, and a corresponding narrowing of the boundaries of the dramatic until it starts to look indistinguishable from social realism, as I will explore in the course of this chapter.

One further consequence of this expansion is that as more and more text-based work is categorised as postdramatic, the terrain of that which is left to the dramatic becomes more and more limited. If the detail of the distinctions that scholars are increasingly making between dramatic texts and postdramatic texts were equally understood and employed in the wider theatre industry, then this might be less problematic. There is, however, a danger that as the scholarly understanding of what the term 'dramatic' conveys narrows, the pejorative associations with the term become intensified. This intensification of the ideological critique of the dramatic is then dispersed into the wider theatre industry, but without the detail of the distinction. Consequently, beyond the rigour of academic analysis, the ideological critique of the dramatic is too often applied to the much broader 'text-driven' definition that Lehmann initially advocated, and which was already under attack by the 'liminal norm' effect of performance studies as described in Chapter 1.

To address the implications outlined above, this chapter will seek to interrogate the premises for the postdramatic's narrative of radicalism – now widely adopted and developed beyond Lehmann's initial analysis – in order to destabilise the ideological binary that it has engendered, and which I do not believe is sustainable under its own terms. Such an interrogation will involve a further 'digging down' into the poststructuralist project of Jacques Derrida, that has substantively provided the philosophical basis for the early twenty-first century's postdramatic challenge to dramatic representation.

Challenges to the dramatic

Lehmann constructs his definition of the postdramatic on the foundations of Peter Szondi's 1965 study of the dramatic model (Szondi, 1987). Szondi outlines the characteristics of 'pure' drama as 'conscious of nothing outside itself', where the narrative is driven exclusively by dialogue between the characters, and 'should in no way be perceived as coming from the author', any more than the drama should be perceived as addressing itself to the spectator, who is rather 'an observer – silent, with hands tied, lamed by the impact of this other world' (1987: 8). Szondi's insistence on seeing 'pure' drama as 'primary', happening only in the present tense with events driven by the dialogue that ensues from moment to moment, leads him to position Ibsen and Chekhov as disrupters of the 'pure' drama. This analysis is substantiated by the dominance of Ibsen's backstory as a driver in the present, and the 'reveries of remembrance and utopian thought' that position Chekhov's events as incidental, and his dialogue as a 'vessel for monologic reflection' (45). The subtleties of Szondi's analysis are rarely taken up by more recent theorists writing on theatre or performance, and his distinctions between 'pure' and 'impure' drama are generally discarded, with Ibsen and Chekhov often seen as the standard-bearers of the classic model of dramatic realism/naturalism to which a postdramatic theatre is regularly opposed. Lehmann undertakes a more rigorous analysis of the dramatic model than most, acknowledging Szondi's distinctions between pure and impure before offering his own analysis, which positions the dramatic model, at possibly its most comprehensive, to encompass not only Chekhov and Ibsen but also the Absurdists and Brecht. Given that Lehmann casts the dramatic net as widely as he does, coupled with the phenomenal influence of his analysis and terminology, particularly in the United Kingdom and continental Europe, we will adopt his initial definition of the dramatic as a starting-point, although, as this chapter will demonstrate, the parameters were soon to shift.

Lehmann continues to identify the dramatic primarily by the characteristics proposed by Szondi: a dialogue-driven narrative closed off from author and spectator; or, in Lehmann's terms, a 'conflict of figures, and totality of plot and world representation' (2006: 54). However, Lehmann argues that *any* piece of theatre which substantively utilises these conventions is more dramatic than not. Thus, despite the non-realism, absence of event, explicit meta-theatricality, and non-consequential nature of dialogue in many absurdist texts, or the alienation techniques through which the spectator is directly addressed in Brecht's epic theatre, Lehmann positions both as dramatic models that may contain certain subversions, but are, nevertheless, primarily situated in that historical tradition. Against this broader conception of the dramatic model, postdramatic theatre is characterised as challenging drama's most widely recognised conventions: the authority of the pre-written text, the actor's seamless representation of character, the dominance of interpersonal dialogue, and the representation of a 'closed' fictional world that hides its author and spectator in order to reflect an originary 'reality', and appear complete in and of itself. As this chapter will detail, such attempts to deconstruct the drama consequently tend to result in performances that emphasise the absence of a pre-written text's authority, the presence of the actor, the predominance of monologues or direct address, and the 'real' time and place of the performance event that acknowledges its audience and explicitly frames any fictional worlds as constructed. In this way, the postdramatic might appear to be the direct descendant of the avant-garde, postmodern and poststructuralist interrogations of the dramatic model. The postdramatic's perceived radicalism, as outlined in Chapter 1, likewise arises from its challenges to the logocentric assumptions of Western philosophy that have long been assumed to underpin the dramatic model of theatre. As proposed in the introduction to this study, the most influential critic of such logocentric assumptions is Jacques Derrida, whose project set out to destabilise the notion of originary meaning upon which all subsequent narratives could validate their claims. In the context of theatre and performance studies, Derrida's poststructuralist project, like Lehmann's postdramatic, has most commonly been used to interrogate the dramatic model, which is perceived to uphold the myth of originary meaning in a number of ways. Under particular examination in this chapter are three of the most common poststructuralist charges levelled at the dramatic model: firstly, that it upholds the origin myth through its mimetic repetition of reality; secondly, that it upholds the origin myth through its dependence on a theological playwright; and, finally, that it offers an illusion of original presence that conceals its reliance on repetition and representation. Each of these charges is echoed in Lehmann's postdramatic critique, which has led to a common conflation of the postdramatic with poststructuralist theory. However, by returning to the detail of Derrida's poststructuralist project, I hope to highlight the potential for misapplication of his theories and, by so doing, undermine the existing and prevalent philosophical and ideological binary of a conservative, logocentric dramatic versus a radical, poststructuralist postdramatic.

The mimetic charge

In 'The theatre of cruelty and the closure of representation' (2001), Derrida addresses Artaud's vision that calls for a wholesale rejection of the classical structure of Western theatre. Artaud's critique focuses specifically on the text-based or literary nature of this tradition, which we will return to, and its mimetic representations of the 'real', with which we will begin. It is worth noting at this point that, whilst Derrida seeks to elucidate Artaud's own criticisms of the Western theatre tradition, there is a key philosophical distinction between Artaud's vision and Derrida's own radical scepticism of presence that can sometimes be overlooked. This distinction is, however, central to the contradictions within certain applications of the poststructuralist critique of dramatic theatre that this chapter seeks to resolve, and so will be highlighted accordingly.

Throughout the article, Derrida draws attention to Artaud's desire 'to have done with the *imitative* concept of art, with the Aristotelian aesthetics in which the metaphysics of Western art comes into its own' (Derrida, 2001: 295, original emphasis), citing Artaud's contention that 'Art is not the imitation of life' (Artaud, 1970b: 310 in Derrida, 2001: 295). This suspicion of theatrical representation as a second-rate copy of an authentic 'reality' is traced, by Jonas Barish, all the way back to Plato, whose anti-theatricalism arose from his understanding of theatre as a mimetic copy of the real world that, in itself, was merely a copy of the 'eternal idea' from the 'kingdom of the forms' (Barish, 1981: 6). Artaud's theatre of cruelty can be seen to belong to this lineage, as Barish and Marvin Carlson (2002) have both observed, in that it refuses the representational, aspiring instead, as Derrida affirms, to be 'life itself, in the extent to which life is unrepresentable. Life is the non-representable origin of representation' (2001: 294).

It is, however, this very notion of 'origin' that is central to Derrida's metaphysical scepticism, as his more extended discussion of mimesis in 'The Double Session' suggests (1981: 193). Firstly, he proposes, mimesis can refer to 'the presentation of the thing itself', a movement through which the thing 'appears (to itself) as it really is'; and secondly, it can constitute 'a relation of *homoiosis* or *adaequatio* between two (terms)' that 'can more readily be translated as imitation' (1981: 193). In both cases, he argues, within Plato's discourse it is 'lined up alongside truth: either it hinders the unveiling of the thing itself by substituting a copy or double for what it is; or else it works in the service of truth through the double's resemblance' (187). On these grounds, Derrida can be seen to critique the anteriority of Plato's discursive framework of mimetic imitation that has been fundamental to the anti-theatrical prejudice Barish outlines. Addressing Plato's analysis, which posits '"reality", the thing itself' against the imitation that follows, 'the painting, the portrait, the zographeme, the inscription or transcription of the thing itself' (191), Derrida notes that, under the 'profound synonymy' of logic, this precisely leads to an order that assumes that 'what is imitated is more real, more essential, more true, etc., than what imitates. It is anterior and superior to it.' (191) Derrida identifies such an order as integral to metaphysics, noting that 'never have the absolute distinguishability between imitated and imitator, and the anteriority of the first over the second, been displaced by any metaphysical system' (192). However mimesis is defined, he argues, 'the presence of the present is its norm, its order, its law. It is in the name of truth, its only reference – *reference* itself – that *mimesis* is judged, proscribed or prescribed' (193, original emphasis). Read through Derridean theory, dramatic representations of 'the real' are undermined not by their inferior status, which renders them a copy of a more authentic 'real' (a criticism that would be upheld by Plato and Artaud), but by the fact that they are working in compliance with the order of mimesis, or 'the process of truth' (193), that Derrida's entire project of deconstruction has undermined. The poststructuralist scepticism of any originary real that is anterior to any imitation of it can be thus seen to support successive critiques of mimetic representations, which implicitly uphold the illusion of the real, and conspire against Derrida's radical deconstruction of the metaphysical order of the truth.

Mimesis and the postdramatic

Lehmann argues that the mimetic tradition of drama is the inevitable consequence of its adherence to an Aristotelean notion of action which, he argues, 'seems to entail thinking the aesthetic form of theatre as a variable dependent on another reality – life, human behaviour, reality, etc' (2006: 36–7). Echoing Artaud, he concludes that '[t]his reality always precedes the double of theatre as the original' (37). Lehmann's most extended discussion of the logocentric implications of mimetic representation is undertaken in *Das Politische Schreiben* in his chapter, 'Wie Politisch ist Postdramatisches Theater' (2002) (How Political is

Postdramatic Theatre).[1] Here Lehmann establishes the political potential of the postdramatic in opposition to practice that offers the 'geläufige Vorstellung von »politischem« Theater' (2002: 12) (current conceptions of political theatre), which seek to offer mimetic representations of the real. The argument that Lehmann advances in this essay is detailed and often persuasive in its critique of a model of theatre that draws its representations from 'real' life. He argues that 'eine theatrale Re-Präsentation von in der Realität als politisch definierten Problemen' (2002: 12) (a theatrical re-presentation of problems that are defined as 'political' in real life) will do nothing to disrupt, and may even confirm, the existing consensus of views we are already bombarded with by the media. Such a theatre, he continues, will inevitably mirror 'die alltägliche (De)formation des Politischen zum Drama, zu pseudo-dramatischen Konflikten und dramatis personae' (2002: 18) (the daily (de)formation of the political into drama, pseudo-dramatic conflicts and dramatis personae) that already circulates in public discourse, and acts to obscure the power relations which occupy a place somewhere between 'Verwaltungs- und Geheimdienstakten, Öl- und Softwareinteressen, Politikerreden, Medienpropaganda einschließlich Menschenrechtspropaganda, politischen Morden, wo nötig, und weiträumigen geopolitischen, imperialen oder auch imperialistischen Strategien' (2002: 17) (administrative and secret-service practice, oil and software interests, speeches by politicians, media propaganda and human rights propaganda, political assassinations and large-scale geopolitical, imperial or imperialist strategies).

Lehmann's analysis holds such practice up to the poststructuralist charge on two counts: firstly, in its adherence to a mimetic structure that complies with the metaphysical 'process of truth' as identified by Derrida; and, secondly, in its propagation of ideological narratives that are made to appear as if they were true and / or inevitable. It might be assumed, given the similarity of terms of reference used in his earlier and seminal study, *Postdramatisches Theater* (1999), that the discredited models of political representations that he describes here are examples of the dramatic model, yet, in this more detailed argument, the work described would more accurately come under the heading of social-realist. The potential reduction of the wider dramatic model to this particular subset of it is also suggested by Nikolaus Müller-Schöll who, likewise, positions the radical potential of postdramatic experimental practice in opposition to a discredited notion of the social-realist model of political theatre, which 'illustrates or doubles the assumed political reality' as noted in Chapter 1 (2004: 42–3). Under such analysis, it is more accurately social-realism against which the poststructuralist charge of mimesis is levelled, not any wider understanding of the dramatic. In turn, this would suggest that not all dramatic theatre is necessarily guilty of the mimetic charge; nor does it necessarily stand outside of a poststructuralist aesthetic, a possibility which is clearly exemplified, as I will now argue, in the work of Howard Barker.

The poststructuralist dramatic?

Lehmann's objections to social realism, as summarised above, are echoed in the theoretical framework that underpins the theatre of playwright and director Howard Barker, which will be examined in further detail in Chapter 3. In the manifesto *Arguments for a Theatre*, Barker reiterates the now familiar opposition to a theatre tradition that trades in mimetic representations, and so subordinates the art of theatre 'to the suffocating principle of *imitation*' (Barker, 1993a: 110, original emphasis). Barker, like Derrida, understands mimesis as 'a project of representation … [t]he essential characteristic of such a form is the notion of truth, a truth which can be validated only by an act of recognition' (109). Like Lehmann and Müller-Schöll, Barker posits his own notion of radical theatre against, what he calls, 'the political play' which shows 'what is', and thus replicates that which is already 'annexed, reproduced, soporific' (23). However, Barker specifically defines such a theatre as naturalistic or social-realist, and understands his own work not as postdramatic but as the return to a historical notion of the dramatic, which was never concerned with mimetic imitation of the real, but a re-imagining of it:

> Decades of naturalistic drama – and the political and social values that attach to it – had taught this individual member of the audience that the sole purpose of showing an action on stage was to achieve the highest proximity to human experience, and that any deviation from it constituted an offence against the collective – was in effect, lying. What I was groping towards … was an emphatic disassociation, a rupture, between stage and reality, in effect a licence to lie … [t]his, of course, is no more than a description of dramatic method before the nineteenth century. (95–6)

Barker acknowledges that '[r]ecognition is the governing principle of the dramatic form which has dominated European theatre practice since the Enlightenment' (109), but where his theoretical critique diverges from the postdramatic critique is in his understanding that whilst it might have been the governing principle, that does not mean that to subvert or ignore such a principle is to necessarily reject the greater potentials of the dramatic form. He thus posits his own work, in opposition to social realism, as a tragic form for our age, which he terms catastrophism. His theatre of catastrophe, as he defines it, possesses the 'classic dramatic values, such as narrative, structure, character or language', but is nevertheless 'irreducible to a set of meanings' (80). In this way, Barker argues for a re-conceptualisation of the potential of the dramatic to deconstruct its own one-time governing principles of 'clarity, meaning, logic and consistency' (43), and to utilize strategies such as the anti-parable or anti-chorus to disrupt the otherwise seductive potential of narrative to induce a clear moral perspective (121–2). In this sense, the poststructuralist heritage of Barker's theatre underpins its aspirations to be 'not a disseminator of truth but a provider of versions' (45).

Barker has been a seminal influence on a significant number of playwrights, including, most notably, Sarah Kane; and the characteristics of his theatre outlined above could also be applied to the texts of Adriano Shaplin, Anthony Nielson and Roland Schimmelpfennig, among others. I will return to Barker and Schimmelpfennig in more detail in Chapter 3, but for now, what is critical to note is that Barker's theatre of catastrophe, in its reclaiming of the tragic form of the dramatic, offers an alternative framework of analysis, which more accurately limits one particular aspect of the mimetic charge, levelled by postdramatic and poststructuralist theory alike, to the dramatic subset of social realism.

The theological playwright

However, whilst Barker's work rejects mimetic representation and disrupts the ideological implications of traditional forms of narrative, it is inarguably driven by his own singular authorship, notwithstanding the richness of his productions' visual and aural scenescapes. The primacy of text in Barker's work is shared by all the writers mentioned above, which might suggest that the wider dramatic form, as I have proposed it, is not immune from the charge of the theological playwright which, as I shall now elucidate, produces its own mimetic order, regardless of the playwright's rejection of any mimetic relation to an external reality, or the contingency of the meanings it provokes.

The identification of the author as theological was established most prominently by Roland Barthes in the 1970s, in his seminal article, 'The death of the author' (1977). In this article, Barthes addresses the literary critical tradition that positions the author, like God, as the origin of meaning in relation to the text. Barthes argues that in order to free the meaning(s) available to a text from the imposition of such unilateral authority, the concept of the 'author' must be annulled. He writes, 'once the Author is removed, the claim to decipher a text becomes quite futile.

To give a text an Author is to impose a limit on that text, to furnish it with a final signified, to close the writing' (147). Barthes goes on to conflate the authority of the author explicitly with the theological authority of God, and advocates instead a writing in which:

> everything is to be *disentangled*, nothing *deciphered*; ... writing ceaselessly posits meaning ceaselessly to evaporate it, carrying out a systematic ex-emption of meaning. In precisely this way ... *writing*, by refusing to assign a 'secret', an ultimate meaning, to the text (and to the world as text), liber-ates what may be called an anti-theological activity, an activity that is truly revolutionary since to refuse to fix meaning is, in the end, to refuse God and his hypostases – reason, science, law. (147, original emphasis)

This rejection of the concept of originary authority is central to the poststructuralist discourse. The shift of authority from the 'maker' to the reader is at the heart of poststructuralism's radical potential, as it mirrors the rejection of divine or metaphysical 'origins' for singular 'meaning', and the turn to subjectively constructed and contingent meanings that are plural and relative. Thus, the radical narrative is allied to performance texts that offer, not the traditional linear and coherent narrative of the dramatic, but fragmented and plural narratives, with no recognisable plot structure to offer up an authorised 'meaning' to the spectator. In such texts, as Sara Jane Bailes observes, '[m]eaning is, rather, viewed as contingent, a thing to be made or arranged, "posited," but as easily abandoned, revised, or renegotiated' (2011: 13). However, Barthes' conflation of literal author and the metaphorical authorship of meaning (which in a literary context makes complete sense) does lend itself to misinterpretation when applied to the field of theatre in which multiple 'authorities' combine in the production of the final work, text-based or otherwise. What is rather required here is the application of Barthes' critique, as Foucault would propose, to the 'author *function*' as it manifests itself variously across artistic models and discourses, to interrogate where, in any model of performance, the authorship of meaning(s) might lie, and to what degree such meanings are originary and singular, or multiple and contingent (Foucault, 1984: 108, my emphasis). It is not sufficient for ensemble, non-dramatic or non-text-based models to merely, as Foucault observes, 'repeat the empty affirmation that the author has disappeared ... [i]nstead we must locate the space left empty by the author's disappearance, follow the distribution of gaps and breaches, and watch for the openings that this disappearance uncovers' (1984: 105). To do otherwise is to reject the metaphorical significance of Barthes' 'death of the author' and apply it too literally in order to explicitly align the author-god with the playwright only, thus substantiating the exclusive alignment of the dramatic model with the theocratic authority of originary meaning.

Such an alignment is often supported by Artaud's critique of the Western theatre tradition that was significantly and explicitly centred on a condemnation of Western theatre's subservience to the pre-written text. Again, it was the recurring notion of repetition that disturbed Artaud, the misuse of the stage to 'illustrate a discourse' that was not in and of the moment, and the consequent subjugation of visual, musical and gestural vocabularies to the 'tyranny of the text' (Derrida, 2001: 297–8). Derrida elucidates Artaud's critique as follows:

> The stage is theological for as long as it is dominated by speech, by a will to speech, by the layout of a primary logos which does not belong to the theatrical site and governs it from a distance. The stage is theological for as long as its structure, following the entirety of tradition, comports the following elements: an author-creator who, absent and from afar, is armed with a text and keeps watch over, assembles, regulates the time or the meaning of representation. (Derrida, 2001: 296)

Derrida's reading of Artaud underlines the latter's critique of the model of Western theatre that was content to merely repeat the 'primary logos which does not belong to the theatrical site'. Regardless of its relationship to the 'real' world beyond the theatre, and regardless of any retreat from the notion of a singular meaning, so long as the subsequently constructed theatrical elements are required to defer, in the first instance, to the originary reference points of the playwright, the performance itself will remain a secondary copy, or repetition, of the text. And while the stage remains governed by the requirement to illustrate or represent the words which came before it, it will continue to comply with the order of mimesis as Derrida understands it, upholding the notion of an original which is anterior to any imitation.

On these grounds, the playtext, even when subversive or open-ended, as exemplified by writers such as Howard Barker, positions the playwright as the originary source for meaning(s), however multiple and indeterminate such meaning(s) might be. Regardless of whether or not the given text offers mimetic representations of a 'reality' beyond the theatre, the performance itself will remain a secondary copy to which the 'original' script is anterior, thus complying with the 'process of truth' as Derrida understands it. If no text-driven work can escape this particular logocentric bind, then is this the charge under which Lehmann's ideological distinction between the (text-driven) dramatic and the (non-text-driven) postdramatic can be best supported?

The theological text and the postdramatic

The exclusive alignment of text-driven performance with the dramatic model has undergone significant developments since it was first proposed by Lehmann in 1999. Lehmann's own analysis of the role of text in the postdramatic is not straightforward; at times he appears to acknowledge that certain playwrights, such as Beckett and Müller, are outside of the dramatic tradition, but contemporary and comparable playwrights, such as Elfriede Jelinek and Sarah Kane, are ambiguously defined as 'retaining the dramatic dimension to different degrees' (2006: 18). However, he does appear to consistently argue that a postdramatic practice should not be text-*driven*, but should assign 'the dominant role to elements other than dramatic logos and language' (2006: 93).

In the introduction to her translation of Lehmann's study, Karen Jürs-Munby already indicates her own divergence from Lehmann's analysis, claiming that the 'turn to performance' in texts by Martin Crimp and Sarah Kane, among others, necessitates that such texts are to be considered postdramatic, 'in the sense that they require the spectators to become active co-writers of the (performance) text' (Jürs-Munby, 2006: 6). The vast majority of theatre scholars to address the postdramatic have followed this lead in broadening the parameters of the postdramatic to encompass certain text-driven work, and it is significant that, in *Das Politische Schreiben*, Lehmann himself highlighted Sarah Kane's *Blasted* as radical practice, in opposition to the representational strategies of social-realist theatre (Lehmann, 2002). In relation to Lehmann's own understanding of the postdramatic–dramatic binary this suggests one of two things. Either his understanding of what constitutes 'dramatic theatre' does indeed extend beyond the representational strategies of social-realism (thus complicating the usual conflation of mimetic realism with the entire terrain of the dramatic, as discussed in the previous section), or he has come to accept that the postdramatic framework can include text-driven practice. The now-widespread consensus among scholars that work can be both text-driven and postdramatic inclines me to conclude that Lehmann, by 2002, is also in agreement with this development. Either way, its current ubiquity as a definition of the postdramatic, regardless of Lehmann's own acceptance or objection, requires that it now stands as the predominant analysis. However, the consequence of such a development is that Lehmann's initial alignment of the radical postdramatic with a poststructuralist interrogation of the originary position of the dramatic playwright no longer constitutes a meaningful distinction, if the same originary position can be found in work categorised as postdramatic.

In order to maintain the radical narrative for such work, additional distinctions need to be identified. This is precisely the project that has been undertaken by scholars of the postdramatic, as I shall detail presently, who suggest that it is the theological nature of the text-driven dramatic model that can be circumvented by the postdramatic text, despite the latter's same upholding of the originary positioning of the playwright and consequent compliance with the 'process of truth'.

Through close examination of this argument I will contend, however, that the theocratic authorship identified by Derrida is not so easy to evade, and that neither the text-driven dramatic nor the text-driven postdramatic can justifiably claim to do so. As my conclusion to the previous section suggested, my argument is not that the dramatic can find a way to escape the binds of this particular authority but that the text-driven postdramatic cannot claim to do so either. The question of radical poststructuralist potential in relation to the charge of theocratic authorship needs to be differently understood.

'Unsettling the heritage to which [it] belong[s]'

Scholars such as Karen Jürs-Munby, David Barnett and Małgorzata Sugiera do not base their radical analysis of postdramatic theatre on its disruption of the originary authority of the written text that pre-dates and informs the making process, but on distinctions they draw between the form and structure of postdramatic text and the form and structure of the dramatic model as identified by Lehmann. In this sense, they substantiate the insight by Martin Puchner that Artaud's legacy of 'antitextual prejudice' has only recently been transformed 'through the influence of a very different understanding of text and writing' (Puchner, 2006: 199). Foregrounded among the distinctions that are said to mark postdramatic models of text are: the lack of identifiable and consistent characterisation, a replacement of dialogue with direct address, an emphasis on monologic or choric structures, and a consequent inclusion of the audience within the world of the performance. Karen Jürs-Munby describes how Elfriede Jelinek's texts 'tend to lack a dramatic plot, psychological characters and often the form of a dialogue or even indicated speakers' (Jürs-Munby, 2009: 46), whilst David Barnett, talking of Martin Crimp's *Attempts on her Life* and Sarah Kane's *4.48 Psychosis* notes that 'character and plot, the mainstays of dramatic theatre, are no longer categories that need enter the stage in an age in which the act of representation has become increasingly untenable' (2008: 23).

As I have argued elsewhere (Tomlin, 2009), and will exemplify and elucidate in Chapter 3, there remain inconsistencies in distinctions that rely on an over-simplistic opposition of character/dialogue/dramatic against absence of character/absence of dialogue/postdramatic. However, even if accepting the limited functionality of the above distinction that is commonly adopted, I will now suggest that it does not follow that the postdramatic forms of text or language identified can avoid the theological or logocentric authority levelled at the dramatic model by certain postdramatic and poststructuralist critics alike.

Lehmann argues that the shift away from dialogue, defined after Julia Kristeva as the '"polylogue" of the new theatre', breaks away from 'an order centred on *one* logos' (Lehmann, 2006: 32, original emphasis); yet such a shift might also be read as better concealing the hidden logos of the still existent author behind a multiplicity of choric voices in the absence of coherent character. Proposing such a reading, Andrej Wirth's argument that 'the figures only seem to be speaking... [i]t would be more accurate to say that they are being spoken by the author of the script' (Wirth, 1980: 19 in Lehmann, 2006: 31), deserves more consideration than Lehmann affords it. Jon Erickson, likewise, argues that, despite the multiplicity of performers, much avant-garde practice, as he terms it, essentially operates from 'a base in monologue' where performers 'are not "people" in the characterological sense' but 'speaking machines for some overall intent of the group or director' (2003: 177). He concludes by wondering

> if splitting one monologue into many vocal parts really does indicate 'multiplicity' or if it ends up indicating the opposite: a weird kind of conformity. One might then view the multiplicities of the fragmented self as conducive to the habitation of an immense totalizing voice, which is everyone's and no one's. (178)

If the polylogue does not guarantee an escape from singularity, perhaps it nevertheless offers a strategy whereby language is able to confront and undermine its own logocentric history. As Karen Jürs-Munby argues, the use of 'polyphonic composition' in Elfriede Jelinek's work offers a reading of language 'as something preexisting the individual who enters it', and further argues that 'ideology... can only be perceived if language is exhibited on stage as such' (2009: 49). Derrida himself claims that all tools of logocentrism, including language, 'are indispensable for unsettling the heritage to which they belong' (1974: 14). Consequently, the capacity for text to be employed against itself in order to undermine its own authority is part and parcel of the potential duplicity of both written and spoken text, as Derrida understands it.

The strategy, referenced by Jürs-Munby, of exhibiting language on the stage in order to interrogate its logos, was first identified as a strategy of Derridean deconstruction by Elinor Fuchs in 1985, and has proved extraordinarily long-lived (Fuchs, 1985). Fuchs identified a trend in the performance of the late 1970s for artists to deconstruct the dramatic tradition by literally revealing the hidden authority of the pre-written text, through presenting the script itself, as a visible object, on the stage. Over thirty years later the prominence of the on-stage text, and the complementary strategies designed to undermine the dramatic model's illusion of spontaneous speech, show few signs of abating. Building on the early experiments of the Wooster Group, and the more recent practice of Forced Entertainment, performance in the twenty-first century continues to abound in performers reading other people's words from scraps of paper, unconvinced by what they are speaking, eschewing ownership and undermining the authority of the words that come out of their own mouths. Even when the explicit signifier of scripted text is absent, much spoken text is coloured with the implication that it doesn't belong to its speaker, communicated through an emotional delivery which bears no resemblance to the meaning of the words, or spoken deadpan, or broken up to destroy its sense altogether. Tim Etchells describes this aesthetic in relation to the work of Forced Entertainment:

> In performance we use the struggle to feel right in the text, and the distance between the performer and her text is always visible. In recent shows this gap is all the more visible because the text features as paper or script – a physical object which can be picked up, handled, subjected to scrutiny, curiosity, indifference, contempt. In the work you can see the performers eyeing up the text, wondering about it, knowing that whatever it is it isn't them. (1999: 105)

In postdramatic theatre, it seems, language is used, not to wield an invisible and ideological authority as in dramatic theatre, but rather to expose its own indeterminacy. Jean-Pierre Sarrazac suggests that it is precisely this vulnerability that differentiates between the old epic voice that authorised, and the 'new' epic voice that undermines its own authority. Cathy Turner and Syrnne Behrndt offer a translation of Sarrazac's description of the new voice as 'the hesitant, veiled, stammering voice of the modern rhapsode … a voice of questions, voice of doubts, of palinodes, voice of the multiplication of possibilities' (Sarrazac, 1998: 201–2 in Behrndt and Turner, 2008: 191). As Etchells confesses:

> Perhaps our first subject was always this inadequacy of language. Its unsuitability for the job it has to do, its failure. And in this failure – by defi-

nition language is not and cannot express what it seeks to describe – an admission of the struggle in everyday life – to get blunt tools to do fine work, to carve out a life in, around, despite of and through what passes for culture in the late twentieth century ... Language transfixed on its own inadequacy. Language at the point of breakdown, at the edges of sense, on the edge of not coping at all. (1999: 102)

Sara Jane Bailes frames this new use of language within a 'poetics of failure' that 'establishes an aperture, an opening onto several (and often many) other ways of doing that counter the authority of a singular or "correct" outcome' (2011: 2). Bailes outlines a series of familiar strategies by which this 'aperture' can be established, including technical mediation of the voice on stage, the 'withdrawal of emotional "triggers"', the refunctioning of language by 'fragmenting and decontextualizing it or by playing with genre, tense, person, syntactical arrangement, often relying heavily on copying passages of text from videos and film' (19). This notion of a performer's failure to 'successfully' represent an 'authentic real' through language or other performance vocabularies recurs insistently in theoretical studies of new performance practices throughout the 1990s and 2000s, and is consolidated in Bailes' *Performance Theatre and the Poetics of Failure* (2011), as discussed more fully in Chapter 1. Arguably, the international influence of Forced Entertainment's work, certainly across the United Kingdom and Europe, and the corresponding theoretical concerns with the notion of failure, have led to an almost exclusive focus on the indeterminacy of language within both postdramatic and poststructuralist discourses of performance. However, this comes at the expense of the acknowledgement that, in order to assert itself as inadequate, language is still wielding its old authority, albeit to maintain a new narrative.

This duplicity of language was highlighted in Vincent Dance Theatre's *If We Go On*,[2] which exhibited an excess of language both to undermine its legitimacy and, simultaneously, to expose its operations of a more covert authority. The structure of the piece was characterised by discrete scores, or units of action, separated by periods of rest, or non-action. The latter were all introduced and referenced as indicated by the following example:

> There will be a short pause before continuing. After which there will be small breaks and gaps until the next rest. Following which there will be intermittent stops and starts to give time to prepare to go again.[3]

Sometimes the introduction would be followed by silence for the duration

1   Scott Smith in *If We Go On.*
Photographer: Hugo Glendinning

of the pause, at other times the text continued, delivered in a monotone by a single performer from behind the sound desk he was operating:

Although it may not be the same kind of pause that we were looking for.

It may, in fact, be more like a gap, which we know has a definite length, and we may slowly start to feel a bit like we are waiting – like we are being a bit dutiful, but we will surrender to the pause from now until then.

[…] Language.

BLOODY LANGUAGE.

The insistence, The sheer bloody insistence – spelling it all out, dragging it all up, stamping all over your hard-earned pause, your hard-won quiet.

[…] Bring back the quiet. Reinstate the silence. Those smart-arsed words, umming and erring all over the place, creeping in, throwing their weight around. It used to be just … – silence and a kind of agreement … no arguments, no misunderstandings, no discrepancies, no indecision, none of that problematising or thematic definition, but at first it's a little bit of *I am not sure what you mean by that* and *we all understand something different when you say* ... and then it's a little bit of *You won't really want to hear this but* [...] and someone in charge is saying *show me, show me* and *could we gather together for a moment* and *has anyone got any thoughts on that* and *shall we share* ... [emphasis in original]

Language is exposed here as something that uses its discursive authority to destroy artistic processes, such as dance, that have traditionally looked to evade its control.

Even as we are being told, in the above text, that language is ruining the productive and creative silence of the pause, the crime language is accused of committing continues to be compounded by the relentless verbalised indictment; the more the indictment is explicated, justified, expounded, the more totalising the offence of language's imposition becomes. In this way, as in much poststructuralist performance, language can be seen as the best medium to undermine its own authority, yet, paradoxically, it necessarily draws on that authority to do so. The relentless imperative of language to author and impose meaning, even to its own downfall, is highlighted in *If We Go On*, but is often overlooked in the analysis of postdramatic theatre. Rather there tends to be an over-riding emphasis on the removal of authority from language which now struggles to assert meaning, rather than a revisiting of the 'old' familiar certainty of language as author and architect of that very struggle. *If We Go On* was notable in its rare exposure of language's capacity to use its still-present authority, precisely in order to assert itself as incompetent for its own ends. Such an analysis of the role of text within the postdramatic framework would suggest that the logos of authority is as ever-present within a postdramatic use of language as it was within the dialogue of the dramatic, but is no longer hidden by the successful illusory presence of 'authentic' speech. Rather, it is hidden by the illusion of incompetence and failure which is, nevertheless, equally intricately and invisibly authored for effect.

The illusion of presence

The illusion of authentic or originary speech that underpins dramatic dialogue is also key to the poststructuralist charge that dramatic theatre offers an illusion of original presence that conceals its reliance on repetition and representation, as Elinor Fuchs first argued in 'Presence and the revenge of writing' (1985). Fuchs proposed that the dramatic model upheld the myths of the phonocentric tradition as it relied on 'the form of writing that strives to create the illusion that it is composed of spontaneous speech, a form of writing that paradoxically seems to assert the claim of speech to be a direct conduit to Being' (1985: 163). Derrida's deconstruction of the phonocentric tradition is laid out in *Of Grammatology*, where he proposes that the spoken word has historically been endowed with originary meaning, through a false recognition of the 'absolute proximity of voice and being, of voice and the meaning of being, of voice and the ideality of meaning' (1974: 12). He consequently argues that this misrecognition of 'a full speech that was fully *present*' has led to the phonocentric hierarchy in which the spoken word is the anterior order to the written word (8). In such a hierarchy writing is seen to be a mere representation, or repetition, of the originary meaning of speech, 'confined within secondariness ... preceded by a truth, or a meaning already constituted by and within the element of the logos' (14). The phonocentric tradition, therefore, can be seen to follow the same 'process of truth' we earlier identified in relation to mimesis and the pre-written playtext (Derrida, 1981: 193), and Derrida's deconstruction of such a tradition consequently aims to disrupt its notion of full and originary speech, so as to disrupt the order of representation that logically follows.

Derrida does this by arguing for the existence of an 'arch-writing' or 'text' on which the 'meaning' of the spoken word is always already contingent. In this way he can overturn the illusion that the 'meaning' of the spoken word is present to and of itself. It is rather a representation of the already written word, which itself is not originary but also a representation, and so forth. All language, understood in this way, gains meaning from an already existing text that, itself, is made up of language, which gains its meaning from an already existing text and so on. Consequently, meaning itself cannot be foundational or originary but always contingent and relative; we are not the originary source of the language we speak, any more than the actor is, but likewise we draw our words, written and spoken, from a pre-existing text that can no longer be understood as having any originary referent or author-god to validate its meaning.

On these terms, dramatic dialogue's illusion of originary speech, which is seen to be both authentic and present, whilst in reality being neither, has been understood as conspiring with the wider operations of language as proposed by the phonocentric tradition and challenged by Derrida. Furthermore, this illusion of presence is achieved, as Artaud argued, through repetition and representation, which removes the theatre from any attempt at accessing the 'true' presence of life itself (Derrida, 2001: 294). Consequently, the avant-garde and early postmodern challenges to the dramatic theatre's illusion of presence was to attempt to evade its representational structures altogether, with the aim of achieving a more 'authentic' presence in the 'real' space and time of the performance event. In one of the most influential essays of the early 1980s, Josette Feral articulates the concept of performance as anti-theatre, claiming it could answer Artaud's demands for a non-narrative and non-representational theatre of cruelty. She defines performance as a rejection of 'all illusion, in particular theatrical illusion' (1982: 171), demanding that the performer no longer represents even him or herself but becomes 'a source of production and displacement' (174). Performance avoids the repetition of theatre in that it 'can take place only within and for a set space to which it is indissolubly tied' (173) and constitutes, 'neither past nor future, but only a continuous present – that of the immediacy of things, of *an action taking place*' (173, original emphasis). Feral claims that 'this is Derrida's *différance* made perceptible' (173, original emphasis), and much perfor-mance analysis that has followed has enthusiastically adopted this premise, although Philip Auslander's cautionary reminders about the reliance of performance art on its own documentary processes of rep-resentation are useful riders to note (Auslander, 2006, 2008: 31). Either way, it is important to be clear that Feral's understanding of 'performance' as defined in her essay, would, thirty years later, be more commonly understood as performance art, or live art practice, which Hans-Thies Lehmann distinguishes from postdramatic theatre, remarking that '[w]hile actors want to realize unique moments, they also want to *repeat* them' (2006: 137, original emphasis). Examples of performance that might be defined as live art practice in their rejection of the conventional spatial and temporal frameworks of theatre are explored in Chapters 5 and 6 of this study. For the purposes of this chapter, however, I would now like to investigate whether postdramatic theatre – that is theatre or performance that is in some way scored, directed, rehearsed, performed and repeated across a series of nights by performers in front of an audience – can claim any real philosophical distinction from the dramatic model which shares the same overall theatrical framework, regardless of their differences in aesthetic form.

Presence, representation and the postdramatic

Theorists writing on the postdramatic often disregard the distinction between live or performance art and postdramatic theatre, and replicate, to a large part, the arguments proposed by Feral, claiming that the postdramatic can, in some way, evade the representational limitations of the dramatic model, explicitly or implicitly realising the 'presence' envisioned by avant-garde artists such as Artaud and Grotowski. As noted in Chapter 1, Lehmann himself positions the postdramatic as 'an intentionally unmediated experience of the real' (2006: 134), and emphasises the turn to ceremony of postdramatic theatre, whereby 'it becomes more presence than representation' (2006: 85). David Barnett also contends that 'the postdramatic proposes a theatre beyond representation, in which the limitations of representation are held in check by dramaturgies and performance practices that seek to *present* material rather than to posit a direct, representational relationship between the stage and the outside world' (2008: 15). Małgorzata Sugiera asks, 'what changes once the events taking place on stage no longer represent reality, while presentation (understood as presence) ousts traditional representation, turning into an interactive act of creation with a pre-planned and active participation of the audience?' (2004: 25). With notable exceptions, the dramatic/postdramatic binary is thus consistently upheld on the perceived distinction between the 'illusion' of the 'present tense' of dramatic fiction where the 'there and then' poses as the 'here and now', and the emphasis within 'non-representational' or 'presentational' postdramatic practice on the present time of the actual event, its liveness, its direct relationship to the audience in time and space. Sugiera argues that 'the basic "as if" convention, upheld in theatre (as well as in the drama written for this theatre), has gradually been replaced by theatre's *differentia specifica*: its "here and now" quality and the temporal immediacy of its media' (2004: 25).

The proposed distinction between dramatic representation and postdramatic presentation serves, of course, to substantiate the ideological binary this chapter is interrogating. The poststructuralist critique of representation, based on the latter's role within the 'mimetic order' or 'process of truth', can then be targeted solely at the dramatic model, enabling the postdramatic to evade the charge and sustain its radical credentials. Within both the postdramatic and poststructuralist discourse this shift towards the 'here and now' of theatre can be read as a response to Derrida's call for a theatre which 'will no longer operate as the repetition of a *present*, will no longer *re*-present a present that would exist elsewhere and prior to it' (2001: 299). However, the postdramatic response does not constitute an evasion of representation but an alternative manipulation of representation in order to shape a theatrical aesthetic which offers a distinct but equally illusory 'presence' to that offered by the dramatic model. As Steve Bottoms categorically states, '*there is no non-theological stage to be had,* no purely present performance in the moment, no escape from representation' (2011: 27). Derrida himself points to Artaud's understanding of mimetic imitation as the 'most naïve form of representation', not in any sense the only form, and goes on to make explicit his own understanding of representation which goes way beyond 'a particular type of theatrical construction'(2001: 295). Whilst Derrida's definition of representation has much wider implications to which I will return, I would like to pause here for a moment to consider the ramifications of this initial cautionary revision in relation to the radical narrative of the postdramatic. If the notion of representation that Artaud's vision would reject is, as Derrida argues, 'an addition, … the sensory illustration of a text already written, thought, or lived outside the stage, which the stage would then only repeat but whose fabric it would not constitute' (2001: 299), might this not equally apply to any kind of performance text, written or otherwise, which was rehearsed and then repeated in performance *as if* for the first time?

Pre-rehearsed strategies to enhance the 'present-time' illusion of performance are a common feature of new work at the turn of the century, yet these are no less 'a text already written … which the stage would then only repeat'. In one section of Vincent Dance Theatre's *If We Go On,* a performer repeatedly attempts to mark the steps of a solo dance in time with music played by a cellist. After several failed efforts, and the increasing irritation of the cellist, he breaks free from what could be explicitly choreographed steps, into a seemingly spontaneous dance that results in him stubbing his toe on the hard blackboard backdrop at the rear of the stage, ending in apparent pain and frustration. This action I would characterise as no less fictional than 'conventional' acting; the 'failure' to mark the steps, the spontaneity of the break-out dance and the stubbing of the toe are all clearly pre-rehearsed elements of the score. Heddon and Milling draw attention to one other such moment of many in their critical history, *Devising Performance*:

Uninvited Guests' *Guest House* (1999) showed the process of constructing their multi-media show, within the show itself. One device used within the performance was that the performers cast and directed each other:

> 'Performer: Can we see that stumble Jo? (Jo stumbles.) OK, let's look at that again, but with a bit more of a look of frustration on your face and a sign or a noise of anger.' (2006: 208)

However, this familiar motif of performing pre-rehearsed 'mistakes' or 'improvements'; whilst referencing them as if they were an on-the-spot disruption or addition to the rehearsed performance, rarely fulfils its original remit of confusing 'the ontological status of the given' (Heddon and Milling, 2006: 209). A characteristic of Bailes's poetics of failure, as discussed in Chapter 1, this strategy can too easily now be read merely as an established comic convention that may be enjoyable to watch but that requires, and often deserves, no deeper analysis. Heddon and Millings suggest that such strategies are a way of presenting and unmasking the process of performance and that the final performance of (probably) pre-rehearsed but seemingly spontaneous elements can be seen, not as a present-tense activity, but as part of a 'representation of a "work in progress"' (2006: 209). This positions this piece, and the conventions it employs, as being no more or less representational than the dramatic model it is too often pitted against. Indeed, as Stephen Bottoms observes, such models may well 'function with *more* duplicity and "illusionism" than do conventional plays' (2009: 70), where the fictional nature of the work is less ambiguous; the fictional action is self-evidently not happening in the present time and place of the theatre. Conversely, strategies designed to give the illusion that we are watching the spontaneous construction of a piece of theatre in the here and now of the theatre event, are, more often than not, minutely observed repetitions of pre-rehearsed actions, and so, precisely, a duplicitous, if playful, representation of a fiction made to appear 'real'. Thus, the distinctions between dramatic and fictional 'world representations', as Lehmann terms them, and postdramatic, but no less fictional, 'representations of the here and now', bear much less philosophical weight, I would argue, than they have generally been asked to carry.

Any suggestion that postdramatic theatre can, by its emphasis on an illusory, present-time immediacy, evade the bind of representation, is further undermined by Derrida's proposal that the order of representation ultimately underpins, not the strategy of any particular theatrical model, but the condition of the world we live in and the ways of knowing we have inherited. Artaud's desire to 'erase repetition' (Derrida, 2001: 310) is, as Derrida expounds at length, an impossible vision that seeks in vain 'a *re*-presentation which is full presence … which does not repeat itself, that is, of a present outside time, a nonpresent' (2001: 313). Conversely, the present that can be perceived in time, that can present itself to us, is always already engaging in the mimetic order of representation, as can be seen by the first of Derrida's two interpretations of mimesis discussed earlier. In relation to Artaud's theatre of cruelty Derrida is clear that:

> [W]hat is tragic is not the impossibility but the necessity of repetition.
> Artaud knew that the theater of cruelty neither begins nor is completed

within the purity of simple presence, but rather is already within representation […] Presence, in order to be presence and self-presence, has always
already begun to represent itself. (2001: 313–14)

If the order of representation necessitates that not even the thing itself
can be present to itself other than via its own representation, as Derrida
suggests, and that consequently, 'contrary to what our desire cannot fail
to be tempted into believing, the thing itself always escapes' (1973: 104),
then any notion of 'present-ness' within a performance aesthetic (never
mind life itself) is always already a representation of 'being-present'
rather than the 'thing itself'.

There is an emerging trend in more recent criticism for this argument
to be advanced. Andrew Quick, in 2009, notes that 'all artistic events are
subject to the operations of representation. They all require the act of
being separated from everyday life otherwise we would not know them as
events' (2009: 32). Stephen Bottoms, likewise, has consistently argued that
'placed within the frame of art, the "real" is always already representational,
and the "self" always already a characterization, however much we might
want to delude ourselves otherwise' (2009: 74). Postdramatic theatre
cannot, consequently, escape, evade or overcome representation, but
can only explore its own representation of the present and/or presence,
within its own representational limitations. The paradox of the discursive
act of evasion I have associated with certain misapplications of poststructuralist scepticism, as Cormac Power astutely notes in *Presence
in Play*, is that it begins to shift uncomfortably close to the modernist
'illusion of ideal immediacy', shared by Artaud and Grotowski, that
would be anathema to the broader poststructuralist discourse (Power,
2008: 114). As Shannon Jackson comments in relation to the Artaudian
influence within the neo-avant-garde, 'such artists proceeded on a course
that was conceptually misguided … attempting to land upon a mode
of being that derived from "before the outset" of representation. Once
again, the "end of representation" was also paradoxically conceived as
"original representation"' (2004: 125). Andrew Quick observes the same
recurring tendency in certain discourses emerging at the beginning of
the 1990s that were distinguished by their attempts to 'resist the operation
of representation, of repetition, of illusion, while somehow being or
presenting "the real" itself' (1996: 12). He concludes that

> the reading or contextualization of these genres of performance (whether
> they are defined as experimental theatre, performance art, or live art)
> which defines and frames them in relation to a pure (idealized) presen-
> tation of the real or reality is severely limited and may, indeed, be un-
> wittingly contradictory. (16)

Cormac Power's study of presence is a timely reflection of a growing realisation that 'the idea of presence – of whatever kind – is itself a kind of fiction, an example of theatre's capacity to create the "powerful illusion" of the "unmediated"' (2008: 114). Drawing on Derrida, and contesting the valorisation of theatre on the basis of its 'presence' in the 'present', Power suggests that '[t]he spatial and temporal parameters of theatrical performance, far from housing a secure and stable "present" experience, should instead be seen as delineating a place of almost infinite possibility in which a "progressive extenuation of presence" can be enacted' (Derrida, 1982: 313 cited in Power, 2008: 194). Power rather offers a plurality of 'presences' and advocates theatre's potential as the capacity to continually put them into play, understanding performance as the ground 'on which presence is explored rather than evaded' (119):

> One of the challenges left to us by theories of phenomenology and post-structuralism is that of appreciating theatre as a representational form that explores the intricacies of presence in particular ways, as we move away from merely privileging theatre as an essentially 'present' phenomenon. (198)

Cormac Power thus concludes that fictional dramatic, or world, representations, hold no less capacity to investigate, destabilise or expose the complex levels of presence which make up the theatre event, than performance which might be said to represent, not a dramatic fiction, but its own, fictional 'present-ness'. In dramatic world representations, Power suggests, the 'fictional "now" often coexists in tension with the stage "now"'. We see the stage and imagine the fiction, and so the whole question of what *is* present is opened up' (2008: 4, original emphasis). Power goes on to argue that an over-emphasis on the 'fictionality' of staged drama to distinguish it from other types of performance leads to a reluctance to acknowledge the common basis of all theatre, which might be characterised as 'a medium that manipulates physical phenomena before a specific group of people' (2008: 19). Replacing the common proposal that dramatic theatre's distinctiveness lies in its capacity to make '*fictions* present', he suggests, should be an acknowledgement that all models of theatre are able to make 'our experience of the present a subject of contemplation' (2008: 16, original emphasis). Power's analysis consequently concludes that 'it is the very potential of theatre to put presence *into play* that enables us to ... reflect upon and question the construction of "reality" in the contemporary world' (2008: 9, original emphasis).

'Always already representational'

If dramatic and postdramatic theatre alike are 'always already representational' (Bottoms, 2009: 74), then the poststructuralist challenge to logocentrism might best be identified in practice that explores ways of exposing and acknowledging its own representational structures and narratives, and examines all notions of the real. Such practice will form the basis of part two of this book, and will demonstrate, through its diversity of form, that poststructuralist interrogation is not restricted to work that might qualify as postdramatic under current prevailing definitions.

Throughout the remainder of this study, I will be interrogating the poststructuralist narrative on its own terms in order to challenge the notion that its deconstructive project inevitably results in radical practice. Poststructuralist practice, I will now argue, must look to deconstruct its own manifestations of originary authority, rather than, as has too often been the case, attempting to evade the charge altogether by a complacent faith in its own potentially totalising conclusions. The rejection, proposed in this chapter, of the ideological basis for the dramatic/postdramatic binary offers up this very opportunity to sustain the self-reflexive imperative of Derrida's radical deconstructive project to ask more rigorous ideological and philosophical questions of a whole range of theatrical structures within their diverse and particular contexts of production.

In Chapter 3, I will examine the poststructuralist deconstruction of identity that can be found in both dramatic characterisation and postdramatic performance personae across a wide range of practice, including Forced Entertainment's *World in Pictures,* the Wooster Group's version of Tennessee Williams's *Vieux Carré,* adaptations of classic texts by Katie Mitchell and Toneelgroep Amsterdam, and playtexts by Roland Schimmelpfennig and Howard Barker. I will identify the common citational aesthetic that underpins contemporary notions of performer and character before addressing the diversity of ideological implications that arise from the notion of a poststructuralist subjectivity that no longer recognises an 'authentic' or 'essential' self.

Notes

1   All quotations from Lehmann, 2002 are translated by Leila Mukhida for the purposes of this study.
2   This analysis is based on the performance of *If We Go On* at Carriageworks Theatre, Leeds, on 8 October 2009.
3   This and all following quotations are taken from the unpublished performance text of *If We Go On,* written by Charlotte Vincent and Wendy Houstoun, made available to me courtesy of Vincent Dance Theatre.

Part II

Apparitions of the real

3

Quoting quotations: citational theory and contemporary characterisation

Erika Fischer-Lichte discusses the historical notion of dramatic character in terms of the transformation of the 'sensual body' of the actor into a 'semiotic one which would serve as a material carrier for textual meaning' (Fischer-Lichte, 2008: 78). In such a context any attention drawn to the physical or phenomenological reality of the body of the actor would inevitably detract from its semiotic purpose of constructing the illusion of character. The avant-garde consequently looked, in its rejection of what it understood as bourgeois dramatic conventions, to precisely foreground the physical reality of the actor's body in a number of ways, most explicitly by removing the notion of character altogether. This particular strategy dominated the practice of the neo-avant-garde, from the Living Theatre's attempts to 'bring a greater level of personal and communal integrity ... by providing the audience with direct access to the actors' (Callaghan, 2003: 25) to the first generation of performance artists who sought to confront audience passivity through performance and body art that was designed to highlight 'the performer(-body)'s fragility, vulnerability, and shortcomings' (Fischer-Lichte, 2008: 82). Across diverse models of performance, the strategy of eliminating character was adopted to enhance the seemingly more authentic presence of the performer who could share real time and space with the audience, whether that was to offer them a more intimate relationship or a radical confrontational act. Autobiographical performance, particularly within the feminist and gay movements of the 1970s and 1980s, was also, to a large part, designed to give a more authentic voice to the politics that were being espoused than the mediation of character and fictional narrative were presumed to offer. In the words of artist Lisa Kron, 'the goal of autobiographical work' was

ultimately 'to use the details of your own life to illuminate or explore
something more universal' (Kron, 2001: xi in Heddon, 2008: 5).

Whilst autobiographical performance, live art and a focus on the
direct performer–audience relationship continued to thrive in new performance practices throughout the 1990s, a growing scepticism towards
the possibility of the real or authentic presence of the body on stage has
productively complicated more recent analysis, as discussed in the wider
concerns of Chapter 2. Cormac Power notes how theatre-makers since
the 1980s have rejected this particular notion of presence that initially
came about as a critique of the illusion of presence that was offered
through representational practice. Subsequent practitioners, he argues,
have rather 'sought to expose the stage as a site of representation and
citation rather than "Presence" and "immediacy"' (Power, 2008: 118).

By the turn of the century, the avant-garde emphasis on the real
body had been reconfigured, for the most part, into a poststructuralist
emphasis on the constructed and authored body, whose hold on the
real may be much more tenuous than previously assumed. Writing on
autobiographical performance in 2008, Dee Heddon comments that the
fact that the 'self' is ostensibly 'present'

> makes performance all the more tempting (and dangerous) a medium
> through which to make claims for the 'real' or 'truthful' self ... We need
> to remember that the presentation of self (in performance particularly)
> is a re-presentation, and often a strategic one ... [T]he performer's task,
> then, might be to harness the potential of the *felt* immediacy of form ...
> for political purposes, whilst simultaneously challenging assumptions of
> unmediated presence. (2008: 27–8, my emphasis)

If the performed self is recognised as a constructed representation or
strategic illusion of unmediated presence, then it offers audiences the
opportunity to reflect on their own representations of selfhood in the world
beyond the theatre. No longer is identity understood as fixed, singular
and authentic, such work suggests, but as fluid, multiple and strategic.
In this way, the rejection of the myth of authenticity, and the emphasis
on the representational basis of autobiographical performance, are
significant in their reflection of, and contribution to, the poststructuralist
shift underpinning the way in which contemporary identity is perceived.
Gubrium and Holstein describe this shift as the rejection of an 'essential,
foundational understanding' of identity which is replaced by 'a plethora of
possibilities for what we can be' (2000: 60). Consequently, they conclude,
contemporary selves 'are in continuous construction, never completed,
never fully coherent, never completely centered securely in experience'

(60). Kenneth J. Gergen also argues that in this historical moment '[e]ach reality of self gives way to reflexive questioning, irony, and ultimately the playful probing of yet another reality' (1991: 7). In this context, it is notable that many companies working with autobiographical premises in the early 2000s do so specifically to complicate the authenticity of the work, rather than to assert it. This can be seen, for example, in Third Angel's *Class of 76* where artistic director and performer Alexander Kelly constructed a series of real and imagined histories of his classmates from an old school photograph, and in Quarantine Theatre's *Make Believe* where a white female performer delivered the autobiographical narrative of her male black co-performer as if it was her own.

If, as Elinor Fuchs asserts, 'each substantial change in the way character is represented on the stage … constitutes at the same time the manifestation of a change in the larger culture concerning the perception of self' (1996: 8), then this chapter will argue that the contemporary understanding of poststructuralist identity, as no longer singular and essential but multiple and constructed, is reflected in a number of related shifts in the characterisation of the performer over this period of study, regardless of whether or not the performer is playing 'self' or an explicitly fictional character. In both instances, there is a significant rejection of the notion of a singular, coherent and essential self and a turn instead to multiple and constructed identities across a wide spectrum of performance models.

Elinor Fuchs' seminal study, *The Death of Character* (1996), offers a rigorous analysis of character development up until the early 1990s, thus providing an essential pre-history to this chapter, which will continue to draw on her conclusions. If character, as understood in a modernist sense, is metaphorically dead by the end of the 1980s, then theatre at the turn of the century, I will argue, is haunted by free-floating, mischief-making apparitions that are concomitant with the contemporary understanding of identity as made up of multiple and provisional selves who create the world that they inhabit. This chapter will thus examine how different models of performance have begun to shift conceptions of our understanding of a real or authentic identity, through representations that remain unconvinced of their own objective reality but are rather intent on obsessively creating themselves and their world out of the material left by a history of previous texts and characterisations. In this sense, the chapter will address the concept and practice of adaptation, but it will also seek to move beyond the usual definitions to ask, through the lens of Derrida's citational theory, what happens to the notion of adaptation once there is no longer any sense of an 'original' to which it can refer. I will initially examine how citational aesthetics can be employed to support Hal Foster's account of a resistant politics, as noted in Chapter 1, in order to expose the workings of the simulacrum from within and thus disable the authority of the illusion of the real. But I will also go on to highlight the potential inherent in such an aesthetic for a new and equally dangerous kind of authority to emerge.

Surrogates and third-rate copies

The sustained influence of the neo-avant-garde's rejection of traditional notions of characterisation can be seen in the ground-breaking practice of the Wooster Group and Forced Entertainment, and the substantial proliferation throughout the 1990s and 2000s of performance which, whilst not autobiographical in content, features the performers 'them-selves' appearing to their audience without the mediation of character. As Sara Jane Bailes confirms, this cannot, of course, be understood as the performer's real self, but as a 'performance persona … that is frequently based on the off-stage "self" and draws on such characteristics' (2011: xvii). Forced Entertainment's 'theatre work "proper"', as defined by artistic director Tim Etchells (Heathfield, 2004: 93), is characterised by such performance personae which, under the performers' own names, appear to be in charge of the show that is evolving before the audience. Productions such as *Showtime* (1996), *First Night* (2001), *Bloody Mess* (2004), *The World in Pictures* (2006) and *The Thrill of it All* (2010), are dominated by what Adrian Heathfield terms 'surrogates', who are only capable of producing the barest bones of a failed characterisation before abandoning it and returning to the predominant representation of 'inept performer' which has also been constructed for purpose. In an interview with Adrian Heathfield, Tim Etchells confirms that

> What we tend to do is to create a set of personas who have then, it appears, created the show. We kind of blame it on them – there is a deferral of authorship […] So we 'blame' the representational strategies and the accidents and the chaotic structures on this set of personas … and in the background we're busy sneaking around and getting all of it, somehow, to work. (Heathfield, 2004: 92–3)

In *The World in Pictures*, Forced Entertainment performer Terry O'Connor introduces herself by name to the audience, and explains that she is going 'to do the talking bit tonight'.[1] There is no clearly distinguishable persona adopted, as she attempts to hold the show together and take us through the history of the world that is being enacted by the other

2   Scene from *The World in Pictures*.
Photographer: Hugo Glendinning

performers who are also referred to by their own name. The surrogate personae of O'Connor's co-performers, however, are explicit, cavorting around the stage in ridiculous wigs and costumes, consistently failing to deliver the kinds of performance O'Connor demands. At one point, performer Bruno Roubicek is told by an irate O'Connor that his acting is 'way too intense' and that he has to 'tone it down' and fit in more with the ensemble, while performer Richard Lowdon spends the entire first half of history with no pants on, exposing himself to narrator and audience, to O'Connor's irritation and embarrassment. The characterisations the surrogate performers manage to muster together are barely even distinguishable as such, beyond the bad wigs and costumes, leaving the surrogate performers as the central point of attention, as in the vast majority of the company's later works.

Etchells distinguishes between the overt self-fictionalisation of the performer-surrogates in the company's 'theatre work "proper"' and the more naturalised representations of self in the company's documentary work, such as *The Travels,* where the performers own 'the content in a straightforward way' (Heathfield, 2004: 93). He also distinguishes the 'theatre work "proper"' from the company's extensive durational work which pushes performers to the kind of exhaustion whereby '[y]ou cannot control the signification of what you are doing and how you are read under these conditions' (Heathfield, 2004: 96). However, even this 'hyper-naturalistic performance style', as noted by Alex Merkimedes, is, as her terminology suggests, still an aesthetic choice and not a revelation of authenticity (2010: 116). As Helmer and Malzacher also caution, in relation to the durational work, '[t]hey are still mainly fictitious and embellished but their creation, or rather, their discovery and presentation, *seem* earnest' (2004: 20, my emphasis).

The play between these levels of presence, from the grotesque fragments of characterisation, to the enhanced surrogate performers, to the 'seemingly' more real performers themselves, is strategically manipulated by the company to interrogate the very notion of authenticity. Through a skilful construction, and then removal, of layer upon layer of artifice, Forced Entertainment continually succeeds in leaving its audience with the illusion of something more essential: '[t]hey told you so many times they weren't acting that when they did act they hoped you'd think it real' (Etchells, 1999: 36). The most evocative moments in the company's work are achieved when a sense of 'the real' is contrived via a constructed slippage of the performance persona, or surrogate, to reveal a seemingly authentic self beneath it. Such episodes would include the moment in

First Night when the lights come up and Cathy Naden looks directly into the eyes of individual audience members as she tells them how they're going to die; or in *Showtime* when the dog's head that Naden has been wearing throughout is removed to enable Naden to take us through a painstakingly detailed account of how she would kill herself. Referring to such moments, Tim Etchells is very clear that 'Cathy plays it *like* she means it. *As if* the mask is gone.' (Heathfield, 2004: 95, my emphasis):

> We like it when those surrogate figures look like they can barely extend or persist any longer, like the mask of them must be abandoned … we like to play as if things got more real. But for the most part, in the theatre works, it is 'just' dramaturgy. (Etchells in Heathfield, 2004: 95–6)

In much of the work that has been influenced by Forced Entertainment's aesthetic, similar layers of characterisation descending from inadequate characterisation, to surrogate performance personae, to the apparently real performer, have become little more than a conclusive postdramatic convention. This most singular influence of the company's methods on younger practitioners has also been arguably supported by numerous analyses of the company's work through a postdramatic lens that foregrounds the relationship between the surrogate performers' failures to represent realistic characters and a critique of the dramatic, or realist, model of theatre, as discussed in Chapter 2. Sara Jane Bailes notes the 'radical amateurism' that characterises Forced Entertainment's aesthetic and lends itself to this mode of analysis:

> Amateurism emerges through a highly developed but intentionally 'poor' delivery style, an affect in performance that they have honed in order to derail stage conventions, the ambitions of dramatic integrity, and the process of spectatorship to often spectacular effect from within the structure and rules of the 'traditional' theatre event. (2011: 56)

It is clear from Tim Etchells's own perspective, as noted in Chapter 1, that the destabilisation of the realist, or dramatic, model is central to the company's work, and that this, as Andrew Quick remarks, is indeed intended to 'undermine the authority of theatre's representational operations' (2004: 163). However, Forced Entertainment's theatre is not a mere parody or easy subversion of dramatic theatre for its own sake, but rather a critical deconstruction which serves a distinctly philosophical purpose that, as I have noted elsewhere, is not necessarily the case with all the practice which borrows an ostensibly similar form (Tomlin, 2008). In his discussion of the work of Impact Theatre, a company producing work in the 1980s that significantly influenced the emerging

Forced Entertainment, Andrew Quick notes the same 'play of fiction' which 'becomes one of the tactical intrusions or manoeuvres within the representational apparatus of the theatre-machine, a play which is seen as an always failing attempt at the recovery of the real' (1996: 20). In this sense Quick positions the same postdramatic playfulness with 'representational apparatus' which was to characterise Forced Entertainment's work, as a means to an end, rather than the end in itself. Quick aligns the inevitable failure of the performers to access the real through dramatic strategies, with a Lacanian analysis which insists on 'the impossible potential of representation … which implicates the limit of the representational apparatus and its ultimate failure to represent exactly: in other words, the very failure, at the locus of representation, the failure of the symbolic to recover the real which renders it only an imitation of life' (1996: 22). Thus, the Impact Theatre or Forced Entertainment performance, perhaps surprisingly, does reflect the world beyond it, but a world that must be understood not only in a Lacanian but also in a Derridean sense. I will return to Lacan in Chapter 5, but it is worth noting at this point that both theorists, in their own distinctive ways, are reflected in the work's failure to achieve any kind of authentic or originary presence through its representations that never get beyond, as Etchells writes, 'third rate copies' or imitations of a real which is forever beyond reach (Etchells, 1999: 32).

Citations and spectres

Derrida's understanding that 'there is no experience of *pure* presence, but only chains of differential marks' (1982: 318), offers, as is now commonly noted, a lens through which all representations of self, both within and beyond the theatre, are recognised as citational, entailing 'an essential break with (and *within*) origins and causal systems' (McKenzie, 2001: 215, original emphasis; see also Jackson, 2004: 182). Derrida's persuasive and highly influential analysis of J. L. Austin's speech-act theory argues that the distinction Austin makes between performative speech acts (that is, those which perform real impact), and citational speech acts which take place, for example, on the stage, and thus have no real impact, is not valid. Not only does Derrida argue for the performative impact of all speech acts but, more importantly in this context, he argues that the citational speech acts that are characterised by Austin as 'infelicitous exceptions' to his rule, evidence, on the contrary, that the underlying nature of all speech acts, utterances, signs and marks is itself wholly citational:

Every sign, linguistic or non-linguistic ... can be *cited*, put between quotation marks; thereby it can break with every given context, and engender infinitely new contexts in an absolutely nonsaturable fashion. This does not suppose that the mark is valid outside its context, but on the contrary that there are only contexts without any center of absolute anchoring. This citationality, duplication, or duplicity, this iterability of the mark is not an accident or an anomaly, but is that (normal/abnormal) without which a mark could no longer even have a so-called "normal" functioning. What would a mark be that one could not cite? And whose origin could not be lost on the way? (1982: 320–1)

Read through the lens of Derrida's analysis, the inadequate characterisations produced by the Forced Entertainment surrogates can be seen to be clearly citational. Not only should such characterisations be read, as is more commonly the case, as intentionally failed attempts to meet the demands of dramatic theatre, but also as productive expositions of citational, rather than essential, readings of identity, as they are demonstrably representations without referent; ostensibly refusing to point to any semblance of an originary reality as would be anticipated within more realistic, or psychologically-rounded, modes of characterisation.

David Savran observes a similar rejection of realistic character development in the work of the Wooster Group, whereby the performers 'do not embody others but allow themselves to be haunted by those absent others whom they reference' (2005: 15). These 'absent others' are the characters, biographical and fictional, whose resurrections populate the reconstructed and deconstructed texts that the company have adapted over their long and influential history. Unlike the vestiges of characterisation in Forced Entertainment's work, those of the Wooster Group do, in this sense, have a character-referent that resides in the original text and ghosts their own absence of realistic representation in the Wooster Group's adaptation. As Savran argues, the company's strategies of characterisation arise from this very absence and are located in the attempts of the performers to give voice to the departed whilst simultaneously dislocating the authenticity or reliability of those they recall. Such apparitions are not copies, even in a radical sense, of the characters in the original texts but, as I will now outline, act as citations that have become divorced from their referent to 'engender infinitely new contexts in an absolutely nonsaturable fashion' (Derrida, 1982: 320).

The enclosure of a number of Chekhov's characters within television screens in *Brace Up*, the company's 1993 reworking of *The Three Sisters*,[2] quite literally serves to remove them not only from the context of the original text but from the stage itself, which other characters continue to inhabit. The flattened out close-ups of the characters' faces offer them no background or location, and their images are interspersed with excerpts from the cinematic work of Japanese film-makers such as Yasujiro Ozu, among other seemingly random (in relation to the original text) references (LeCompte, in Quick, 2007: 107). As conversations cross from live actors to television images and back, the television characters are cut off from the physical space of those to whom they are speaking, and are placed as much in temporal and spatial relation to the video sequences which regularly obliterate them as they are to the characters or narrative of either the present reworking or the original text. This is not to say that there are not a number of ways in which this production can be read as an analysis of, or commentary on, the concerns of the original text, as Phaedra Bell persuasively suggests (2005), but to suggest that the spatial and temporal juxtaposition offers the viewer an indefinite choice of possible other readings, exemplifying what Derrida refers to as the 'essential iterability' of the sign that is always, by definition, able to be 'cut off from its alleged "production" or origin' (1982: 317–18).

In the adaptations of the Wooster Group, as in many of the companies influenced by them, the characters, or signs, are uprooted in this way from their original context and reframed in ways that offer the spectator multiple rather than singular potential referents. In this sense they are signs that do not consist of a signifier (character in the present) coupled with a signified (character in the original) but are now free-floating signifiers open to multiple interpretations. In addition to the distancing device of the television screen characters in *Brace Up*, the *mise-en-scène* generally favours isolating from each other the characters who are on the stage. Liz LeCompte describes how she was influenced by the patterns of Noh Theatre, dividing the space up into background, middleground and foreground with different rules for each (LeCompte in Quick, 2007: 110). This is evident in the isolated work of individual performers that dominates, and is only sporadically interrupted by bursts of choreographed ensemble dance sequences. The characters speak Chekhov's dialogue in sequence, but rarely directly 'to' each other, often framed in their own distinct playing space, enabling them to be read outside of any narrative context, and in physical juxtaposition with other elements of the scene that might be totally unconnected to the narrative at that point in time. Moreover, all characters are continually located as free-floating signifiers by the narrator who, through her meta-theatrical questioning of the text and prompts to other performers, constantly breaks up the faintest illusion of any underlying reality of fictional character.

The meta-theatricality, fragmentation of performers and deliberate clashing together of seemingly unrelated aesthetics (in this instance Noh Theatre and the Chekhov text) is common to most of the Wooster Group's work, which made their 2010 production of Tennessee Williams's *Vieux Carré* (1977) seem, on the surface, somewhat anomalous.[3] Many of the reviewers commented on the 'surprisingly faithful adherence to the Williams text' (Shaw, 2011), the consistent characterisation, and the development of the on-stage relationships in the spirit and shape of the original. The performers disappeared behind their characterisations, the television monitors and non-realistic movement sequences were very much secondary to the on-stage dramatic interaction, and there was no meta-theatrical commentary from the company, all of which permitted the work, ostensibly at least, to maintain the shape of Williams's broadly dramatic theatre in a way that earlier work such as *Brace Up* had resisted. However, the nature of the characterisation in *Vieux Carré*, I will now argue, was not a break with the Wooster Group's practice but a development of an aesthetic which now begins to offer an extended notion of the very concept of adaptation itself.

The Wooster Group's analysis of *Vieux Carré*, undertaken through research into Williams's plays and journals, and the company's own visits to New Orleans, foregrounded the thematic emphasis on sex, death, despair and loneliness which pervaded Williams's text, but did so through grotesquely highlighted signifiers that placed the internalised, psychological characterisation of the original within external quotation marks. This was exemplified in the character of Nightingale, the dying artist whose sexual appetite was signified by a large strap-on dildo which protruded from his kimono, and whose fatal consumption was signified by a blood-stained white cloth which hung next to the dildo throughout. Although certain exchanges, notably the seduction of the Writer by Nightingale, were conveyed in a relatively realistic manner, much of the dialogue was emotionally heightened and/or delivered deadpan to divorce it from the naturalistic guise of its original emotional colouring and highlight it as citational.

The non-naturalism of the delivery was supported by a technique introduced into the process, though not visible in performance, whereby, through earphones, each performer was fed a soundtrack that was not the text they were required to deliver, thus impacting on the rhythm of their spoken text and the impossibility of focused emotional engagement with their words. Such alienating strategies were enhanced by technical effects

3   Kate Valk and Ari Fliakos in The Wooster Group's version of Tennessee Williams' *Vieux Carré*.

Photographer: Nancy Campbell

such as the canned laughter which embellished the performer's own, and the occasional use of screens and projections to enable characters to be dissected into two parts; a live head above a projected body that became decapitated when the performer moved out of position, or a cartoon face providing the head for the live performer's body which stood behind the screen. In such ways, the identification with character that Williams would have sought was consistently blocked even as the coherence of the narrative and the relationships between the character-citations were maintained. The distinctive result of this combination of dislocated character within a more or less coherent framework was that we were no longer so much encouraged to sever the relationship between the character in the present and its referent in the much-distanced original text, as in *Brace Up*; rather, due to the upholding of the original dramatic framework, we were being directed towards a severance of the relationship between character-quotation and its referent of internalised, psychological self. Whilst this deconstruction of singular and coherent identity is also suggested by the fragmented characterisation of *Brace Up* and other productions, the retention in the Wooster Group's *Vieux Carré* of the dramatic framework of the original text suggested that Williams's play itself was vital in offering the Wooster Group the very philosophical lens through which such questions might be further developed.

Williams's *Vieux Carré*, like his better-known text *The Glass Menagerie* (1944), is a memory play, both in that it draws on Williams's experiences in New Orleans as a young writer and in that the piece is structured around the character of the Writer who introduces the boarding house at the beginning of the play from a future perspective and directly narrates sections of it in the past tense throughout. In the Wooster Group's version, much of this narration occurs as typeface on an overhead projection, and the motif is extended from Williams's original to encompass the writing of a certain section of dialogue between characters Jane and Tye which, in Williams's text, is presented as live dialogue, rather than narrated. In this sense, the original text offers the Wooster Group both the meta-theatrical framework that they themselves would more usually construct and the 'site of memory' which David Savran recognises as central to the company's work. What Savran observes in relation to the centrality of technology in much of the Wooster Group's work, is equally applicable to *Vieux Carré*, despite the more secondary role played by modes of mechanical reproduction in this piece:

> Live performance is set next to modes of mechanical reproduction to pro-
> vide a sense not of ontological transparency but of instability and evanes-

cence. This move means that the site of performance is the space not of the now, but, to borrow Paul Auster's words, of 'memory: the space in which a thing happens for the second time' (Auster, 1988: 83, cited in Savran, 2005: 16)

In memory, as in history, the past cannot exist beyond the construction of those in the present, and so the Wooster Group's long tradition of performers who are 'haunted by those absent others whom they reference' is here taken to a series of complex levels. The primary 'absent others', the original Williams characters, are themselves ghosts conjured up in the memory of the fictional writer, ghosts which, in turn, are spectres of the 'absent others' whom Williams himself has reconstructed from memories of his own past. In the Wooster Group's version, what is implicit in Williams's text becomes explicit on the overhead screen as we see the scene between Jane and Tye being furiously written by the Writer; the characters now theatrical creations of the Writer, who himself is created by Williams, all without essence of their own. Here, indeed, we can see the logic of Derrida's claim that 'the signified always already functions as a signifier' (Derrida, 1974: 7), as we try to trace this series of quotations back to an originary meaning or referent which, the Wooster Group's version suggests, can never be located. As the typing gets faster and faster, so that we can no longer read the words appearing on the screen, the text momentarily breaks apart, the whole becomes inconceivable, the illusion of authorial meaning impossible to retain. Not only does this reflect a familiar self-deconstruction of the authorship of the company towards the meaning of their work but it simultaneously suggests that Williams, the playwright who hides behind the fictional Writer, can be understood as no more coherent, no more stable in his identity, than his fictional counterpart. Williams's plays may be populated with characters who adopt fantasy roles to protect them from the harsh reality of their lives, such as the two old women in *Vieux Carré* who insist on their dinner invitations by rich relations with chauffeur-driven cadillacs even as they gather rotting food from the garbage pail to keep themselves from starvation. But his work invests, nevertheless, in the concept of an inner truth of character that the Wooster Group's citational aesthetic exposes as being no more authentic than the fantasy roles Williams's characters adopt.

Quoting the dramatic

The quotation marks which the Wooster Group place around character are widened out in the work of Katie Mitchell's adaptations to incorporate discrete scenes of dramatic action in which psychologically rounded portrayals of character and detailed observations of scenic location are played out. Unlike the companies examined so far, Mitchell's work with performers, as discussed in her handbook *The Director's Craft*, is heavily influenced by key elements of Stanislavskian theory and is designed to produce naturalistic performances of character relationships that clearly reference an originary reality beyond the theatre (Mitchell, 2009: 225–32). In common with much of her work at this time, *Some Trace of Her* (2008),[4] Mitchell's adaptation of Dostoevsky's *The Idiot* (1869), features close-up scenes drawn from the original that are filmed live on stage and simultaneously projected onto large overhead screens, a technique that effectively serves to place her quotation marks around the dramatic scenes in their entirety. Because the audience are watching the exquisitely detailed close-ups on screen at the same time as they are watching the construction, set-up, and location of the live shooting of that scene on the stage beneath, the representation of the original text's reflection of reality is shown explicitly, and simultaneously, as construction. The artifice that underlies the construction of the representation is made explicit by Mitchell's use of foley art, sound effects which are created live on stage by everyday objects in order to enhance the theatricality of the process. The sound of horses' hooves might be made by a man's shoe heels on a wooden board, or the sound of fire by the rustling of crisp packets held next to a microphone. The visual effects are likewise created in a deliberately lo-tech manner, a woman's hair being wafted by a flat sheet of wood to give the impression of wind and movement, water sprayed directly onto the actor's face from a plastic atomiser to signify driving rain, or the actor, shot from a low angle, kneeling on a desk and leaning out with his shirt wafted from behind to give the impression of Myshkin's expressionist flight in the darkness of his epileptic seizure. This kind of explicit theatricality of effects has featured for many years in the work of the Wooster Group and Forced Entertainment, but in Mitchell's work the simultaneous image of the successfully mediated illusion of the real offers a new dual-perspective for the spectator. Watching the scene on film, the sound and visual effects are absolutely convincing, yet just below the screen we can see a fragmentation of all its elements now completely out of context.

Often the hand on the table holding the glass that we can see being filmed is not the hand of the actor who is on the other side of the stage speaking the internal monologue into a microphone. On the screen the hand belongs to the voice; on the stage the two elements are dislocated from each other and their context within the narrative that is being

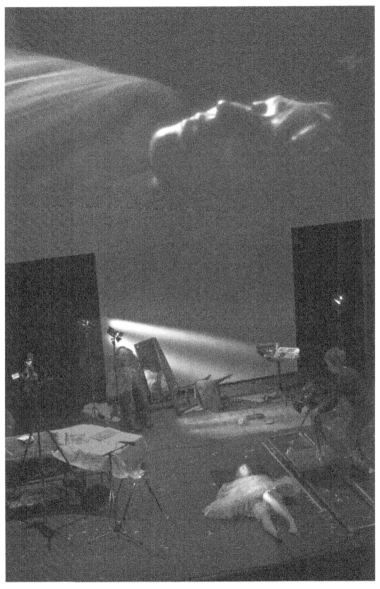

4   Scene from *Some Trace of Her.*
Photographer: Stephen Cummiskey

constructed. Two people who are in conversation on screen, the camera moving conventionally from a close-up of one face to another, are shot on opposite sides of the stage, with no spatial relationship to each other. Cut-aways to a hand holding a cigarette, presumed to belong to the speaker, may be provided by yet another actor in yet another set-up somewhere else on stage. In this sense, the stage action bears similarities to the dispersion of narrative elements and characters already noted in the Wooster Group's *Brace Up*. The construction of each shot is isolated from its part in the whole, a free floating signifier on a vast stage where the *mise-en-scène* is constantly shifting, as cameras and actors (who also operate all the technical and stage management tasks throughout) move continuously around the stage to the location of their next set-up.

The capacity for the spectator to move between, on the one hand, the performance of construction on the stage and, on the other, the filmic performance on the screens is a highly charged strategy for deconstructing the representation of the real whilst highlighting its powerful and ideological potential for persuasion. In the former, the choreography of the movement, the relationships between the actors and the intrigue of the foley art and visual set-ups all offer possibilities for selective attention and interpretation, whereas in the latter, the evocative mood and lyricism draw the spectator emotionally and consensually into the illusion, even knowing as they do, the work which is happening below.

Using entirely different theatrical strategies, Toneelgroep Amsterdam's 2009 production of *Roman Tragedies* similarly situated a series of dramatic extracts within quotation marks over the course of a six-hour performance.[5] The production, which encompassed abridged adaptations of Shakespeare's *Coriolanus, Julius Caesar* and *Antony and Cleopatra*, was staged on a massive playing area, filled with sofas, desks and television cameras and monitors, giving the impression of a series of open-plan news offices and television studios overlapping one another. Down each side of the stage were bars where refreshments were sold to the audience in the regular two- to seven-minute breaks at approximately every half an hour. The audience was also invited, in the first and subsequent breaks, to come up onto the playing area and sit on the sofas, or hang out by the bars, to watch the next section of action from the stage itself. Consequently, you could watch one scene from the audience's seating bank, focusing either on the live action on stage (which encompassed audience members dispersed throughout) or on its live-feed close-up on the overhead screen; and the next from a sofa on the stage, again choosing either to focus on the live action that might be occurring right next to you

5   Scene from *Roman Tragedies*.
Photographer: Jan Versweyveld

on the sofa or over at the far side of the stage, or to follow its transmission onto one of the smaller television monitors positioned to offer each sofa a good view of the action.

The choice of perspective mirrored that of *Some Trace of Her,* but the disjunction wasn't highlighted in the same way; what was seen on the screens was simply what was seen on the stage, only in close-up. This mode of dual viewing, now commonplace in football matches, concerts and other public events, no longer seems to undermine a sense of the real as challenged by representation but rather corresponds to a familiar way of reading and accepting the real *through* representation. In *Roman Tragedies* the citational quality of the performance came rather from the temporal and spatial structure of both live and mediated action and the shifts from fictional time/space to the present time/space that were orchestrated. For the thirty minutes or so of each segment of dramatic action, the actors played out a modernised adaptation of the Shakespearian political power struggles without direct reference to the audience who sat among or before them. Even when actors were cast against gender, the performances remained realistic and psychologically persuasive and the narrative thread of the original was relatively consistent and undisturbed. During the intermissions, however, the actors immediately abandoned role, politely asking audience members to move along on sofas, for example, if they needed more room for the next scene. This, coupled with the constant relocation of spectators, succeeded in suspending any absorption into the dramatic world that was being presented within the segments of fictional action. As the production stopped and started, at one moment a court in Rome transposed to a contemporary news room, at the next, a social space where audience mingled with actors, the ontological basis of the world remained a fragmented and acknowledged theatrical fiction, retained in the quotation marks of the production's spatial and temporal structure.

Deconstructing adaptation

The proliferation of strategies designed to frame representation as citation in adaptations of this period begins to undermine the distinct notion of adaptation itself. If, as Derrida argues, everything is citation, then there can be no sense of a pure or authentic original to which the notion of adaptation can refer. If, as Linda Hutcheon suggests, we interpret adaptations through a Barthesian lens, 'not a "work", but a "text", a plural "stereophony of echoes, citations, references"' (Barthes, 1977: 160 in Hutcheon, 2006: 6), then the same philosophical lens would expose

6   Cathy Naden and Richard Lowdon in *Void Story*.
Photographer: Hugo Glendinning

our experience of the real itself as a comparable text. Thus, not only can
the adaptation no longer find an originary authority in the text it cites, as
we have discussed, but that text itself can now be seen to be drawing from
a 'real' which is no less another text, consisting of an infinite multiplicity
of citations. Thus, the adaptations discussed so far are not distinct from
that which they adapt, but are merely the latest manifestations in an
endless chain of signification without origin. If every signified is also
a signifier, as Derrida claims, then Derrida's rejection of the binary
opposition proposed by Austin – between performative speech-acts
which perform real impact and speech-acts which are mere citations of
the former – can be equally applied to a poststructuralist reading of the
act of theatrical adaptation. This, to borrow from Derrida, is now also
'concerned with different types of marks or chains of iterable marks, and
not with an opposition between citational statements on the one hand
[i.e. the adaptation], and singular and original statement-events on the
other [i.e. the original text]' (Derrida, 1982: 326). In other words, the
characterisations in the adaptation, the original and the 'real' world

referent of the original, become merely 'different types' of citation, rather than ontologically distinct.

This interrogation of the notion of adaptation, I have argued, is embedded in the Wooster Group's retention of Williams's dramatic framework of *Vieux Carré* to underline not only the citational nature of his characterisations but also the inevitable textuality of the playwright's own autobiographical narrative. Likewise, the work of Forced Entertainment can be read as establishing an aesthetic of citation without an 'original' text performing the role of referent. In *Void Story* (2010),[6] the characters are visualised only as graphic novel images projected onto a screen, described on the company's website as 'a storyboard for an impossible movie-version of Tim Etchells' uniquely unsettling text'. Their voices are disembodied from the images, provided by performers sitting at tables beneath the screen through microphones that often serve to distort the voices with cartoon-like effects, thus isolating the voices not only from the images but also from the performers themselves.

Void Story follows two protagonists through an apocalyptic world, unfolding a narrative which moves between poetic lyricism and a deliberately and ironically excessive catalogue of every conceivable filmic disaster convention. The citational aesthetic underlines the characters' own scepticism of the 'truths' they re-iterate from filmic and other sources. 'In situations of danger', one protagonist says to the other, 'only hope can keep people alive'. To which his partner responds, 'and do you believe that?' to be told, 'I read it somewhere, a fortune cookie, maybe'. *Void Story* is not an adaptation as such, but its citational strategies constantly underline the fact that it is created out of recognisable narratives and conventions that now circulate in our culture without any specific referent point or origin. If the very notion of an original text has been discredited by poststructuralist theory, then it becomes difficult to distinguish the notion of an adaptation, as previously understood, from the citational aesthetic of work like *Void Story* which might, through a Derridean lens, be said to be likewise drawing on the multiple texts of contemporary culture where no text, or sign, can be read as originary.

The signifying self

This application of Derridean theory results in a productive tension, not only in respect of the distinction between traditional notions of the adaptation and the original but also in respect of the binary distinctions between the actor/performer on the one hand and the character on the other. In her discussion of presence and representation, Erica Fischer-

Lichte focuses on the spectator's process of 'perceptual multistability', that is, the continual shifts made by the spectator to enable them to perceive, on an alternating basis, either the actor or the character (2008: 148). Fischer-Lichte's approach echoes Stanton B. Garner's concept of 'phenomenological complexity' that Cormac Power defines as the balance between the semiotic textuality of the character and the corporeality of the actor's body (Garner, 1994: 43, in Power, 2008: 176–7). However, as Power rightly cautions, such bifocal models tend 'to privilege the phenomenological as more "actual" than the semiotic, without fully recognising that the "actual" or the "real" when framed on the stage, is itself also signified' (2008: 180). We have already seen how the surrogate performers in the work of both Forced Entertainment and the Wooster Group are no less signified, no more authentic, than the characterisations that they adopt, but Derrida's radical poststructuralism would suggest, furthermore, that the actors behind the surrogates – even if those two different orders could be perceptually distinguished by the spectator – are also, in their own way, semiotic/textual signifiers of themselves.

Such a reading is entirely consistent with the philosophical developments in conceptualisations of self and subjectivity at the turn of the twenty-first century. In *The Self We Live By,* Gubrium and Holstein trace the trajectory of the modern self, beginning with the 'transcendental self' of Descartes and the European Enlightenment, which was 'disembodied, separated, and distinguished from the very corporeal body upon which it otherwise philosophically mused and cast judgment' (2000: 18). They locate the radical advent of the 'social self' in the early part of the twentieth century when the self was to become recognised as 'an other-seeking agent, one who directs behavior toward others, whose responses, in turn, provide definitions of who one is' (2000: 10). As Gubrium and Hostein note, this notion of the self became integral to Erving Goffman's concept of the presentational self in everyday life that has been so influential for twentieth-century performance theory (Goffman, 1959), but which was soon to be confronted by the advent of poststructuralist scepticism. Kenneth J. Gergen writes that, at this point, 'the very concept of an "authentic self" with knowable characteristics recedes from view' (1991: 7). Those advocating the social-self may already have relinquished the notion of transcendence from the Enlightenment conception of subjectivity, thus acknowledging the relativity and malleability of a self that is shaped by its interaction with, and performance to, others, but this was nevertheless still a self that could be understood as a single agent and held as a discrete reference point for the purposes of identity and responsibility for its actions. The hyper-reality of postmodernism, as Gubrium and Holstein conclude, 'puts an end to the story of the social self':

> The crisis of an embattled self is over, because any sense of a central point or fulcrum for being or from which to evaluate experience has disappeared. The metaphysics of presence, which orientated us to experiential time and space, is no longer meaningful; the self has no location as such, no witnessable presence to which we can coherently respond …The self appears in myriad locations, untamed by criteria of authenticity. (2000: 67)

This is the notion of self that is reflected in the citational aesthetics of the work we have discussed so far. What used to be understood as an authentic inner self, however this might have been influenced by its social environment, is now recognised, through a postmodern and poststructuralist lens, as a construction made up of materials that can only be drawn from the common hyper-reality of which it is part. Demonstrated by the explicit quotation marks that contemporary artists, in their different ways, have sought to draw around the reality of their characterisations, it also inevitably reflects back on the performers themselves who appear, through the same lens, as merely a different order of iteration from the fragmented and free-floating constructions of character that they offer up.

If a contemporary understanding of the constructed nature of the 'self' has replaced the notion of the 'authentic' reality of the performer on stage, then it might be expected to follow that, in other models of theatre, more sustained engagements with characterisation would also be designed to mirror the constructed nature of contemporary selfhood, rather than drawing on the psychological understanding of the self that informed the Stanislavksi tradition. In this next section, I will examine a selection of work in which the notion of the performer who constructs a particular version of 'self' in the space and time of the performance event is now transposed to characters who likewise seek to write and perform 'themselves' in the present space and time of their own fictional reality.

'Consumed by their own fictions'

Roland Schimmelpfennig's *Arabian Night* (2002) diverges from the models of performance we have explored so far in that the performers are never made explicitly visible behind, or in between, the characterisations. In this sense, his work upholds the dramatic conventions noted by Erica Fischer-Lichte that might be said to subjugate the presence of the actor to the semiotic realisation of the character. However, the subversions of the dramatic model within *Arabian Night* have been noted by Małgorzata Sugiera (2004), amongst others, primarily in response to its form of presentation in which the characters narrate what would more usually be the stage directions, alongside their more conventional participation in dialogue.

> FRANZISKA: I don't know – I was on the sofa, having a lie down.
>
> LOMEIER: Her key's still in the door. I take it out of the lock and give it to her.
>
> FATIMA: He gives me the key, I wedge it against one of the shopping bags with a finger. Thanks again and do pop back later about the missing water.
>
> LOMEIER: Yeah, I might do that. Well have a nice evening – (Schimmelpfennig, 2002: 15)

In this way Schimmelpfennig's fictional world is not interspersed with the real time and space of the event as we have seen in the work of Katie Mitchell or Toneelgroep Amsterdam. The quotation marks that underline its citational aesthetic are not drawn by the actors, or directors, in this sense, but by the very characters that inhabit the fictional world. At just the moment when illusory presence threatens to establish itself through the dramatic convention of characterised dialogue that takes place in a fictional world, so this presence is disrupted by the characters' digressions into narration of their own actions. Schimmelpfennig's script leaves it open to the production as to whether these stage directions are addressed to the audience in the real time and space or maintained as narration between the characters themselves within the fictional world of the play. In either case, the digressions serve to encompass the dialogue as self-citation; the quotation marks which would be present in a novel are invisible but explicit. The characters are not offering their audience the illusion of 'whole speech' in Derrida's terms but are speaking implicitly 'written' texts within a meta-text of narration. In this sense, the characters are writing the story, and within that story, they are quoting their own text. The fact that the narrated information is often superfluous, as we can see in the above extract, adding nothing that could not simply be enacted, also offers a director the option of having the actions on stage contradict the narration that is given, in order to disrupt the veracity of the characters' versions of events and so underline further the constructed nature of the narrative. The sense in which the characters are also the authors, reliable or not, of the very story that frames them is strengthened by Schimmelpfennig's use of self-consciously artificial over-exposition. This gives his characters an echo of the children's story-teller who is making clear in the present time of telling her own foreknowledge of events to come:

> FATIMA: She won't wake again now till dawn. Then she'll be wide awake, she'll make Turkish coffee, wake me up, Good Morning Fatima, my Oriental princess, I've got to dash I'll be late for work, but listen, I must have gone to sleep on the sofa again last night, why didn't you wake me up? I wonder what would happen if one night she did wake up.
>
> [...]
>
> If someone succeeded in waking her.
>
> [...]
>
> Maybe someone'd need to come and kiss her awake.
>
> [...]
>
> If someone did come and kiss her maybe that would mean the end of these nights, nights with her sleeping on the sofa while I sit beside her watching TV or I'm with Kalil. (24–5)

Schimmelpfennig's strategic quotations around what would otherwise be the illusory presence of his characters' speech, serve to offer a formal framework for the ambiguous world of the play that likewise offers no illusions of metaphysical certainty. Situated, initially, in the familiar location of a high-rise tower block, the narrative of *Arabian Night* suggests, in the first instance, that it is obeying the rules of the conventional narrative structure of the thriller. Franziska follows the same pattern every day; returning home from work, having a shower, and falling asleep on the sofa, whilst her entire memory of the day's events, and even who she is, evaporates. On this evening, from his window in the opposite block, Karpati watches Franziska taking a shower in her seventh-floor flat. Lomeier, the caretaker, is preoccupied with the problem of the water that has stopped running from floor eight upwards and the memory of the woman who has left him, and consequently neglects to put an 'out of order' sign on the faulty lift door. Franziska's flatmate, Fatima, is expecting her boyfriend, Kalil, who gets stuck in the lift while Karpati mounts the stairs to the flat, obsessed with meeting Franziska. Fatima, concerned that Kalil hasn't arrived at the flat despite having heard his motorbike arrive, leaves the flat to see what has happened. She leaves the flat's door ajar and accidently locks herself out of the block. As she rings the bells of other flats in an unsuccessful attempt to be let in, the coast is now clear for Karpati to enter the flat and put his fantasy into action. However, once he kisses the sleeping Franzisca, the ontological basis of the world that the characters are constructing, already undermined by the digressions of direct narration as noted above, now breaks down completely. Karpati finds himself in the bottom of a half full bottle of brandy, only a few centimetres tall, while Franziska continues to dream out loud:

> FRANZISKA: I am the lover of Sheikh Al Harad Barhadba, but the Sheikh loves me kindly, like a daughter, I am a virgin. I have been living in the harem inside his palace in the desert city of Kinsh el Sar ever since I was kidnapped in Istanbul [...] But Kafra, the Sheikh's first wife, is so jealous of me, the blonde child, last night she cursed me in front of the whole harem [...] For this the Sheikh has had her beheaded. [...] But even disembodied, lying in the dust, her sinister skull still shouts after me one last time: This is your curse. You shall be destroyed. You shall be one of the lost. You shall remember nothing of what you once were. Misfortune is what you shall bring to anyone who kisses your lips. (38–40)

Despite this world's first appearance as a dream, the events of the play progress in accordance with the curse, and the more familiar dichotomy of reality/fantasy is ambiguously undermined by Lomeier's entry into the Arabian desert and his subsequent meeting with Franziska's father. The father substantiates the backstory of Franziska's kidnap, thus repositioning the 'reality' of Lomeier's own world of the flats, and implicitly himself, as belonging to the fantasy world of Franziska's nightmare, which was induced by the curse of the Sheikh's first wife in what increasingly appears to be the 'real' world.

Arabian Night is not a representation of any one foundational reality on the basis of which fantasies can be defined but a construction of possible, multiple realities, which are contingent on one another for their meaning and thus remain ontologically inconclusive. Schimmelpfennig's explicit presentation of such worlds as fictions-in-the-making is achieved, in form, through characterisations that place quotation marks around their own dialogue that might otherwise be taken to be whole speech in Derridean terms. In *Arabian Night,* as in the work of Forced Entertainment, we are confronted with stage figures, be they characters or surrogates, who are attempting to create worlds, even as those in-construction worlds are falling down around their heads. Cathy Turner's analysis of *Arabian Night* could apply equally well to the work of Forced Entertainment:

> While … it draws attention to the construction of stage reality through language, we are not at all certain that these narrators know more than the story knows – rather, they seem consumed by their own fictions, at once authors and prisoners of the story they are telling. Images of imprisonment, disempowerment and disorientation create a sense of helpless thraldom or enchantment, even while the 'spell' seems to be woven by the very subjects of the tale (2009: 108)

Just as Derrida would argue that we are spoken by already existing texts, rather than the author of original speech, the stage figures in the work discussed so far are spoken by the very texts they believe to be subject to their authorship. Likewise Martin Crimp's *The City* (2008), on which I have written at length elsewhere (Tomlin, 2009), is populated by characters who only believe they are real, and who continue to act as if they are real even after the character Clair has revealed her diary in which they are created.

> I invented characters and I put them in my city. The one I called Mohamed. The one I called the nurse – Jenny – she was funny. I invented a child too, I was quite pleased with the child. But it was a struggle. They wouldn't come alive. They lived a little – but only the way a sick bird tortured by a cat lives in a shoebox. It was hard to make them speak normally – and their stories fell apart even as I was telling them. (Crimp, 2008: 62)

Yet, even this ontological disruption is undercut by Clair's own admission that she, herself, may well not be real, throwing into doubt her own claims of authorship even as she imposes her narrative on the others. The persistence of Crimp's characters to continue to exist to the bitter end, even as their existence is pulled from under their feet by the revelations of the diary that may or may not exist, is testament to the nurse Jenny's often repeated assertion that the people who are clinging on to life are the most difficult people to kill. There are strong parallels that can be drawn between the philosophical concerns of Crimp and Schimmelpfennig, and those of Forced Entertainment, whose performers often enact similar desperate attempts to fulfil the obligations of dramatic characterisation and coherent narrative in the face of their own scepticism that such things can be any longer sustained. Referencing Crimp's strategies throughout the piece, Jenny identifies the 'signs of people clinging onto life: rags, blood, coffee cups – and the stink of course – … the particular stink people make when they're clinging and clinging on to life' (2008: 23). This is the 'stink' of the death throes of the classical order; the evaporating characters who for so long have carried all the implications of logocentric authority and enlightenment faith in the rationality of a coherent world.

Such work would seem to uphold Elinor Fuchs's prediction of the death of the character that is now reduced to haunting our stages through the apparitions of its ghostly remains. Fuchs chronologically aligns the death of character with the 'brilliant layerings' of the Wooster Group's 'former dramatic and theatrical presences folded back on themselves as text' and '[t]he appearance of these kinds of textualities on many different stages' (1996: 88). Yet what we might also be witnessing in the 1990s and 2000s is the resurrection of a very different order of character – such as those of Schimmelpfennig and Crimp – whereby the notion of textuality that Fuchs notes above is explicitly displayed in the work of the Wooster Group is now embedded in the character's own self-conscious construction and performance of self. The texts that the Wooster Group displayed and from which they cited can, in one sense, be seen to be the forerunners of the invisible meta-texts that are drawn on by increasingly performative characters in order to write and enact their own identities.

'Seduced by their own articulation'

Nowhere is this aesthetic more explicit than in the work of Howard Barker, which is renowned for the protagonists' 'compulsions to excavate, explicate and perform their selves' (Rabey, in Barker, 1993a: 143). Barker's self-defined theatre of catastrophe begins to evolve in the late 1980s, although the seeds of his philosophy can be seen throughout his earlier work. Thus, by the beginning of the 1990s, he was trailblazing a distinctive and unique approach to characterisation that was to significantly influence later writers such as Sarah Kane and Adriano Shaplin, among many others. If the characterisations of Forced Entertainment, Schimmelpfennig and Crimp reflect a degree of existential despair at the poststructuralist condition that has chronicled 'the demise of a self that can no longer stand as a grounded source or object of experience' (Gubrium and Holstein, 2000: 68), the characterisations of Howard Barker offer a distinctly different perspective. Barker refuses to accept the debilitating consequences of alienation predicted by Guy Debord, who warned back in 1967 that 'the individual's own gestures are no longer his own, but rather those of someone else who represents them to him' (1995: 23). Refusing to accept the reduction of the self to a mere citation of free-floating signifiers within the discourse in which it circulates, Barker sees the 'crisis of an embattled self' (Gubrium and Holstein, 2000: 67) as the possibility 'to forge new meanings out of the fractured ruins of … identity' (Price, 1993: 7). In *Arguments for a Theatre* Barker asserts '[c]atastrophe in my theatre is willed, as opposed to simply endured …

What lies behind the idea of catastrophe is the sense of other varieties of the self repressed or obscured by politics, social convention, or simple fear' (1993a: 143–4).

The notion of society that informed the development of the social self can here be seen to be anathema to Barker, as he reads the realist text of social interdependence as an ideology that restricts the will of the individual to create themselves in accordance with their own will and desire. This underpins his rejection of naturalism which he believes, along with Hans-Thies Lehmann, encourages easy empathetic identification with the protagonist, leading the spectator to confirm, rather than challenge, the ideological meanings that already saturate media circulation. Barker's protagonists are rather required to reject the commonplace preconceptions of moral behaviour, such as pity, charity, love and other related familial and social bonds, in order to 'consciously create themselves as a work of art' without limitation (Price, 1993: 10):

> What the characters do in rupturing these bonds is to create morality for themselves, as if from scratch. They insist on a carte blanche, however impossible. It is as if they were seeing their own lives as theatre, and demanding the right to invent themselves.' (Barker, 1993a: 149)

This process of self-invention can be seen through the self-conscious construction of narrative that underlines the 'written' text that belies the illusion of whole speech. As Charles Lamb observes, 'the characters, through using language, can be seduced by their own articulation ... there is a sense in which perhaps the words speak the character rather than vice versa' (Lamb, in Barker, 1993a: 162). Katrin, a character from *The Europeans* (1993), can be seen here giving an account of her rape by Turkish soldiers, but her constant self-corrections, like the stage directions in *Arabian Night*, act as quotation marks to dispel the illusion of whole speech, and highlight a meta-text of self-conscious narration.

The character's key objective is not, as would be expected in the case of the naturalistic actor or psychologically coherent self, to express shame, pain or anger, but rather to construct the narrative that might best define her role in the official history of the war:

> It's you who are ashamed not me but I forgive in all directions then one of them threw up my skirt excuse me – (*She drinks.*)

> Or several of them, from now on I talk of them as plural, as many-headed, as many-legged and a mass of mouths and of course I had no drawers, to be precise – (*Pause*).

> I owned a pair but for special occasions. This was indeed special but on

7   Judith Scott in *The Europeans.*
Photographer: Leslie Black

rising in the morning I was not aware of it, and I thought many things, but first I thought – no, I exaggerate, I claim to know the order of my thoughts what a preposterous claim – strike that out, no, among the cascade of impressions – that's better – that's accurate – (Barker, 1990: 4–5, original emphasis)

This denial of naturalistic emotion is consistent with Katrin's rejection of the consolations and comfort of her sister's home, recognising it as 'the instrument of reconciliation' (1990: 7) that will stifle her journey to a self-knowledge that requires the continuing pain of her ordeal. She chooses instead to display her body, from which her breasts have been hacked

off, to be painted and distributed throughout Vienna, along with a future
image which she constructs for the painter:

> KATRIN: And another, later, like this …! (*She pretends to feed a child.*) I
> raise my infant, who is crying for his feed, but to the absent breasts, where
> no milk flows! His arms reach out, his tiny hands …! Imagine my expres-
> sion! Imagine his! (1990: 14)

She further enacts her own public spectacle of private pain by insisting
on giving birth to the child of her violation unassisted and framed
specifically as a public performance not unlike that of the radical avant-
garde performance artist. When the Emperor Leopold holds the baby
aloft and christens her 'Concilia', he threatens to rewrite the conclusion to
Katrin's personal narrative of pain, as historical and political reconciliation
between the Muslim and Christian empires, but Katrin refuses the role
and, ultimately, transcends the bonds of motherhood to hand her baby
over to the Turks, thus rejecting Leopold's authorship of her own and her
baby's history.

The imperative to subjectively rewrite the official version of history
is paramount to the radical narrative of poststructuralism, as defined in
Chapter 2, which seeks to challenge logocentrism by promoting multiple
and contingent readings, putting 'presence *into play*' and destabilising
any sense of a coherent or originary real (Power, 2008: 9). The citational
strategies explored in this chapter all seek to place their representations
of the real within quotation marks of some kind or another in order to
underline the constructed nature of self and the real that reflects the
shifting understanding of identity and reality in the world beyond the
theatre. The radical reading of citational characterisation, as outlined
by Philip Auslander's reading of Hal Foster introduced in Chapter 1,
would be that it exposes the workings of the simulacrum from within.
What this chapter has hopefully demonstrated, in addition, is that this
exposure of illusion through self-conscious acts of construction can be
undertaken either by more or less explicitly surrogate performers or by
the foregrounding of performative characterisations, as both are merely
different orders of citation when read through Derrida's theory. There
is no philosophical or ideological distinction, no authentic real of the
performer as opposed to the illusory real of the character, as has been too
often suggested by the theatre/performance or dramatic/postdramatic
binaries. Whatever the particular method, through highlighting the
constructed nature of all illusions of the real, citational aesthetics can
disable the ideological power of such illusions to sustain their authority.

The artist-tyrant

The role that citational aesthetics has been called upon to play in the radical narrative of poststructuralism is not, however, immune from further ideological interrogation. By disabling the authority of an objective real, a new kind of authority inevitably emerges that is now relative and subjective, as each individual becomes, in potential, the Author-God of their own narrative, resulting in the contestation of micro-narratives described by Lyotard whereby 'to speak is to fight, in the sense of playing' (1984: 10). The playing field, however, as cautioned in Chapter 1, is not a level one, and there are losers as well as winners in the absence of objective authority, however illusory this may have been proven to be, as a closer look at Barker's theatre of catastrophe will reveal.

In a previous article (Tomlin, 2006), I argued that the ideological implications of Barker's protagonists' acts of self-definition could not be assessed without reference to the philosophical theories of Nietzsche, whose influence is ever more apparent in Barker's later work. In *Thus Spoke Zarathustra*, Nietzsche's prophet rejects the compensations of a limited humanity, and calls for an 'Übermensch' who will take on the task of challenging the barriers of conventional morality and move beyond a mortal concept of good and evil to create a heroic self whose will to power will raise himself and mankind to a divine greatness (Nietzsche, 1969). In *The Will to Power*, Nietzsche expands on his vision of a 'new vast aristocracy, based upon the most severe self-discipline ... artist-tyrants' (1913: 365) who, as Ansell-Pearson comments, 'look upon man as a sculptor works upon his stone' (Ansell-Pearson, 1994: 149).

This would suggest that Nietzsche's 'artist-tyrants' are fully realised in the protagonists of Barker's tragic theatre; artists who work first and foremost on shaping themselves; yet also, inevitably, tyrants who will coerce others to bend to the shape of their created world. Ansell-Pearson summarises Nietzsche's 'new aristocracy', as defined in *The Gay Science* (Nietzsche, 1974), as 'new conquerors who love danger, war, who refused to be reconciled to, or compromised and castrated by the present' (Ansell-Pearson, 1994: 150) and who, above all, realise that 'every strengthening and enhancement of the human type also involves a new kind of enslavement' (Nietzsche, 1974: 338). In *Beyond Good and Evil*, Nietzsche writes further:

> The essential thing in a good and healthy aristocracy is, however, that it does *not* feel itself to be a function (of the monarchy or of the common-wealth) but as their *meaning* and supreme justification – that it therefore accepts with a good conscience the sacrifice of innumerable men who *for*

its sake have to be suppressed and reduced to imperfect men, to slaves and instruments. Its fundamental faith must be that society should *not* exist for the sake of society but only as foundation and scaffolding upon which a select species of being is able to raise itself to its higher task and in general to a higher *existence*. (1990: 193, original emphasis)

Thus, in Nietzsche's philosophy, the mass of humanity becomes no more than the raw material on which the privileged 'artist-tyrant' draws. This particular subject/object dialectic occurs in Barker's work when the tragic protagonist seeks to determine the making of a world that requires particular contributions from the characters which refuse, or are unable to countenance, such aspirations of their own.

In Barker's *Ten Dilemmas in the Life of a God* the protagonist is Draper, a land-owner who craves a sustained separation from Becker, the woman he worships, to prolong the impotence she inspires in him, thus preventing the consummation of his idealised desire. It is, he pronounces, 'more beautiful ... to rot in celibacy' (Barker, 1993b: 358), than to accede to mundane sexual comfort, and he achieves this desired separation through his random and arbitrary murder of a visiting musicologist, a guest of Becker's:

PLAYDEN: ...Why me?

DRAPER: (*taking him gently in an embrace*): Why not you? By the same token, why not?

PLAYDEN: I did no wrong to you.

DRAPER: Oh, the irrelevance of that! The pathos of such a calculation, as if murder could follow only on offence! You do offend me, but how innocently, no, nothing can attach to that, you were chosen by her beauty, as I was. Her beauty sank your life, as your death will sink mine ...

PLAYDEN: I refuse to be an element of your degenerate life ...

DRAPER: Yes ...

PLAYDEN: I refuse ...!

DRAPER: Yes, and how appalling it is nobody knows but me I require no pity and you are petulant to quarrel like this, isn't he, when my mind is. I must be locked away and you're the means. (1993b: 363)

In the reduction of Playden's humanity to an 'element' of Draper's 'degenerate life', we can glimpse the Nietzschean implications of Barker's tragic vision. Such moments, which are many throughout Barker's work, suggest that the self-construction of the tragic protagonists may well be achieved through the oppression, appropriation or manipulation of the raw material at their disposal; their privilege as artists, in other words, may be bought by their tyranny.

If Barker's characters succeed in resisting their slide into simulacra, by taking control over their own construction of self, this is an affirmation of autonomy which bears little relation to progressive sociological theories of the postmodern self. One such theory, as advocated by Gubrium and Holstein, would, in common with Barker's philosophy, no longer reference 'an experientially constant entity, a central presence or presences', but would rather stand 'as a practical discursive accomplishment' (Gubrium and Holstein, 2000: 70). However, such a theory would also, unlike Barker's vision, seek to regain a revised notion of subjectivities that could be held 'practically and morally responsible for our actions' (2000: 71). I would argue rather that Barker's characters revert to the pre-social, 'transcendental self' of the romantic protagonist, but in full celebration of the imperialist implications that were the underbelly of the 'transcendental pretense' which, as Robert Solomon reveals, was 'no innocent philosophical thesis, but a political weapon of enormous power' (Solomon, 1988: 6). Just as the notion of colonialism was integral to the self-realisation of European identity, so does contemporary self-realisation, as Barker's work demonstrates, come too often at the expense of the appropriation of the other to the self's narrative desires. If the transcendental self of historical times, as exemplified by Lord Byron, Friedrich Nietzsche or Oscar Wilde, was available only to the privileged elite, it has now become, through the neo-liberalist narrative that underpins Barker's philosophy, available to all who aspire to its imperatives. For this reason it is vital, in any ideological analysis of poststructuralism, to bear this less progressive consequence of radical self-determination in mind.

In the following three chapters I will examine models of performance where this consideration becomes particularly critical. In Chapters 5 and 6, I elaborate on the neo-liberalist narrative of self-authorship in relation to performance models that seek to enable the spectator to become the author/participant in order to subjectively 'rewrite' their own 'real' and the reality of others. But firstly, in Chapter 4, I will interrogate the process of verbatim practices that require artists to construct and stage, neither themselves nor fictional characters, but a 'real' other. The metaphorical exploration of citationality, as explored by the artists in this chapter, is employed as an actual methodology by artists who are working with verbatim strategies and, quite literally, constructing their work from the citations of people who have offered their testimony of self as source material for the text of the production. Given the scepticism outlined in this chapter towards the authenticity of the real performer and the truth of autobiography, Chapter 4 will ask how contemporary verbatim practice might maintain the necessary quotation marks around the testimonies it uses, without reducing the testifiers to fictional elements of the artist's own narrative. I will examine, moreover, how it might do so without merely reverting to discredited notions of truth and authenticity.

Notes

1   This analysis is based on the performance of *The World in Pictures* at the Lyceum Theatre, Sheffield, on 13 October 2006. All quotations are transcribed from documentation of the performance recorded at Nuffield Theatre, Lancaster, October 2006.

2   This analysis is based on documentation of an assemblage made from three performances of the company's revival of the production in 2003. *BRACE UP!* DVD (The Wooster Group, 2009).

3   This analysis is based on the performance of *Vieux Carré* at the Royal Lyceum Theatre, Edinburgh, on 23 August 2010.

4   This analysis is based on the performance of *Some Trace of Her* at the National Theatre, London, on 18 October 2008.

5   This analysis is based on the performance of *Roman Tragedies* at the Barbican, London, on 20 November 2009.

6   This analysis is based on the performance of *Void Story* at the Crucible Theatre, Sheffield, on 26 May 2010.

4

Representing the real: verbatim practice in a sceptical age

Emerging out of the prevailing climate of scepticism in the final decade of the twentieth century was the revitalisation of documentary forms of theatre in the first decade of the twenty-first. This particular wave of documentary theatre tended to draw, most of all, on the tradition of verbatim or testimonial performance which can be seen to permeate all manner of theatrical practice across this period. Verbatim performance texts are created entirely from extracts of interview transcripts or testimonies, offered by a selected body of contributors, to be edited by the artists concerned and delivered by performers. The strategic use of such texts in this period is widespread, evidenced in the German documentary renaissance highlighted by Thomas Irmer (2006), the Tricycle Theatre's series of Tribunal Plays in the United Kingdom, the inclusion of verbatim accounts by political dramatists such as David Hare (2003, 2004), and the turn to verbatim by internationally renowned companies as diverse as DV8 (*To be Straight With You,* 2008) and the Tectonic Theatre Project (*The Laramie Project,* 2000). Such a wealth and diversity of practice suggests that verbatim strategies were offering something significant to a broad spectrum of artistic production at the beginning of the twenty-first century. For companies such as Forced Entertainment and Uninvited Guests, the strategy has offered the potential to undermine the singularity of authorship from the poststructuralist perspective addressed in Chapter 2. The material for Forced Entertainment's *Instructions for Forgetting* (2001), defined by Tim Etchells as 'one of the group's intimate, fragmented, and at times semi-fictional documentary performance works'(2006: 109), was pre-gathered from members of the public who might be future or past spectators of the work, 'who often imagine the kinds of material that they might have contributed had they been asked' (2006: 111). This particular use of verbatim strategies to enable audience participation in the collaborative making of art is explored, in that context, in Chapter 6, but here I will focus on the much more widespread use of verbatim strategies to address issues of political and topical concern in the world beyond the theatre. This chapter will consequently examine a range of performance models drawing on verbatim strategies for more or less explicitly ideological ends and will seek to address the apparent paradox of a form that is required to rely on the real for its political authority, whilst simultaneously remaining suspicious of the very notion of the real as dictated by the poststructuralist scepticism of this particular historical moment.

Verbatim practice in this period arguably stems, on the one hand, from the epic documentary theatre of Brecht and Piscator in the 1920s (Weiss, 1971: 41 and Paget, 1990: 44), and on the other, from more ancient traditions of oratory, as proposed by Carol Martin (2009). In Derek Paget's historical study of the 'broken tradition' of documentary theatre, he traces the innovations of Brecht and Piscator through the work of Joan Littlewood and Peter Weiss to the new wave of verbatim practice emerging in the 2000s (Paget, 2009). It is significant that Paget locates the emergence of the earliest wave of modern documentary theatre at the beginning of the century in which 'facts and information' had begun to 'supply religion's place as a provider of certainties' (Paget 1990: 18). With this in mind, the resurgence of documentary methods at the turn of the twenty-first century, and their increasingly widespread influence over the first decade of the new millennium, seems somewhat paradoxical given the prevailing scepticism towards 'facts' or the 'real', as highlighted in previous chapters. It is, however, significant that it is verbatim strategies, above all else, which most often characterise the documentary theatre of the early twenty-first century. Paget observes that:

> Testimony and witness have increased in importance as former certainties
> – and faith in facts as understood by the likes of Weiss – have drained away
> [...] Documents have become vulnerable to postmodern doubt [...] But
> the witness's claim to authenticity can still warrant a credible perspective.
> (2009: 235–6)

Correspondingly, Carol Martin locates the roots of twenty-first century verbatim practice in the tradition of orature: 'a system of transmission and repository of cultural knowledge wholly equivalent to literature' but without literature's 'fixed, authentic and authorised texts' (2009: 83). Thus, there can be a certain licence accorded to the use of verbatim strategies that liberates such practice from the truth claims of earlier periods of documentary theatre; truth claims that would be less sustainable in the sceptical climate of the twenty-first century. Where Martin argues that documentary devices such as 'stage acting, film clips, photographs, and other "documents"' still function to 'attest to the veracity of both the story and the people being enacted' (2006: 9), I will propose that the increasing use of personal testimony over 'film clips, photographs and other documents' in twenty-first century verbatim practice significantly limits the 'truth claims' of the work, as much of its source material is derived from private narratives, as opposed to public documents which are more accessible to verification processes. Moreover, the shift from public information to private narratives raises the stakes for the ethics of performance because the citation of testifiers, as distinct from the citation of testimony, can too easily become the representation of testifiers, whereby the 'self' of the other is reconstructed by the performer for the purposes of the artistic project. In the previous chapter we noted the risk of the subjective authority which has the power to undertake a rewriting not only of 'self' but also of 'other', and this risk becomes an ethical concern when the 'other' is a person who exists in their own right and identity beyond their function in the performance text.

This chapter will consequently examine a range of different approaches to the representations of testifiers in verbatim performance, from predominantly naturalistic portrayals of character within a dramatic narrative framework to intentionally inadequate citations of character that never succeed in dislodging the performer personae from the centre of the theatrical narrative. An ideological examination of these various choices will demonstrate how the radical poststructuralist aesthetic, in the contexts described in Chapter 3, may read very differently once the notion of a 'real' that is distinct from a 'representation' is no longer something that can be so easily dismissed. In this sense, the surge in popularity, in such sceptical times, of a performance practice that stakes its credibility on its alleged relationship to a reality beyond the theatre clearly requires some investigation. I will thus begin by outlining some of the possible reasons that might explain why documentary theatre has re-emerged at this particular point in history, before going on to look at the complex negotiations that poststructuralist scepticism has necessitated within the form itself.

The irruption of the real

Stephen Bottoms (2006) and Carol Martin (2006) are among those who suggest that the events of 11 September 2001 are central to the subsequent rise in popularity of the verbatim form, although Bottoms does note that the thematic material pertaining to 9/11 and the subsequent political events is particular to the United Kingdom (57). This perspective would suggest, as does Derek Paget, that it is in heightened political times that documentary methods are revitalised (Paget, 2010: 173), and it may well be, as Bottoms observes, that 'mere dramatic fiction has apparently been seen as an inadequate response to the current global situation' (2006: 57). The ongoing suspicion of dramatic representation, outlined in detail in Chapters 1 and 2 of this book, might further explain the shift away from the 'state of the nation' dramatic texts of the 1970s and 1980s and the rising popularity of verbatim strategies as used to address more recent political events. In *The Problem of Speaking for Others*, Linda Alcoff suggests that there has indeed been a 'crisis of representation' that has, in the wake of poststructuralist, feminist and anti-colonialist theories, raised political questions regarding the artist's right to engage 'in the act of representing the other's needs, goals, situation, and in fact, who they are' (Alcoff, 1991–92: 9). The perceived problematics of dramatic representation, in particular, may thus have been influential in the shift away from the political dramas that fictionalised marginalised 'others', to a preference for a political verbatim practice that enabled those 'others' to speak for themselves. That this is not without its own ethical challenges will be addressed throughout this chapter, but the promise of self-authorship that verbatim practice ostensibly offers might suggest one possible reason for its recent rise in popularity. However, if verbatim practice shares some common ground with a postdramatic theatre practice in its rejection of the illusory, fictional world representations of the dramatic, it diverges significantly from the majority of new performance practices in the 1990s in its address to explicitly political and topical 'real' events. If the prevailing tendency at the close of the twentieth century, as I have argued, was to interrogate the conceptual possibility of the real, the poststructuralist project may have been given pause for thought by the attack on the twin towers, which was characterised by Jean Baudrillard as a 'singularity' that had the power to rupture the totality of the integral reality which he defined as the advanced stages of the simulacrum (Baudrillard, 2003: 96–7). It seems plausible that the irruption of an act that shattered the illusion of the capitalist consensus that had risen from the ruins of European Communism at the close of the 1980s might have called for a return to the 'reality' of the global political situation which, from a Western perspective, was arguably the most threatening that a new generation of artists had experienced in their lifetime.

Beyond such theoretical propositions, what is beyond doubt is that the attack on the twin towers set in process the strategic and pre-emptive invasions of Afghanistan and Iraq that intensified public scepticism in the United States and the United Kingdom towards the testimonies of their political leaders and the media-driven representations of events. UK Prime Minister Tony Blair's attempts to 'sex up' official documents in order to fabricate evidence of the direct threat to Britain posed by Iraq's alleged weapons of mass destruction, and President George Bush's spin designed to connect Al-Qaeda and Saddam Hussein in the minds of the American public, were transparently employed to 'justify' a war on Iraq to which the rest of Europe, and significant percentages of Bush and Blair's own populations, were vehemently opposed. Such levels of political corruption and deception undoubtedly re-awakened the ideological imperative for a theatre practice that might, once again, seek to demystify the 'official' version of events, as the early Marxist documentary theatre had advocated. Work that engaged directly with the events that followed 9/11 included *Justifying War* (2003) and *Guantanamo: Honor Bound to Defend Freedom* (2004), produced by London's Tricycle Theatre, David Hare's *Stuff Happens* (2004), produced by the National Theatre, Robin Soans' *Talking to Terrorists* (2005), commissioned by Out of Joint, and Steve Gilroy's *Motherland*, which toured the United Kingdom in 2009. In addition to productions that drew on the subject matter of these specific political events, the fallout from 9/11 can also arguably be said to have shaped a historical period of enhanced political awareness and agitation that may have contributed to the increase in the use of verbatim to demystify the official version of events across a wide range of subject matters. Examples of such work, amongst many more, would include David Hare's *The Permanent Way* (2003), which investigated the privatisation of Britain's railway system in the wake of a number of fatal accidents; the Tricycle Theatre's *Bloody Sunday* (2005), a tribunal play made of up edited transcripts from the official enquiry into the 1972 shooting of thirteen Catholics by British soldiers in Northern Ireland; *My Name is Rachel Corrie* (2005), produced by the Royal Court Theatre and created from extracts of text written by Corrie before her death at the hands of the Israeli army during her protests for peace in Gaza; and *Katrina* (2009), produced by Jericho House and composed of accounts provided by both survivors and those responsible for the failed relief effort following the hurricane which destroyed the city of New Orleans in August 2005.

As Stephen Bottoms has observed, explicitly political verbatim practice in the United States over this period cannot be likewise aligned with the events of 9/11 (2006: 57). The groundbreaking work of Anna Deavere Smith predates the period of this study, beginning in the early 1980s but coming to prominence with *Fires in the Mirror* (1992), following the race riots in Brooklyn, New York, a year earlier; and *Twilight: Los Angeles 1992* (1993), which followed the acquittal of the police officers caught on camera during their violent assault on Rodney King. *The Laramie Project,* first produced in 2000 by New York's Tectonic Theatre Project, also predates most of the work under discussion in this chapter, introducing a particular use of verbatim to a new generation of international artists, whereby a company of actors self-referentially performs a series of, sometimes conflicting, direct address testimonies to the audience around a central event, in this case the homophobic murder of student Matthew Shepard in the town of Laramie, Wyoming, in 1998.

Throughout the diverse range of forms and subject matter that verbatim practice can be seen to take in this period, a recurring imperative, expressed by both artists and critics, is that of challenging the dominant historical account of the subject matter in question. In this sense, verbatim practice remains committed to the objectives Peter Weiss set out for documentary theatre in the 1960s under the headings: 'critique of concealment', 'critique of distortion' and 'critique of lies' (1971: 41). Whilst the political narratives foregrounded in more recent work are rarely explicitly Marxist, they do also share with the early documentary theatre an allegiance to those groups which are marginalised by the dominant economic, social and political systems of the time. Such concerns define a contemporary verbatim practice which is also testimonial, characterised by Linda Ben-Zvi as

(1) a desire to reinstate the voices and experiences of those written out of history; (2) a belief that the words of individuals telling their stories can provide a powerful corrective to the mediatized versions of reality claiming legitimacy; and (3) a recognition of the power of performance to challenge the master narratives and discourses of history (2006: 45).

Yet, in spite of the evidence that a diverse range of performance was making a return to 'real' and explicitly political events at the turn of the century, with much the same ideological motivation as its documentary predecessors, the prevailing scepticism of the climate ensured that such a return to the 'real' was accompanied by critical imperatives unique to its own time. Despite the epic tradition's rejection of mimetic or naturalistic reflections of a questionable reality, a conviction nevertheless lay at the heart of early documentary theatre that there was a truth at the core of its overt constructions; a belief that Marxism could and would offer the necessary alternative to a capitalist future. By the beginning of the 1990s, however, the remainder of those particular ideological convictions were crumbling along with the Berlin wall. The failure of Soviet communism, the totalitarian invasions of Eastern Europe and the atrocities of the Stalinist regime had arguably combined with the rise of poststructuralist theory to make the singularity of the Marxist ideology of the earlier documentary theatre an impossible position to sustain.

Consequently, there is a tension at the heart of twenty-first century verbatim practice and reception that is the result of seemingly irreconcilable conflict between, on the one hand, the drive for political change that necessitates both a relationship with the 'real' world and an ideological commitment to a particular political discourse, and, on the other, a philosophical scepticism of the 'real' world, and a consequent discrediting of truth claims or ethical imperatives that seek to distinguish any one narrative as authoritative. Nels P. Highberg argues explicitly that 'a core value of documentary theatre […] is the extent to which it encourages audiences to recognise the damaging effects of singular impositions of truth within society'(Highberg, 2009: 167). To address this, one of the most common strategies in this later period of verbatim practice is a pluralistic approach that seeks to offer a number of different versions of the event, none of which can claim, in its own right, to be authoritative, but all of which, taken together, will contest the authority of the dominant interpretation of the event over other possible interpretations. This results in a multiplicity of, often conflicting, testimonies, delivered either by a single performer, as in the case of Anna Deavere Smith, or by an ensemble such as Tectonic Theatre or DV8. Yet, despite the adherence of such practice to pluralist forms that ostensibly advocate a poststructuralist understanding of the political, such a framework most often remains paradoxically in tension with the ideological aims of the practice. For artists working within a testimonial verbatim practice almost always hold a commitment to a particular narrative of opposition. As noted by Wendy S. Hesford, they might strategically seek to move 'away from the creation of a single protagonist', but the 'creation of a communal voice' that replaces the single protagonist remains, despite its plurality, most often singular in its political objective (2006: 35).

In the *Epilogue to the Laramie Project* (2009), members of the Tectonic Theatre Project returned to Laramie to research public opinion ten years after the death of Matthew Shepard. Readings of this new piece were performed in 120 theatres around the world on the eleventh anniversary of Matthew's death. One of the key motivations for the Tectonic Theatre Project to return to Laramie, and featuring heavily in the *Epilogue*, was the influence of a mediatised version of the murder that had been screened on the ABC newsmagazine *20/20*. Shot in a similar format to the Laramie Project, and presenting interviews with many of the same people, the *20/20* team was offering a very different hypothesis for the murder. Rejecting the conclusion of the Laramie Project (and, significantly, of the original court hearings) that this was a gay hate crime, the *20/20* analysis concluded that the murder was the result of high levels of methamphetamine in both perpetrators and victim; a drug- fuelled crime that got out of control. In the *Epilogue*, we heard convincing arguments that suggested that this verdict was categorically untrue. Nevertheless, the Tectonic Theatre Project was not concerned with merely disproving one verdict; rather, it was dedicated to re-enforcing another: that this had, indeed, been a hate crime committed against Matthew Shepard because of his sexuality, and no other reason. In the UK staged reading I attended at the Lowry Theatre in Salford, the performances of the British company offered up a plurality of narratives that offered a multiplicity of positions on the verdict. However, the project ensured, through judicious editing and representational strategies, that its own conclusion was foregrounded to claim a greater veracity, or credibility, than all other possible narratives. The representations of high-status individuals who were supporting the 'hate crime' verdict, such as Professor Catherine Connelly, were given correspondingly serious and rhetorical modes of delivery, with American accents of the educated class. Also delivered naturalistically and empathetically were the heroic police officers who had been converted from their previous prejudice by the experience of this particular case. Conversely, the republican senator arguing against same-sex marriages, and the local newspaper editor who had decided it was 'time to move on', were treated parodically, thus undermining the credence of anything they had to say. Members of the anonymous public were often caricatured by performance and accent as rednecks who clearly knew no better. That a poster-boy image of Matthew Shepard closed the piece only confirmed his status as the icon of an international gay-rights movement, and confirmed the singularity of the ideological agenda of both the original production and its epilogue. Such singularity of narrative is common amongst verbatim practice of this period, which, for the most part, employs pluralistic strategies, not simply to undermine the authority of the dominant narrative by repositioning this as one among many possible narratives, but to actively offer a more or less coherent position of challenge that becomes implicitly authorised by the production as 'the truth'.

The sceptical climate, in which twenty-first century verbatim practice has paradoxically flourished, has subsequently ensured that academic debate and analysis are rarely focused on the issues raised by the source material but are rather compelled to interrogate the validity of the form itself, particularly in relation to any implicit or explicit truth claims it might be seen to be making. The tension that exists 'between objective shards or fragments of reality and subjective treatments of it' is consequently characterised by Janelle Reinelt as 'a structuring fault-line' of the representations of documentary theatre in general and, I will now argue, verbatim practice in particular (2009: 8).

Treating the marginal

In Chapter 3, I highlighted the potential dangers of the poststructuralist shift towards self-determination, when less powerful 'others' were employed as raw material in the imperialist narrative ventures of the sovereign self. Verbatim practice intensifies such dangers, as the 'others' who are being cited or represented in the theatrical narrative constructed by the artists are not fictional characters and, furthermore, as earlier noted, are often speaking from positions of marginality or disempowerment. For the remainder of this chapter, I would like to turn my attention to the particular ideological issues raised by the artistic treatment of 'real-life' testimonies and testifiers, who are placed within theatrical frameworks to serve as raw material for the narrative of the artists involved.

Peggy Phelan argues in *Unmarked,* her seminal study of the representation of marginal identities, that 'there are serious limitations to visual representation as a political goal … it provokes voyeurism, fetishism, the colonialist/imperial appetite for possession' (1993: 6). When the visual representation of one subject is authored by another, such dangers are intensified. Quoting John Beverly, Maryrose Casey observes that 'if the narrator is only perceived as a witness, then the narrator does "not have the power to create their own narrative authority and negotiate its conditions of truth"'(Beverly, 1996: 276, in Casey, 2009: 136–7). Even when the pluralist model is adopted and deliberate attempts are made to collate a number of conflicting narrative voices, the ultimate framing, editing and shaping of the work lies in the hands of the artist(s) rather than the testifiers. It is the artists who will design the framework of the process; be that specific questions or simply recording over a period of time whatever is said; and it is they who will decide what material to use and how. Unlike the court of law – used as a comparative model for verbatim practice by Carol Martin (2006: 11) – where the 'argument' is essentially dialogic, the verbatim text, despite its plurality of voices, is fundamentally monologic, as the perspective of the artist holds the ultimate authority, both over the political conclusions of the piece itself and over the representations of the individuals involved. Despite the best intentions of the majority of artists working in this field to speak on behalf of the testifiers, or give voice to the testifiers' own agenda, Helen Nicholson cautions against 'the coercive function of gift-giving', first identified by Marcel Mauss, arguing that a rigorous acknowledgement of the power relations at work in such a process is always required (2005: 161).

Such power relations do not only exist between artists and testifiers but, likewise, between testifiers and audience. The aims of documentary theatre have always included, at their core, the desire to raise awareness or to educate the audience, but the more recent emphasis on verbatim strategies and the testimonies from marginal communities requires a reassessment of the potential political consequences of such an aim, which can no longer be taken as unproblematically progressive. Traditionally, documents and facts were researched by the artists, and edited and performed for the benefit of the audience. The audience as primary beneficiary only becomes problematic when the documents and facts are replaced by the testimonies of human beings, commonly already holding positions of less cultural power than those who are gaining from exposure to their narratives. There immediately arises a conflict between those who already have less, and are held of less value, giving freely to those who have more and are held in more value. This might be applicable to either or both artists and audiences depending on the different contexts of production. In a previous article, I have described how, in DV8's production of *To Be Straight With You*, the performers may well have been speaking on behalf of and to their own community about the issues of homophobia in Asian and African cultures (Tomlin, 2010). Likewise, many of the audience at the West Yorkshire Playhouse in Leeds were of the same ethnic background and sexual orientation, creating a sense of a shared community of which testifiers, artists and spectators were all a part.

The difficulties arise when this is not the case, in those, more common, instances where marginalised communities are offering their testimonies to be presented and received by those who are outside of the direct experience of such communities and hold far greater cultural power. As Maryrose Casey's research highlights, even when the performers themselves are from the community in question, the wider production and reception parameters of such work are often designed to be of benefit to the dominant, rather than the marginal, community. In her discussion of Aboriginal documentary theatre she cautions that such practice is

> consistently reduced to a form of testimony of oppression for non-Indigenous critics and audiences to witness as a gesture of good faith. On this basis, non-Indigenous audiences have interpreted and received Indigenous theatre work as produced for the educative and consciousness-raising function for white audiences in the limited sense of witnessing past oppressive actions and practices. (2009: 133)

In this sense, the marginal experience once again becomes incorporated into a dominant narrative of absolution, in which its role and function are fixed and exploited for the benefit of the dominant culture. For this reason, its potential political efficacy to shift the experience from the margins to the centre of social discourse is diffused, its only remaining power being, as Casey suggests, 'to affirm and recuperate the virtue of White Australians' (132) through a pathological aesthetic which 'is intrinsic to framing Indigenous voices as testimony' (136). In such a way, the indigenous voices remain exoticised and 'other', employed as a means of self-flagellation and self-congratulatory absolution that is of benefit to the audience, rather than to the testifiers, shoring up existing social relations as opposed to challenging them. Where audiences are offered new insights into the experiences, or histories, of a marginal community, the work perpetuates the tradition of documentary theatre as a tool of education, or means of 'consciousness-raising'. However, if the existing social power relations are left unchallenged, then any conviction that a spectator's increased awareness, in itself, 'is likely to contribute towards ameliorating problems' is, as Derek Paget suggests, naïve and generally unsubstantiated (1990: 90). Moreover, as Wendy S. Hesford argues with reference to Susan Sontag's *Regarding the Pain of Others*, 'identification, like compassion, is an unstable rhetorical stance that can function as an alibi for *lack* of action' (Hesford, 2006: 38, original emphasis). In Sontag's own words, 'so far as we feel sympathy, we feel we are not accomplices to what caused the suffering. Our sympathy proclaims our innocence as well as our impotence' (Sontag, 2003: 91). In short, consciousness-raising that leaves the existing power relations intact is likely to restrict the role of the audience to that of the cultural tourist.

Dramatising the real

In Alecky Blythe's *The Girlfriend Experience* (2008),[1] a predominantly naturalistic dramatic text created from verbatim recordings of three women who run their own brothel, we hear how the prostitute behind the character 'Tessa' wishes to raise the consciousness of her audience. Through her testimony we hear that she hopes that:

> people w-will appreciate that we're not all crackheads, an', an' – an', you know w-what we're *painted* as, what these people like Jerry (*Beat.*) – Jeremy Kyle (*Beat.*) – you were, you know, you say the word 'prostitute' 'Oh so you're *scum*'– you know, 'you've wasted your *life*, you're – y'you know, you're *noth-ing*' (Blythe, 2008: 69) (original emphasis)

Here, 'Tessa' hopes that the negative media connotations of 'prostitute' as exploited by daytime television shows can be counterpointed by her own 'real' experience that will be exposed to an audience who will be, in the main, oblivious to the reality of her marginal existence that is not otherwise visible in their world. However, as the conclusions of Peggy Phelan's *Unmarked* (1993) and Tessa's own reference to Jeremy Kyle make clear, visibility in itself is not necessarily a positive thing; the reading of the 'object made visible' is dependent on the framing that will determine the gaze of the audience and, in turn, a particular perception of the viewed object. I would now like to suggest that the dramatic model chosen in this instance as the vehicle for the verbatim strategies not only was unable to challenge the prevailing reading of prostitution but also actively fixed the existing power relations between the testifiers and the audience by placing the latter in a superior position to the characters throughout, as the *Guardian* review confirms:

> What Blythe brings out best is the self-delusion that afflicts even these supposedly hard-headed sex workers. They insist their job is like stacking supermarket shelves and that their only function is to make their clients happy without getting personally involved. But the more we see of 58-year-old Tessa, who owns the flat-cum-sex parlour, and her 42-year-old colleague Suzie, the more we realise they are yearning for permanent relationships. (Billington, 2008)

As members of an audience who were inevitably familiar with basic dramatic convention, we could already read in the women's adamant declarations of independence at the opening of the piece the journey of self-revelation which was to follow. We knew, better than the characters (and thus the testifiers), where this was going to lead. In this sense, the piece not only placed us in a position of superiority to the testifers but

8   Lu Corfield and Debbie Chazen in *The Girlfriend Experience.*
Photographer: Alastair Muir

also validated the dominant morality that would position romantic and domestic love as the ultimate aim, and prostitution as something that was simply a fearful denial. As 'Tessa' looks to turn away from prostitution, 'educated' by her lover to realise that 'i-it makes me (*Beat.*) – be able to disappear (*Beat.*) – I said, "Because I don't, like (*Beat*) – the *real me*' (81) she is only now admitting what the predominantly 'normative' audience has suspected all along.

The dramaturgy of the dramatic narrative thus clearly shaped the selection of material into a recognisable arc. From her beginnings as an overtly comic, self-assured 'character' who would never date a client, the arc moved on to Suzie's fatal flaw of falling in love, and then to the resolution where she discovers that 'he kinda fell in love with Suzie – he – didn't fall in love with the real me. (*Beat.*) Cuz 'e expected me to be up to sex the whole time' (71). Tessa, who had mocked Suzie behind her back throughout her dating, then falls for Corey and giggles like a teenager as she recounts how they 'held hands' (74) and as she plays

Suzie their 'love song' (80). That these were presumably 'real' journeys of the women involved is not in question, but the skill of the dramatic shaping of the piece, in order to make these journeys coherent and central to the narrative, placed an inevitably fixed and fictional frame around presumably more fluid and less coherent realities. Each woman's 'journey' was portrayed as single and linear, but, given the long history of the women's activity, was likely in reality to have been much more multiple and circular; it was hard to imagine that this was the first time the two women in their forties and fifties had been through this cycle of denial, hopefulness and disappointment. In this way, the complex 'realities' of the women involved were harnessed to a specific theme: the denial of the need for love that was shown to be an illusion. In itself, this narrative framed the women, against Blythe's intentions, to be ultimately self-deluded, and their lifestyle to be less fulfilled than the normative alternative of romantic monogamous relationships and domestic partnerships.

The representational acting techniques also served to reduce the reality of the testifiers to precisely the media stereotypes the piece might have wished to undermine; the women defined by the *Independent* review in terms such as 'the tart with a heart' and 'warm hearted hookers' (Jones, 2008). Technique was particularly visible in all the actors' sense of comic timing and use of gesture, and especially acute in Debbie Chazen's performance of Tessa, which was reminiscent of Dawn French. The beats, within the comic material, were sharp and perfectly timed, and gestural motifs included fanning of the face, two hands held palm up to the audience to indicate resistance, a fist stuffed into the mouth to indicate excitement, and a bathetic mimed drum roll during the playing of 'her' love song. The 'real' woman behind the characterisation was undoubtedly theatrical in her own right, although from the small amount of original recording the audience were invited to hear, the accent seemed slightly more accentuated by the actor than it was in the original. Nevertheless, the gestures were not available to the actor, and even if these had been relayed by the writer rather than created, they took on a distinctly clichéd form to increase the audience's recognition and comic appreciation. There is also, of course, the possibility that the very fact of being recorded for performance, even when the writer wasn't herself present, may have increased the levels of self-performance, and even self-parody, of the women themselves. As Richard Kilborn details in *Staging the Real*, when people who were being filmed for fly-on-the-wall documentary series 'became aware of how they were "coming across" as television personalities, they consciously began to shape their behaviour according to the roles they imagined they were being called on to perform' (2003: 92).

Even in a piece such as the Tectonic Theatre's renowned *The Laramie Project,* the potential dangers of creating 'characters' from 'real' people have been noted. Despite the self-referential aesthetic, the Brechtian staging, and a performance style that was predominantly episodic and non-dramatic, with most texts being monologic and addressed directly to the audience, Amy L. Tigner observes how the very process of editing 'reconstructs the interviews with real people into a theatre with consistent characters in a through-line narrative'(2002: 145). She describes how one of the testifiers, Harry Woods, 'found watching himself as a character troublesome, precisely because this short narrative, which he related in autumn 1998, begins to stand in for who and what he is as a person' (152). As Tigner concludes, 'the character is, after all, not the person, but a theatrical construction, which is fixed in time, controlled, and contained – that is, a rhetorical creature, embodied for the time and space of the performance' (151). If this is the case in a piece that was working against dramatic models and naturalistic performance techniques, how much greater must the danger be of constructing a theatrical character that can 'fix' the 'real' in the rhetorical, in a verbatim piece that is modelled on dramatic form?

Admittedly, the fourth wall was ruptured at certain points by the women's occasional direct address to Alecky Blythe, for whom the audience now stood in, and our momentary access, at the opening of the piece, to the original recording of the text that was played to the actors through headphones throughout. However, these gestures to Brechtian demystification were not sufficient to prevent the dramatic conventions of this particular piece from subsuming the 'real' of the testifiers into the rhetoric of their 'characterisations' in a way that served to re-enforce, rather than to challenge, the testifiers' marginal status in relation to dominant cultural values. As the conventions and familiar signs of situational comedy took precedence, the 'reality' of the women behind the representations retreated further away from audience perception, making it easy for us to laugh, not only with the women but also at them. At some points, the piece succeeded in forcing us to confront such laughter, as in the section where Poppy, the young, inexperienced prostitute, gets taken for a ride by 'Groper', who gets his turn-on for free, before pushing her into agreeing to sex without a condom. At this point, the hesitant laughter at the comic framing of the action quickly died out and there was a sense of the returning realisation of the reality behind the fiction. The juxtaposition of the banal detail that accompanied their far from banal occupation also afforded comic moments that you would imagine the women would have appreciated, if not contrived, such as Suzie's line – 'Oh, I'm gonnoo 'ave a sandwich. (*Beat.*) And I bet you, soon as I 'ave a sandwich (*Beat.*) – the door will go' (15). However, in other sections, such as the one where Suzie admires Tessa's new light bought from Wilkinsons (8–9), there is an audience laughter which is distinctly middle-class, a joke that the women themselves would not have recognised or intended. This is the laughter of the cultural tourist who finds humour in the naivety or taste of the 'other' who does not share their levels of sophistication; a laughter that serves, as Peggy Phelan cautions, to turn the 'other' into a 'fetish' for the dominant subject of the audience (1993: 6). At such moments, the reality is effaced by the comic performances that make the laughter feel easy, but if the reality is recalled, the piece becomes uncomfortably voyeuristic. Despite Blythe's belief that 'these women see my play as a genuine opportunity to show the outside world a side of prostitution that is rarely seen', and her declaration that 'they are [...] assertive and mature, and they see themselves as independent businesswomen' (Hammond and Steward, 2008: 82–3), the material chosen, the narrative arc and the technical performances ultimately reduced the reality of the women to a familiar dramatic fiction.

Fact and fiction

The reduction of one person's reality to a dramatic representation is particularly problematic when the testimony itself is fused with additional material, thus further blurring the line between the fictional and the real. Whilst many of the early documentary-makers combined facts with fiction, the citational nature of the representations and the epic structures of the work enabled clear distinctions to be made between the two. Once those distinctions disappear, through the seamless coherence of dramatic structures and/or characterisation, there is a danger that the 'real' people in question can be rewritten to fit the narrative of the artist, without the audience even being aware that such a transfiguration has taken place.

The fusion of reality and fiction in Pol Heyvaert's *Aalst* (2005) resulted in legal, as well as ethical, challenges. Produced by the Belgian theatre company Victoria, and later translated and adapted for the Scottish National Theatre by Duncan McLean (2007), *Aalst* is based on the trial of two parents for the murder of their children in a hotel room in the suburban town of Aalst in Belgium in 1999. In an interview for the Scottish National Theatre, Heyvaert explains that sixty per cent of his text was taken directly from the televised trial footage, ten per cent from a French documentary of the case, and the remaining thirty per cent from original text contributed by Flemish writer Dimitri Verhulst (Heyvaert, 2007). There is no way of telling, from the finished script, which sections are creations of Verhulst or the documentary-makers and which are taken verbatim from the parents' own testimonies at the trial, except for the one clearly fictional piece of text with which the piece concludes:

> MICHAEL: And we thought it would be better to wipe out the whole family. It isn't fair, sir: there are people who *make* a baby to save their marriage, no one objects to that … But when someone wipes out their kids to finally get *out* of the misery, they're hauled up before the courts! Everyone picks on us.
>
> *The lights dim.*
>
> MICHAEL: How was it?
>
> CATHY: It was perfect. Very convincing. That's five years off your sentence, I'm sure. (McLean, 2007: 46–7, original emphasis)

This twist can be read in two ways. Given that nothing we have heard up until this point has suggested that anything that we are hearing is not what was heard in court, then one reading is that this clearly fictional conclusion reads as the director's comment on the veracity, or otherwise, of the defendants' testimonies throughout. Alternatively, it might make us realise, for the first time, that we are not hearing only verbatim material, and so lead us to question how much of what we have heard is actually from the testimonies of the defendants at all. This latter is Stuart Young's reading of the play, supporting his analysis that 'by commingling fact and fiction, it cunningly and subtly moves from *recording* to *reporting* the drama – this is, it shifts the focus from "(the illusion of) direct *speech*" to the process of "*writing*" itself' (Young 2009: 74, original emphasis). Helena Grehan observes, on the contrary, that

> [a] number of people who saw the play commented that the moment the 'trial' was revealed to be a sham (or a performance) they felt the work became overtly manipulative and that the question of the playwright's mo- tivation emerged as an important one. There was a sense that they were being toyed with and that the work was perhaps using these horrific events primarily for entertainment, and that the slippages between stories ran the risk of rendering spectators or witnesses as voyeurs. (Grehan, 2010: 7)

There is little in the director's own account that would support Young's reading of the play as consciously self-reflexive about the ambiguities of its purported truth-telling. Despite the fact that the legal challenge identified one of the key problems as being 'not with the actual performance, but with the fact that it is neither an objective rendition of the story nor total fictionalization' (Hilliaert, 2005), Heyvaert, like Young, seems reluctant to acknowledge that the fusion of fact and fiction in the piece might give just cause for ethical concern. However, unlike Young, Heyvaert views the fictional additions as politically beneficial for the real people behind the characters the text has partially rewritten. The theatre's claim, in defending Heyvaert, that 'through this use of fiction we give these people their voice' (Hilliaert, 2005) was one that Heyvaert reiterated time and again in his recorded interview for the Scottish National Theatre. Here, he suggests that the writer, Dimitri Verhulst, had created material which constituted 'a defence ... that they didn't try to do in court', enabling the accused 'to say things which I believe they could have said in court but they didn't say' (Heyvaert, 2007). The artistic director of the company, Dirk Pauwels, proposes that, in this way, the piece offers a critique of the judicial process, arguing that 'we gave the two convicts a voice that they didn't have during the trial. The way an Assises Court case is held, is thereby questioned' (Pauwels in Van der Speeten, 2005). This may well be the case, but for the vast majority of the production's audience, who would not know in any detail what was or wasn't permitted to be said at an Assises Court, this did not alter the fact that an audience would be totally unable to distinguish between what had actually been said and what Verhulst had fabricated, making it impossible for anyone in the audience to assess the facts of the case, or the personalities involved. Heyvaert is clear, when questioned, that the mother's claim that she had also been a victim of child abuse was something that had been said in court, and stresses: '[there were] no major things that we invented', expressing surprise that the mother was taking legal action against the play when she had granted rare permission for the trial to be televised (Heyvaert, 2007). But there is a strange lack of awareness on Heyvaert's part that there are significant distinctions between the two: namely, that in the play the mother is not permitted to speak for herself but only appears to be speaking when, in fact, a fictional character has taken her place and is saying things that an audience are very likely to ascribe to the 'real' character behind the fiction.

In his interview for the Scottish National Theatre, Heyvaert explains that he didn't want to meet the couple or their family as he didn't want to

9   Kate Dickie and David McKay in the Scottish National Theatre's
production of *Aalst*.

Photographer: Richard Campbell

'make something together with them' (Heyvaert, 2007). I would suggest
that he preferred to re-create them, to re-imagine them as characters
to which he could freely impute psychological causes, motivations and
complexities that he felt the trial and the media had perhaps suppressed.

However laudable his motivation, the fusion of fact and fiction in
Aalst, and the director's own lack of reflexive critique on the ethical
ambiguity of his process, leads to a conflation, in the audience's minds, of
the real person and the character they see on stage, as this review extract,
and its seamless slippage from the actor to the real person he embodies
(see italics) demonstrates:

> But the performances of *Dickie and McKay* are quite the opposite. *They*
> are not evil, but vulnerable, heartbroken and perplexed, as if the enormity
> of *their* crimes is as much a mystery to *them* as to us. With wide eyes and
> touching honesty, *they* are like children themselves, struggling not to deny
> the wickedness of the deed but to explain the circumstances that made it

seem rational. 'We wanted to wipe out our problems,' says *the father* at the end of the play and it is with a sense of alarm that we can see what *he's* driving at. (Fisher, 2007, my emphasis)

This slippage from the actor to the unwitting testifier highlights the potential dangers in representing the 'real' person through coherent psychological characterisation, particularly when elements of the representation that are entirely fictional have been seamlessly grafted onto the real. In Chapters 2 and 3, I highlighted the poststructuralist imperative to disrupt the presence of traditional dramatic characterisation in a purely fictional context, but the need to underline the distinction between the actor who is constructing and the character who is being subjectively constructed becomes acute in verbatim practice to prevent representation – an always-ideological illusion of the real – from overwriting the 'real' itself.

'Interrupting the satisfactions of theatrical presence'

Within the traditional critical framework of documentary practice, for this very reason, characterisations were rarely approached through naturalistic techniques but were presented by the actors through Brechtian methodologies. The character would be played 'in quotation marks' in order to frame its construction, and there would be a constant switching of roles that prevented any consistent identification on the part of the audience, or depth of psychological representation on the part of the actor. These quotation marks did not perform the same philosophical function as the more radical extremes of poststructuralist scepticism inherent in the citational aesthetic discussed in Chapter 3, but were correspondingly political in their distancing of the 'characterisations' from the 'real' people themselves. Furthermore, they foreshadowed the poststructuralist aesthetic in their refusal to draw on the capacity of naturalism to offer the illusion of reality; a capacity which Brecht and Piscator recognised as inherent to the social ideological fictions their work was designed to demystify. Both were well aware that any exposure of society's representations had to go hand in hand with a theatrical form that instructed its audience in reading representations as ideological constructions, not as the natural way things were. This necessitated a theatre form that underlined its own constructions of narrative through epic models and alienation techniques, establishing, as Derek Paget describes, 'a tradition opposed to realism […] in which access to the means of production is granted to an audience expected not to consume passively, but to engage actively with the material being presented' (Paget 1990: 42).

Naturalism's emphasis on the journey of an individual protagonist, designed, when accompanied by in-depth psychological characterisation, to induce empathy and identification on the part of the spectator, is noted by Paget as inherent to the ideological dangers of the televised documentary form. Writing that his book, *True Stories,* 'opposes the "natural" collapsing of the collective object or event into the individual subject' (1990: 27), Paget refers back to the revolutionary traditions of documentary theatre that 'needed to be able to make connections not governed by the temporal and spatial logic of a single individual's experience', and asserts that 'montage supplied that capacity' (1990: 43). In this way, Paget argues, the source material of the documentary 'becomes the *true* protagonist in the drama' (1987: 318, original emphasis).

Likewise, in 'Staging Terror', an analysis of the use of the Abu Ghraib photographs as source material for artistic displays, Wendy S. Hesford proposes that in order to avoid replicating the original 'spectacle of violence', the artist needs to find a way of interrupting 'the mimetic consumption of violence' by highlighting 'the cultural framing of visual evidence' in order to rupture the traumatic repetition of the original abuse (2006: 33). This echoes Elinor Fuchs' description of a radical post-metaphysical practice which is characterised by its intent on 'interrupting the satisfactions of theatrical presence' (1996: 71), and moves the philosophical consideration of any mimetic replication of a questionable reality into explicitly ideological territory.

For these reasons, many of the artists working with verbatim strategies seek to resist the psychological characterisation identified in *The Girlfriend Experience*, and the docu-fictional representations in *Aalst,* thus disabling the potential for the audience to capture and objectify the testifiers within a dramatic frame that reflects an already ideological real. Linda Ben-Zvi describes how Nola Chilton's work seeks to rupture, rather than replicate, the dominant power structures of, in this instance, Israeli–Arab relations:

> In Chilton's documentary play, rather than stage Israeli bigotry and Arab acquiescence, which she believed would only reinforce what she wished to change, or exploit Arab pain and turn the audience into voyeurs – something she refuses to do – she chose to have Jewish actors represent the Arab other. With the auditorium lit, five Jewish actors, dressed in their ordinary clothes, performed the text on a bare stage with only a row of chairs. They did not try to imitate the Arab men whose words they spoke, for fear of making them caricatures rather than individuals. The audience was always aware of each actor's presence; his individuality was never erased. In this way Chilton underlined the theatricality of her documentary theatre: a

performance that is fiction, which seeks to call attention to itself (as de Certeau noted that theatre always does), and at the same time points to the performative construction of all nationalities and religious identities. (Ben-Zvi, 2006: 48–9)

Chilton's emphasis on presentational delivery, rather than imitative characterisation, and the overt visual distinction between the performer and the testifier, combine to support an aesthetic that rejects the creation of a dramatic character whom the audience can, at best, too easily empathise with, at worst, too easily consume. The emphasis, as in the traditional documentary form, is firmly on the material as protagonist, and the theatrical (and ideological) structure presented as contingent. Whilst Anna Deavere Smith's method of performance differs from that advocated by Chilton, in that Smith re-creates the precise details of the interviewees she represents, she, too, emphatically asserts that

> Mimicry is not character. Character lives in the obvious gap between the real person and my attempt to seem like them. I try to close the gap between us, but I applaud the gap between us. I am willing to display my own unlikeness. (Smith, 1993: xxxvii–xxxviii)

Smith's practice of performing across multiple genders and cultural identities also prevents any consistent character from emerging, keeping the focus on the complexity and multiplicity of testimonies. In this way, the performance becomes, as Jill Dolan observes, 'an embodied chronicle of ever-shifting positionality, of the impossibility of seeing such a moment and its consequences from an omniscient point of view' (2002: 512). Dolan further proposes that the multiple-character solo performance, or 'monopolylogue', model holds a unique political potential, not only in that it can 'stage various cultural identities on the same body in ways that highlight difference' but also that it 'perhaps points toward commonalities among people' (2002: 499). This notion of 'commonality' that can connect testifier to actor and, subsequently, testifier to testifier and testifier to audience, through the actor's multiple embodiments, is vital to Dolan, and she advocates the embodiment of the 'other' as the model that affords verbatim practice the greatest political efficacy. For Dolan, the more meta-theatrical methodology of Tectonic Theatre's *The Laramie Project* fails to achieve the same commonality but rather emphasises 'the perspective of outsiders *for* outsiders, with the danger of condescension to the local using such a technique involves' (Dolan, 2005: 117). For myself, both approaches would appear to hold the potential to highlight the performative nature of social identity in ways that should induce a critical capacity within their audience towards the ideological

construction of identity both within the performance and, most importantly, beyond it. In this way, the testimonies should rupture any potential
repetition in performance of their testifiers' social marginality, and rather
gesture towards a repositioning and reconstruction of their testifiers'
'real' identities within social and political discourse.

The real in retreat

Without this careful foregrounding of the citational nature of representation, and a corresponding emphasis on the subjective construction
of narrative, it becomes all too easy for an audience to forget, as Carol
Martin cautions, that 'those who make documentary theatre interrogate
specific events, systems of belief, and political affiliations precisely through
the creation of their own versions of events, beliefs, and politics' (2006:
9). Martin's pertinent interrogation of the truth claims of documentary
theatre goes beyond questions of form and the ideological processes
by which material is transferred from the archive into performance.
She rather exposes the ideological nature of the archive itself which is
'already an operation of power', due to the choices that have led to its
specific inclusions and omissions (2006: 10). The awareness, at this point
in history, of there being no absolute truths or foundational knowledge-
base from which to begin, that everything we 'know' has already been
edited and selected from everything which we might know, poses a
particular problem for a theatre practice which is in constant negotiation
with the 'real' world, 'real' people, and events which 'really' happened.
Consequently, verbatim strategies are increasingly becoming employed
in this period, not to offer a particular version of the truth but to self-
reflexively ask questions of the form itself:

> At its best, documentary theatre complicates the idea of documentary and
> of the real, of a document, and even what it means to document; docu-
> mentary theatre troubles our already troubled categories of truth, reality,
> fiction and acting. (Martin, 2009: 88)

When self-reflexive commentary provides a critical framework for its
source material, it responds to the historical and ideological demands of
the documentary form, by ensuring that its own constructions are made
visible and open to question. As Steve Bottoms discusses in detail in
relation to the tribunal plays of the Tricycle Theatre, and as we have seen
with the dramatic model of *The Girlfriend Experience* and the misleading
representations in *Aalst,* an absence of sufficient self-reflexivity can
result in productions that are 'manipulative and worryingly unreflexive
regarding the "realities" they purport to discuss' (2006: 67).

There is a danger, however, that the valid call for poststructuralist self-reflexivity might result in an over-emphasis, in both analysis and practice, on anxieties about the form itself, at the expense of the political potential of its source material. Such a danger is illuminated by Stuart Young's article 'Playing with Documentary Theatre', where Young problematically conflates the documentary form with plays designed primarily to explore or critique such a form (2009). Concluding that the testimonial performance *Fallujah* (Holmes, 2007), 'essentially follows the same model as other British documentary plays' (Young, 2009: 75), Young contrasts such a model with *Aalst* and *Taking Care of Baby* (Kelly, 2007), which, he argues,

> effect a more complex, reflexive intervention in the genre by emphasizing the process of writing or reporting, thereby drawing attention to the methods of construction in documentary theatre and to the problematic issues inherent in those methods. (Young, 2009: 75)

Whilst I disagree with Young's analysis of *Aalst*, as detailed above, there is no doubt that Dennis Kelly's *Taking Care of Baby* is designed to offer a critique of verbatim practice, as Young claims. However Kelly's is not a verbatim piece itself but an entirely fictional drama that uses the appearance of verbatim strategies to structure its critique of the genre of verbatim practice. The original projection, its familiar words presented unscrambled and authoritative at the beginning of the play, disintegrates throughout, until the final scene when it barely makes sense:

> Te foling has beelown takhen wormed for wspoord frondrm intews and cughorrevieence. Nothything has been odded and evering is in the subjts' awn wongrds, tho sam editing hoes keplan tace. All nas havece been chaed. (Kelly, 2007: 97)

The invisible author's voice is heard throughout, conducting his interviews with Donna McAuliffe, a young mother accused of killing her two infant children; McAuliffe's family; and the 'expert' Dr Millard. Through this technique, Kelly highlights the way in which leading questions can manipulate the subject's answers and asks important questions about the role of the writer and audience in their consumption of other people's stories. To compare such a piece with *Fallujah* is unhelpful, as *Taking Care of Baby* had no 'real' story to tell; its intervention in the verbatim genre was undertaken from a critical vantage point located outside of the form itself. More important than the generic confusion is Young's failure to acknowledge that documentary theatre cannot be called to account for not sharing the same intentions as fictional texts that are designed to critique the documentary form. The aim of *Taking Care of Baby*, as

Young observes, is to manipulate the audience in order to 'highlight the relationship between representation and reality, and, therefore, notions of "truth"'(2009: 75). Kelly's play might well be invaluable in a wider analysis of the use of verbatim strategies in the practice of this period, but if his focus on 'highlighting the relationship between representation and reality' is to be taken as some kind of benchmark for the sophistication of verbatim practice, then the potential political efficacy of the verbatim form is put into jeopardy. In such an instance, the danger is not that the fusion of the 'fragments of the real' might over-ride an acknowledgement of their subjective treatment, as in the predominantly dramatic framework of *The Girlfriend Experience*, but, conversely, that the 'fragments of the real' become subsumed by the subjective treatment that ultimately becomes the subject matter of the piece at the cost of the 'fragments of the real'. Such a development risks pushing verbatim practice fearfully away from an engagement with 'the real' and into a potentially totalising poststructuralist self-referentiality, where all attempts to interrogate how 'the real' might be understood, re-figured or represented in the age of scepticism are abandoned.

In a Thousand Pieces, a production devised in 2008 by UK company Paper Birds following a period of research in Poland, was marketed as 'visual physical verbatim theatre exploring Eastern European girls forced into British sex trade' (Edinburgh Fringe Programme, 2009).[2] However, the verbatim element of the piece was restricted to a cross-sample of British people's views on the sex trade, and extracts evidencing their complete lack of knowledge about Eastern European countries. The voices of those involved in the sex trade were not recorded; instead we listened to the voice of the performer, her imagined experiences of exploitation and brutality recorded onto a crackling tape recorder and offered to us, apologetically, as the closest to the voices of the East European women we were going to get. The dramaturgy of the entire piece was shaped around the difficulty of finding those whose trade made them invisible, and the self-referential inadequacy of the company's subsequent contemplations of what such lives may be like. This would fall under, what Linda Alcoff terms, the 'retreat response' to the problem of speaking for others (1991–92: 17). She characterises this response as the tendency 'to retreat from all practices of speaking for and assert that one can only know one's own narrow individual experience and one's "own truth" and can never make claims beyond this' (17). Whilst this can seem like, and arguably sometimes can be, a progressive political stance, Alcoff cautions that it can also mask 'a thinly veiled excuse to avoid political work and indulge one's own desires' (17). Jon Dovey is among those who highlight the same self-referential trend in documentary film-making whereby the documentary, rather than being about the 'facts' of the story, becomes focused on the incompetent process of the apologetic and unsuccessful film-maker. Dovey comments that 'since "nobody believes in objectivity any more", this opening out of the process serves as a new source of authority' (2000: 50), highlighting the danger that too much self-conscious emphasis on a failed personal process might further silence the already-marginalised voices we are still not permitted to hear (2000: 50).

This danger was to be fully realised in Paper Bird's subsequent production, *Others* (2010),[3] which was 'based on a six-month exchange of letters and emails with a prisoner, a celebrity and an Iranian artist', in order to engage with women whom they considered 'other' to themselves. The publicity material further emphasised the company's 'attempt to represent three absent women' and their intention to 'question if it is possible to better understand "other" women or indeed ourselves'. The television personality they had selected as their 'celebrity', Heather Mills, had never responded to the original request for participation and her presence in the piece consisted of a filmed interview with her on daytime television and the performers' humorous attempts to engage with her silence, bombarding her with questions and constructing their own answers. The other two participants, however, had seemingly responded to the letters sent out by the company and committed to an ongoing correspondence, extracts of which were offered by the performers throughout the performance. We were to hear much less from them, however, than we were to hear from the performers themselves, and we were to learn much less about the 'realities' of the 'other' women than about the performers' own misconceived preconceptions about those with whom they were corresponding. The company were not only aware of this imbalance, they had clearly decided that their 'failure' to fully engage with the 'otherness' of these women should become the subject matter of the piece itself, much as had been the case with *In a Thousand Pieces*.

It was consequently not the 'real' performers themselves who were foregrounded, but surrogates in the mode of the performance personae discussed in Chapter 3. Where the surrogates in Forced Entertainment's work were intentionally failing actors, the surrogates here were intentionally failing documentary-makers whose ignorance of their subject was exposed through their adherence to a series of absurd myths concerning the 'other'. The performer who was given the 'role' of Naseem, the Iranian artist (in the first performance I saw, the performer herself was of Iranian descent) was shown to get increasingly outraged and frustrated by her co-performer-surrogates' instructions to act out the life of the stereotype they had created. Such instructions included her 'washing clothes in the river', 'fetching the grain' and 'selling her daughter in the marketplace to an old man on a camel'. She was also instructed to 'beat the washing' in fury with the West, and be 'sombre in the bedroom' as her husband beats her. The performer begins to argue back, telling her co-performers that her husband couldn't have a drink problem as Muslims don't drink, and, in response to constant references to the war, that it's not 'Iraq or Afghanistan'. The difficulty with this self-parody of ignorance, as Shannon Jackson explains, is that it enables the audience to be let off the hook by the ease with which they can remove themselves from the critique. As an audience we can laugh at the type of Westerner (the 'white unlike me') who holds these ludicrous beliefs, safe in the knowledge that our own understanding of Iran is far superior (Jackson, 2004: 210). Thus, our knowledge about the Iranian 'other' is not extended beyond a confirmation that stereotypes, which most of the audience will not actually hold in the first place, are not true.

The inadequacy of the surrogates not only showed itself in their inability to impart any significant information about 'the other' but also encompassed their own lack of self-awareness about their egotistical motivation for making the work. This was demonstrated by the ironic refrain that recurred throughout the show and ultimately concluded it, the repetition and emphasis clearly intended to underline the falsity of the statement: 'this isn't about us' (Paper Birds, 2010). In reading out to the audience the initial letter she had written to the women, performer Jemma McDonnell was consistently interrupted by her co-performer-surrogates with humorous qualifications to her pledges. So 'we will answer your questions' was undercut with additions such as 'some of them, not all of them'; and 'we will cut and condense very sensitively' was undermined by the more honest admissions, 'we won't use it all', 'we'll have to edit it if we want to get a good show'. This could, of course, be read as a light-hearted framing device that was legitimately seeking, as Carol Martin advocates, to trouble 'our already troubled categories of truth, reality, fiction and acting', but the sense I had on both occasions I saw the performance was that in offering these asides to their audience, but not to the women involved, there was a danger that the piece, by self-referentially undermining its own authority, was also undermining the women who had, in good faith, committed to the expressed aims of the project. As a result, the show spends far more time and theatrical energy on its self-parody of the performers' desire to know why Sally was imprisoned, than on Sally's own story. In a critique of the exploitative potential of the show the surrogate performers, having repeatedly and emphatically reassured Sally that it's none of their business what she's in prison for, physically move in an oppressive, invasive mass, as if cornering their victim, until they are screaming through a picture frame, 'What did you do? We need to know ... we need to know for the play'.

The political difficulty with this emphasis on 'self' as opposed to the 'other', however ironically it is framed, is that it can only read 'otherness' in generalised relation to the self. Consequently, none of the 'others' in the piece are presented as particularly and uniquely 'Other', but merely as examples of 'Not-Self'. This was starkly clear in the touring version of the show, where the performer of Iranian descent had been replaced by a performer of Israeli descent who defined her affinity with Naseem as coming from a 'Middle Eastern' background and not being white British. 'I am their other', she says to Naseem, referring to her co-performers, 'so I can't be your other'. The obvious distinctions between an Israeli and Iranian cultural identity were not referenced or explored. The refusal to engage with the real of the 'other', and the corresponding focus only on the narrative processes of the self, would thus support Linda Alcoff's assertion that the problem with the 'retreat response', however well intentioned, is that it

> assumes that one can retreat into one's discrete location and make claims entirely and singularly based on that location that do not range over others, that one can disentangle oneself from the implicating networks between one's discursive practices and others' locations, situations, and practices ... The declaration that I "speak only for myself" has the sole effect of allowing me to avoid responsibility and accountability for my effects on others; it cannot literally erase those effects. (1991–92: 20)

Consequently, the over-riding danger is that a poststructuralist verbatim practice that is self-referential to the detriment of the voices it effectively appropriates will result in an oppressive silencing of such voices and their possibilities, in an absolute reflection of the marginalisation of such voices in the world beyond the theatre. *Others* does not say nothing about otherness; it is not neutral, but it implicitly argues that the failed efforts of 'people like us' to engage with people who aren't like us are more interesting, and of more relevance, than the 'other' lives which are destined to remain forever on the margins of our own self-concern. *Others* goes beyond self-reflexivity to parody the value of documentary practice and implicitly dismisses any attempt to listen to and learn from the others in our world, consuming the potential of their stories in yet more narratives of 'our' failure. To return to Stuart Young's demand that sophisticated practice requires more, not less, scepticism, I would counter that a move too far in this direction might undermine the efforts of those artists who attempt the more difficult task of finding ways to engage with 'others' that now have to contend not merely with the fictionalisations of their realities within dramatic frameworks but also with the capacity of poststructuralist self-referentiality to silence them altogether. It seems that almost as soon as verbatim performance resurged in response to the 'real' political events of the twenty-first century, the latent scepticism of the previous decades resurfaced in defence, striving to reassert the authority that no claim to the 'real' could hold value. The turn to more explicit self-reflexivity in verbatim practice of this period may be ideologically necessary under the terms of the poststructuralist imperative, but I would argue that the form will lose its historical political efficacy if such a turn replaces, rather than reconfigures, documentary theatre's original emphasis on the 'real' events and voices that have been omitted from the dominant narratives of the time.

My examination of the rewriting of the real throughout performance practice in this period is continued in Chapter 5, where I will turn my attention to the theories of Jean Baudrillard. Through the lens of Baudrillard's radical scepticism of any objective reality I will explore a series of performances that intentionally seek to enable the spectator-participant, as well as the artist, to write their own narratives over existing realities. Such models of performance purposefully lose the 'actor' and reposition the 'spectator' in order to avoid the dangers of representation which this and previous chapters have addressed, and empower the spectator-participant to construct and experience their own order of the real. However, despite this move away from the traditional representational frameworks of theatre, I will suggest that such work cannot always avoid the imperialist impositions of self-determination identified in Chapter 3, and explored throughout this chapter in relation to certain models of verbatim practice.

Notes

1   This analysis is based on the performance of *The Girlfriend Experience* at the Young Vic Theatre, London, on 8 August 2009.
2   This analysis is based on the performance of *In a Thousand Pieces* at the Pleasance Theatre, Edinburgh, on 26 August 2009.
3   This analysis is based on two performances of *Others* at the Pleasance Theatre, Edinburgh, on 23 August 2010 and at the Crucible Theatre, Sheffield, on 15 November 2010.

5

Re-membering the real: experiential challenges to the medium of theatrical representation

As outlined in Chapter 1 of this study, Jean Baudrillard's theories converge around his notion of the simulacrum, which posits that our culture is now at the point whereby the real itself is constructed by the simulated which, in turn, is a copy of 'the real', resulting in a mobius strip of simulations that make up the totality of our contemporary reality. As all conceptual positions are thereby also within the simulacrum, there appears to be no position from which it can be either accepted or denied. Baudrillard's theories have been a seminal influence on the discourses of the real in performance practice and theory, assuming such critical importance that Baudrillard stands alongside Brecht himself in Baz Kershaw's *The Radical in Performance: Between Brecht and Baudrillard,* where Kershaw playfully indicts him of 'banishing the real' (Kershaw, 1999: 17). Hans-Thies Lehmann's concept of 'hypernaturalism' as a postdramatic performance aesthetic is directly drawn from Baudrillard's 'hyperrealism' and comes into play when 'the real cannot be differentiated from a perfectly functioning simulacrum in any way' (Lehmann, 2006: 116). The most consistent radical position that theatre artists and scholars have proposed, granted Baudrillard's analysis, is an exposure of the simulated nature of our entire contemporary reality. Such an exposure results in the sceptical deconstruction of 'the real' and an insistence on the artificial or citational nature of all representations of reality, both of which have thus far been identified as the seminal features of performance practice during this period.

In this chapter and the next, however, I will explore an alternative mode of poststructuralist resistance which seeks to reconfigure contemporary notions of reality, rather than merely highlighting the simulated nature

of all representations of the real. This mode of resistance draws on Baudrillard's critique of 'mediatisation', which argues that the mediation of information through mass media representations, rather than 'causing communication', more accurately *'exhausts itself in the act* of staging the communication; instead of producing meaning, it exhausts itself in the staging of meaning' (Baudrillard, 2007: 101, original emphasis). In other words, the very process of mediation threatens to consume its own content; the staging comes to replace that which is staged.

This chapter will thus conduct an examination of specific performance models that attempt to circumvent the mediation process inherent in the representational practice discussed so far, in their rejection of a theatrical framework that 'stages meaning' and thus mediates between its material and its watching audience. The alternative models of performance which are the subject of this chapter rather seek to engage the participant (now neither performer nor spectator in any conventional sense) in a more direct and experiential relationship with their own subjectively constructed reality. The notion of any kind of return to the real might seem to constitute an outright rejection of Baudrillard's theories, but I will now argue that Baudrillard's later writings, contrary to popular opinion, do offer us a distinction between two different orders of the real; the real as mediated representation as distinct from the real as directly experienced. I will propose that such a distinction can offer us a useful lens through which to analyse the ideological implications of performance models that would seek to evade the limitations of theatrical representation by offering their participants a more direct and experiential access to a reconfigured reality.

The image and the event

As I noted in Chapter 1, Baudrillard is concerned throughout his work with a double-implosion of the real that has sometimes been over-simplified by those drawing on his ideas. The first implosion is that of a perceived political or social reality, the simulacrum arising from the spectacle that Debord first identified as the construction of an ideological illusion of the real, and that Brecht, through his work, sought to demystify. The second is the implosion of epistemological or metaphysical certainty that the simulacrum attempts to cover over. Thus, the distinction between Debord's spectacle and Baudrillard's simulacrum is one not just of degree but of metaphysical significance. Unlike the spectacle, the simulacrum, as Baudrillard explains, 'conceals not the truth, but the fact that there isn't any' (2008: 102). The greatest crime of the simulacrum, which, in its final stages, is defined by Baudrillard as 'integral reality', is that it offers us a hyper-real that satisfies our craving for certainty and prevents us from having to confront the metaphysical fact, as argued by Jacques Derrida among others, that the objective reality of the world itself, and our existence within it, is more accurately the result of our subjective construction of what we perceive the world to be:

> So the world, then, is radical illusion. That is, at least, one hypothesis. At all events, it is an unbearable one. And to keep it at bay, we have to realize the world, give it force of reality, make it exist and signify at all costs ... This gigantic enterprise of disillusionment – of, literally, putting the illusion of the world to death, to leave an absolutely real world in its stead – is what is properly meant by simulation. (2008: 17)

The 'illusion of the world' is thus obscured from us by the simulacrum we have constructed and complied with to hide the absence of a metaphysical real. In this sense, for Baudrillard, the radical act is not to accept the predicates of the simulacrum that offers a false, yet absolute, reality, through its effacement of any ontological distinctions between representations of the real, but to rupture the simulacrum, or integral reality, to confront the metaphysical illusion of the real.

The rupture called for by Brecht and Debord, in the historical period characterised by the society of the spectacle, was a radical act to break the public's belief in the spectacle by exposing it as ideological construction. What Baudrillard's later work points to is the fact that, at a more advanced stage of global capitalism, when the simulacrum has successfully established itself as integral reality, the most pressing problem might not be that the public erroneously accepts given representations as reality, but rather that it is more likely to be convinced that all that is seemingly real is, in fact, mere ideological simulation. In *The Spirit of Terrorism*, Baudrillard draws attention to the prevalence of the conspiracy theory which proposes that it was the US government that staged the terrorist attacks of 9/11, and posits this as evidence of a growing cultural tendency to refuse to believe that anything has the power to act independently of, or to rupture, the simulacrum of the 'new world order' of global capitalism (2003: 79–81). Rather than acknowledge the attacks, as Baudrillard does, as a rare 'singularity' that might rupture the seemingly hegemonic global narrative, many prefer to see it as another illusory simulation, constructed by and within the simulacrum for its own ideological ends. What this theory suggests is that a consensus of belief in the reality of the simulacrum's simulations is no longer the most pressing problem. To perceive even the extremity of a terrorist act as a constructed fiction that is only *disguised* as a 'singular' and radical rupture must suggest that the proliferation of mediatised representations that make up the simulacrum of our cultural existence have led, not to a situation whereby all appearances are, erroneously, recognised as real, but to one where all appearances are assumed to be simulated. That is to say, we are already living in an age of ultimate scepticism or, more accurately, cynicism, in which reality-television shows, news reports, documentaries, eye-witness statements and statistics given by state and opposition groups alike are all treated as commensurate narratives with little credence given to the reality or truth of any one version over any other.

A cynical reading of all appearances of a mass-mediated reality as ideological simulation is far removed from the sceptical understanding, advocated by both Derrida and Baudrillard, of all human perceptions of the real as subjective construction. As Baudrillard insists, the mystification of the simulacrum intentionally prevents us from perceiving the absence of a metaphysical real. However, the potential confusion between the two that can be discerned at this point in history points up the following risk: it becomes difficult to distinguish performance practice that, through its reduction of all narratives to ontologically equivalent representations, intends to be a sceptical rupturing of metaphysical illusion, from performance practice that, through an ostensibly similar process of reduction, merely replicates the workings of the simulacrum by adding credence to the existing cultural cynicism that there is no way of distinguishing between one narrative, or representation of the real, and any other. The blurring of the boundaries between fact and fiction, which has been such a consistent motif in new performance practices throughout this period of study, can thus just as easily operate to sustain the relativity promoted by the simulacrum as to offer radical challenge to its predicates by exposing the absence of a metaphysical real.

As the danger of credence in the spectacle has retreated, to be replaced by the threat posed by the widespread cynicism of the real, the nature of the radical act now also needs to be reconsidered. If the radical potential of the exposure of the mechanics of representation was, in Brecht's time, to reveal the truth that lay behind the spectacle, and in the postmodern period, to reveal the illusion of the world, then such a potential, in either case, becomes weakened in an age where a cynicism of the hyper-real perceives everything as constructed and equivalent in the first place. In such an age, the radical act might rather be to re-instate distinctions between different orders of the real in order to combat the disempowering relativity of the simulacrum. Examples of such distinctions can be found within Baudrillard's own writing which attempts, at certain points, to conceptually distinguish between the reality of the event that was directly experienced and the reality of the simulated event that was received through mediation. Baudrillard's claim, in *The Spirit of Terrorism,* that 'the image consumes the event, in the sense that it absorbs it and offers it for consumption' (2003: 27), ambiguously acknowledges the existence of an independent order of reality even as it simultaneously transforms the event into simulated spectacle. In *The Intelligence of Evil,* he likewise speaks of the sphere of information as 'a space' that empties 'events of their substance' (2005: 122), thus confirming the conceptual distinction between events and the spectacle which transmogrifies them. 'The event of news coverage,' he explains, 'substitutes itself for coverage of the event.' (2005: 133) There is displacement here, but, more critically, there is acknowledgement that it is *access* to the actual event that is blocked, not its conceptualisation. The actual event is not covered and does not exist to our perception, so all we can perceive is the 'event of news coverage', but this does not deny the existence of another order of event which has been occluded from our perception. Baudrillard's use of 'event' corresponds here to the philosophical definition proposed by Hans-Thies Lehmann as 'the moment of incommensurability' (2006: 105), which signifies that such events should be somehow distinguishable from the simulations that they seek to rupture.

A radical practice, then, at this point in history, should perhaps find ways, not to merely reveal the simulated nature of all representations, which is already common knowledge under the prevailing cultural cynicism, but to distinguish between whichever orders of the real we are able to conceptualise, given the absence, post-Derrida, of any singular metaphysical foundation. This chapter will consequently focus on performances that attempt to distinguish the experienced real from the mediated real; that is, the event as it is experienced or owned, from the mediation of the event as it is constructed or consumed. Whilst wishing to avoid distorting Baudrillard's position of total metaphysical scepticism by claiming that he would necessarily hold to a superior ontological status for any one order of reality over any other, I would nevertheless suggest that, by seeking ways to uphold the order of the experienced real as fundamentally distinct from the order of the mediated real, a radical performance practice might begin to challenge the very predicates of the simulacrum, and the widespread and politically regressive cynicism that it has engendered.

The experiential real in performance

In Chapter 2, I argued that neither dramatic nor postdramatic models of theatre were able to escape the bind of theatrical representation, as they were both tied to a form where certain events were constructed, rehearsed and repeated to an audience *as if* for the first time. Such limitations have been addressed by performance models that have rejected not only the concept of rehearsal but also the framework that necessitates that performers make the spectacle for an audience who then witness it. This framework, of course, is central to the concept of mediated representations of the real, and the rejection of it is intended to offer the spectator, who now becomes the participant, access to an experiential real of their own making, as a more radical alternative. This can be clearly seen in the concept of the performance walk, one popular model of this type of practice, which became increasingly common in UK and European performance over the first decade of the twenty-first century. The notion of the performance walk can manifest itself in pedestrian performance which includes a performer as a guide, and so shares a similar framework to the wider field of site-specific performance, or it might simply feature a soundtrack played through headphones which, among other textual and musical prompts, designates a specific route for the walker to take. I would like to focus here on the latter, also known variously as sound art (Gorman, 2010: 167) or the audio tour (Fischer-Lichte, 2008: 113), to examine its more explicit rejection of the performer/spectator relationship so central to representational performance practice.

Carl Lavery suggests that the value of the performance walk 'is not to be found in the way it supposedly unveils the truth of the world, but, on the contrary, for its ability to highlight the essentially performative quality of landscape' (2009: 46). For, as the lone figure wearing headphones becomes the actor of their own performance, she simultaneously becomes the active spectator, or author of meaning, who evokes the narratives that the surrounding landscape is now required to perform. Thus, the performer/spectator roles of the representational theatre framework are fused into one, only the role of director, played on the audio tour by the soundtrack, remains distinct. Lavery identifies the 'avant-garde heritage' of the form in the distinction it makes between the mediatised and experiential orders of the real, 'its ultimate purpose … to replace vicarious experience (reading someone else's account of space) with actual experience (producing one's own spatial map)' (2009: 45). Sarah Gorman describes her own experience on the audio tour of Janet Cardiff's *The Missing Voice (Case Study B):*

> The process of following a prescribed journey, and of having to negotiate the conflicting information of 'real' environmental sounds of traffic and voices, alongside binaurally pre-recorded environmental sounds, appears to displace or disorient traditional viewing conventions. Through a process of defamiliarization and disorientation it appears to ask the viewer to consider his or her place within the context of the changing environment. (2010: 171–3)

This concept of framing the real in order to perceive it differently was a recurrent one in the work of the neo-avant-garde, and one which aimed to, as Mike Sell observes, 'dematrix everyday life, rendering it into something uncanny, both familiar and unfamiliar' (2006: 171). The radical potential of this is the opportunity for the individual to author and viscerally experience their own narratives of reality, rather than merely spectating and passively consuming the ones already circulating in the simulacrum. Michel de Certeau is one influential theorist who advocates that hegemonic authority can be circumvented by discovering 'innumerable and infinitesimal transformations of and within the dominant cultural economy in order to adapt it to [our] own interests and ... own rules' (1984: xiv). This is a key strategy that can be aligned with the discourse of resistance identified in Chapter 1, but de Certeau develops it in important ways. He identifies the danger that to accept the premise that the hegemonic order is all-pervasive and beyond transgression is to remain caught in the terms set out for us by that very order. In short, where we once answered to a narrative of progress, we are now being compelled to answer to a narrative of catastrophe (1984: 96). De Certeau therefore refuses to merely expose the workings of the simulacrum as all-consuming and inescapable, thus concurring with its catastrophic narrative, but seeks ways to reconfigure the world from within, proposing that whilst we may all be subject to a hegemonic order that none can escape, the individual still has the freedom to choose what they 'make' or 'do' with the circulating simulacra of twenty-first-century life (xii). He suggests that we need to place less emphasis on what the system presents the individual with, and more on how the individual might subvert what they are given:

> Rather than remaining within the field of a discourse that upholds its privilege by inverting its content (speaking of catastrophe and no longer of progress), one can try another path ... one can analyze the microbe-like, singular and plural practices which an urbanistic system was supposed to administer or suppress. (1984: 96)

By turning his attention to the tactics of consumption (1984: xvii), de

Certeau reconfigures the hitherto 'passive consumers' of the system, as 'unrecognized producers' in their own right, 'poets of their own acts, silent discoverers of their own paths in the jungle of functionalist rationality' (1984: xviii). In this way, de Certeau identifies the radical potential of seemingly everyday practices such as walking, whereby the individual is able to imaginatively reconstruct their own route through a shifting landscape to recreate, from the patterns which city planners and economic developers have established, a subjective and experiential reality over which they have sole authorship. In this, de Certeau's thinking follows that of the Situationists who, as Carl Lavery notes

> rejected conventional forms of artistic expression and instead explored alternative, non-alienated modes of creativity [...] The principal technique used was la dérive or drift, a planned walk in which a small group of adepts would consciously set out to register the psychogeographic effects or ambiences of certain areas and sites in the city. Drifting exemplified what the Situationists called détournement, a way of subverting the logic of the system by using the tools of the system against itself. (2010: 92)

Whilst the work under discussion in this chapter would have accommodated the aesthetics of artistic practice too far to have constituted radical action in Situationist terms, the influence of both 'the drift' and '*détournement*' as political strategies are clearly evident in the structures and objectives of the performance walk and related models of practice. As Lavery suggests, '[i]nstead of passively registering the world of images and spectacles, drifting allows the individual to encounter and to imagine the world actively. The drifter or *dériviste* is thus a producer – and not a consumer – of meaning' (2009: 47). This, Lavery notes, recalls the subversive nature of the nomad, characterised by Mike Pearson and Michael Shanks as the walker who seeks to resist the state's desire to 'take the space and enclose it and ... create fixed and well-directed paths', by deliberately forging their own routes and emphasising the movement through, rather than the marked-out destinations. (Pearson and Shanks, 2001: 149)

Lavery also draws attention to important objections to the narrative of radicalism he is outlining, most notably that of Patrick Keiller, who reads the imaginative rewriting of urban areas in particular as an attempt to 'poeticise our relationship with dilapidation', and abandonment of our responsibility to materially reconstruct the space, in the actual terms of regeneration (Keiller, 2001: 66, in Lavery, 2009: 45). Doreen Massey also holds objections to de Certeau's 'imagination of power (central bloc versus little tactics of resistance)' that results in an understanding of 'the city structure versus the street' (2005: 46). Massey's overall thesis is concerned with challenging notions that posit 'space' as the fixed, unchanging binary opposition to 'time', and in this context she discredits de Certeau's conceptualisation of 'the space of the city' as 'immobility, power, coherence, representation' (47). Massey's objections are relevant to this study as they underpin, as she argues, masculine notions of a romanticised 'resistance' to the concept of 'the city' under which such activities as 'rushing about down dark passages, dreaming of labyrinths and so forth' can be categorised as radical actions (47).

These are important and related qualifications to any over-simplistic ideological analysis of the performance walk, and serve to caution against an over-estimation of its potential political efficacy. Moreover, the potential to romanticise, in literary and prosaic understandings of the term, the experience, as underlined by both Keiller and Massey, suggests a level of self-absorption in the world one is creating, to the possible detriment of the external reality that now merely serves as backdrop to the personal narrative. Such a possibility raises the historical spectre of Baudelaire's *flâneur*, as characterised by Pearson and Shanks as 'at once a bohemian and producer of written commodities', who, in his contemporary guise has come to represent the 'gazing, grazing, consuming' of the 'contemporary urban dweller' (2001: 149). Picking up from concerns raised in Chapters 3 and 4, I would now like to examine the very real possibility that, within the framework of the performance walk, one person's radical and experiential construction of reality might also hold the potential to appropriate existing orders of the real through a process that recalls not only the aestheticising habits of the *flâneur* but, more pertinently, the simulacrum's appropriation of the experienced event by the mediating image as described by Baudrillard. To return to de Certeau, the question here arises as to what the 'author' of a subjective reality chooses to 'make' or 'do', not only with the simulated real of the dominant discourse but also with the independent realities of other individual subjects. Through the theoretical lens of this chapter it might be said that performance walks, whilst offering an experiential reality to the walker, do so by enabling the walker to alter the order of the reality of the surrounding landscape by transforming it into a representation of itself.

In this way 'real' objects become signs of something else and 'real' people become characters in a performance which is imposed upon them by the imagination of the walker in response to directions and ambient prompts from the soundtrack. Describing her experience of this during Janet Cardiff's *Missing Voice*, Sarah Gorman confesses that the sight of a suited young man in an otherwise empty church, his head bowed, had made her feel voyeuristic, as if she was 'somehow exploiting this young man's feelings and enjoying the fact that they added an emotional depth to "my" narrative' (173). The very power of subjective authorship that the performance walk upholds as a radical subversion of the consumption of the spectacle, can also, it seems, hold its own temptations to consume the reality of others.

Taking part in *En Route*,[1] a performance walk devised by the Australian company One Step At a Time Like This, I was aware that I was continuously appropriating images of the 'real' people I passed on the streets of Edinburgh, including a man fixing a window, a woman sitting on a deckchair in the middle of an empty courtyard, and an ex-soldier protesting against the involvement of Scottish troops in the wars in Iraq and Afghanistan, to serve as fictional representations in a now-mythical and performing cityscape. As the independent realities of the city are written over by the representations it is now required to serve, such realities are appropriated to furnish the walker's own subjective narrative experience, the city reduced to a mirror which gives, as the soundtrack reminded me, 'reflection to your dreaming'. In this sense, the experiential real of the walker can be seen as a potential challenge to the mediated realities of the simulacrum, *only if* this subjective order of the real resists from mirroring the strategies of the simulacrum that transforms the independent realities of others into narrative simulations for its own ends. As Alan Read cautions, 'despite the propensity of the last decade to "read" the city like a book ... the city remains what it is – significant for its difficult realities as well as signifying imaginative possibilities' (1993: 18).

The most radical aspect of *En Route* was thus its commitment to re-conceptualising the act of looking in a way that rejected the more common imperative to consumption and appropriation. The following fragment of text, taken from a letter written by Rainer Maria Rilke in 1899, was communicated through the soundtrack towards the end of the walk:

> For in our gazing lies our truest acquiring. Would our hands were as our eyes are, so ready in grasping, so bright in holding, so carefree in letting all things go, then we could become truly rich. But we do not become rich by having something dwell in our hands and wither there. Everything is meant to stream through their grip [...] to wander on beyond our hands, sturdy and strong, and we are meant to retain nothing. (Rilke, 1997)

Rather than the more common conflation of the look with the act of physical and tangible possession, the company draw on Rilke and Merleau Ponty to offer the look as a more radical way of conceiving of the ways in which we might use the things we hold, as well as the things we see (Merleau-Ponty, 1968: 130–55). A mutual relationship is established throughout *En Route* that rejects the polarisation and power differential of the watcher and the watched, and rather posits that 'we who see cannot possess the visible unless we are possessed by it, unless we are of it'. At the very point when I am instructed to lean against a wall for a moment, my gaze takes in the man across the other side of the courtyard who is busy fixing a broken window, and I hear the words 'in the act of seeing I am being seen'. At that moment the man looks across at me, a lone figure in a backyard of small-scale industrial enterprises, wearing headphones and watching him, and it becomes clear that I, in my watching, am also a spectacle for the gaze of others. When later passing through the private courtyard of a block of flats, and smiling at the woman sitting on her doorstep who greeted me, I wondered if I was appropriating her habitual reality to perform for my spectatorship, or if she was only sitting there in the first place to enjoy the spectacle of performers in headphones walking through her courtyard at half-hourly intervals. None of us are, as the soundtrack cautioned 'outside seeing' and we can all, at any time, be the subjects of others' narratives, watched and speculated upon as we go about our own experienced realities of the everyday which are not threatened by serving dual purpose in the imaginations of others. If we 'look' in the way *En Route* invites us to, then we will not write over the independent reality of the city or those who pass us by, but merely borrow the external appearance only, to act simultaneously as its own real and one particular representation of that real, for a temporary moment of shared and uniquely experienced time. For 'the act of walking', as de Certeau reminds us, is like the 'space of enunciation' (1984: 97–8); it takes place in time only and then is gone, leaving nothing behind it that can be either possessed or retained. Speaking more broadly of site specific practice, Miwon Kwon confirms that '[t]he art object or event in this context [has] to be singularly *experienced* in the here and now through the bodily presence of each viewing subject, in a sensorial immediacy of spatial extension and temporal duration' (Kwon, 1997: 86, original emphasis). The reciprocal nature of the bodily presence of watcher and watched (who are simultaneously watched and watcher) during the performance walk is vital to its radical potential because, as Lavery notes, 'it compels the walker to be physically present in the space s/he observes' (2005: 152).

10   Scene from *En Route*.

Photographer: Jane Barlow

The divine spectator

Such reciprocity enables a very different order of looking from that described by de Certeau as he conceptualises his gaze from the summit of the World Trade Center down onto New York City below:

> his elevation transfigures him into a voyeur. It puts him at a distance. It transforms the bewitching world by which one was 'possessed' into a text that lies before one's eyes. It allows one to read it, to be a solar Eye, looking down like a god' (1984: 92).

This panoptic mode of looking signals the point at which the experiential and subjective order of reality construction, positioned by de Certeau as a radical opposition to the given narrative of the simulated real, threatens to assume the divinity of the author in a Barthesian sense. In other words, the would-be radical transition from passive consumer/ reader to active creator of meaning is more accurately, when the reader is not also 'of the visible', a less radical transition from passive consumer/ reader to active producer/author/god with all the implications that such Barthesian authority brings. In their discussion of landscape, Pearson and Shanks remark on the tensions inherent in the gaze that requires 'separation and observation ... distant horizons and distanced vantage-points' (2001: 151), and offer one definition of landscape as 'a pictorial construct, something to be apprehended by looking, something available for the appreciation and consumption of the visitor, a commodity: viewpoint, perspective, vista, frame' (141). *En Route,* through the context and positioning of its participants, upheld the reciprocity that is vital to hold the divine look at bay. We were always in and of the city streets on which we were inescapably a part of the community, especially at festival time. We were 'of the visible' of others even as we looked, participating in a shared network of narrative exchange on streets that were populated, in the main, by transient visitors and people at work, often, like myself, both at the same time. We may have been led down alleyways and into the quieter interstices of the city at times, but these spaces were not owned by anyone and there was no sense of trespass. We also looked, and were looked at, face to face and one on one with the passers-by. We were asked to make ourselves as vulnerable, or not, as those we encountered. This enabled a potentially radical interchange whereby a plurality of the acts of looking and imagining formed a network of narratives which intersected with each other, contested each other, and reflected on each other without any one version of the real holding authority over any other.

However, as I cautioned in Chapter 1, proponents, such as Lyotard, of the radical potential of such contestations of narrative, do not always consider the material and economic context in which they are played out. There is too often an unspoken assumption that the freedom of narrative construction extends equally to all contestants in the wake of the collapse of a foundational authority or objective real. Lyotard claims that '[n]o one, not even the least privileged amongst us, is ever entirely powerless over the messages that traverse and position him at the post of sender, addressee, or referent' (1984: 15), and this could relate directly to the walkers and inhabitants who are both authoring and authored simultaneously as they move through the cityscape. What Lyotard fails to fully confront, however, is the varying capacity for subjective authorship that each 'contestant' may have at his or her disposal in any particular context. De Certeau, admittedly, appears more aware of this, emphasising that subversive rewriting, or re-use, of the dominant narrative 'is related to social situations and power relationships' (1984: xvii). Yet, it is precisely this kind of qualifying materialist analysis that is so often occluded from the poststructuralist discourse of radical subjective authorship. In *The Fate of Place*, Edward Casey proposes that 'the importance of place' to poststructuralist theorists – and also, I would add, artists – lies in 'a conviction that place itself is no fixed thing: it has no steadfast essence' but is 'part of something ongoing and dynamic' (Casey, 1997: 286). To challenge the radicalism of practices that seek to enable individuals to 'write over' one reality of a place with another subjectively constructed reality is often taken to be a return to essentialism, a re-assertion of the very possibility of an objective truth which should be protected from misrepresentation. Responding to my previously published analysis of Forced Entertainment's *Nights in this City* (Tomlin, 1999), Sara Jane Bailes reads my own ideological interrogation of this performance in just this way, as an upholding of 'a fixed reality' and a rejection of the political potential of the aesthetic strategies of subjective reconstruction (Bailes, 2011: 88). But it was not the postmodern remapping of space or the construction of alternative realities that concerned me, as I shall now again detail, but the occlusion of any kind of complementary materialist analysis of the power relations between the narrating and the narrated who were the 'contestants' in this particular game.

Nights in this City (1995)[2] was a variant on the performance walk, constituting a guided coach tour where the audience were driven through the city of Sheffield accompanied by Forced Entertainment performers as the guides. Here, as in *En Route*, the people we were to pass as we drove down the streets were to become representations of themselves for our own narrative constructions:

> All the people you can see from here are ghosts. And the cars that are driving are cars being driven by ghosts. And all the houses you can see are the houses of ghosts, and all the windows you can see are windows on the houses of ghosts.

An assumption of ideological equivalence based on the comparable structure and shared poststructuralist imperatives of each production, however, would be to ignore a number of distinctions between the two, which are more comprehensively explored in my previous article. In the context of this chapter, the most significant distinction was that we were not 'of the visible' during *Nights in this City*, but looking *at* the visible through the mediating frame of the coach windows, the cinematic resonance accentuated by John Avery's haunting soundtrack and the seductive voice-overs of the performers, aestheticised by handheld microphones. Our 'looking', in this performance, appropriated the visceral physicality of the people on the street and their own order of experiential reality, to serve as our mediatised spectacle. My sense of unease at this order of appropriation was heightened when the coach left the city centre to drive through an economically deprived housing estate two miles outside Sheffield, where I suspect none of the audience would have been willing to walk alone, as darkness fell, with headphones on and staring, through the streets which the coach drove down in safety. That is to say that we would not have felt comfortable to look at these passers-by face to face, or one on one; and this fear on the part of the watching to meet the watched and be watched by them on equal terms instinctively signals that at this point we are no longer 'of the visible' but looking from outside it, no longer lookers in a shared network of narrative-making but voyeurs taking the vantage point of the divine. The coach, of course, was also 'looked at' by those whom it passed, on streets where no buses ran, but its fifty or more occupants looking out of its windows, to consume the spectacle of individual figures framed by their own front-room windows, or walking alone down the street, imbued our spectatorship with a numerical and cultural dominance that is closer to replicating the strategies of imperialism than those of radical practice. In the words of Barbara Kirshenblatt-Gimblett:

> [L]ive exhibits tend to make people into artefacts because the ethnographic gaze objectifies [...] To make people going about their ordinary business objects of visual interest and available to total scrutiny is dehumanizing [...] Semiotically, live displays make the status of the performer problematic, for people become signs of themselves. (1991: 415)

This framing of 'the other' as spectacle is defined by Kirshenblatt-Gimblett in her description of the West's historical preoccupation not just with the ethnographic other but also with the dispossessed, and she identifies the need of the privileged to view the lives of those who populate the margins of dominant society and to explore the forbidden territory whose danger is best enjoyed from a safe vantage point:

> [T]he panoptic approach offers the chance to see without being seen, to penetrate interior recesses, to violate intimacy. In its more problematic manifestations, the panoptic mode has the quality of peep show and surveillance – the viewer is in control. (1991: 413)

The panoptic mode, as Kirshenblatt-Gimblett outlines above, comes into being only when the objects of the viewer's gaze are not looking back, when they are unaware that their experienced reality is being consumed and assimilated; when the roles of watcher and watched are fixed and not reversible. Those defined by the local press as the 'stars' of *Nights in this City* – 'two girls carrying an electric cooker across the Norfolk Park tram lines and a solitary drinker staring out of a pub window at his travelling audience' – had no control over the ways in which their realities were being manipulated, nor any capacity for self-authorship (Highfield, 1995: 26). Their ignorance of their own role in the narratives that were unfolding as a result of their context posited them as characters in a fiction. They had no recourse to any self-reflexivity that might disrupt the narrative process, nor were they able to assume autonomous behaviour within it. The nature of their representations was guided by the performance text that framed them; their lack of consent or awareness strengthened their narrative impact within a text that favoured ghosts and lonely travellers who had lost their way. But most significantly, the actual situations and often difficult social contexts of these people were mythologised by those who held the cultural power and were not 'of the visible' on which they looked. The potential danger of the discourse of radical poststructuralism is that in undermining all alleged objectivity to destabilise the illusion of the hegemonic narrative of the real, it can inadvertently and simultaneously leave subjective, yet, in this instance, culturally dominant, narratives like that of *Nights in this City* too often beyond challenge, as they utilise their own narrative strategies to 'write over' the experienced realities of others. Such realities are unable to compete on an equal cultural or artistic level to act as counter-narratives and, furthermore, have no recourse to their own independent order of reality for validation, since they have now been made commensurate with the fictions that have consumed them. In such instances, the scepticism of the performance event is no longer operating as a radical challenge to the hegemonic reality of global capitalism, but as a reflection of its strategic practice, whereby the experienced realities of others are made commensurate with its own simulated narratives and assimilated and mediated accordingly.

The absent real

Conversely, in the case of Graeme Miller's *Linked* (2003), we can see the model of the performance walk employed not to encourage audiences to write over the urban realities of others but to enable a community to write their personal narratives over the absence left by the destruction of their homes for the construction of the M11 link road in 1994. Miller produced a soundscape made up of testimonies from local citizens and road protestors, which were gathered by himself and a team of researchers. These are broadcast from twenty transmitters that line the route of the link road that is now transformed into a 'site of disappearance', with all the political resonances which that holds (Pearson and Shanks, 2001: 155). The radical potential of *Linked* is explored in depth in the article, 'The Pepys of London E11: Graeme Miller and the Politics of *Linked*' (Lavery, 2005), where Lavery describes *Linked* as 'a form of resistance, a sonic memorial to the families who lived in the five hundred houses that were forcibly requisitioned and demolished so that commuters could reach the nearby City of London in time for work' (Lavery, 2005: 149). In this way, the performance can be seen to rupture the constructed reality of global capitalism, of which the link road is an economic symbol, in order to revalidate the experienced realities and memories the motorway link road has effaced. The sounds and voices of the exiled community enable the walker to imaginatively re-member a past order of reality that has been literally effaced by the construction alongside which they are walking. The walker is enabled to assert, against the scepticism of the times, the validation of her subjective and experiential reality that challenges the present visible order of the real with the subjective realities of those who are now gone. As Miller explains, '[i]t's hard these days to know if something has actually happened, and I thought by making *Linked* I could prove that something did happen in East London in 1994' (Miller, 2005: 163). Despite its innovative framework, *Linked* puts its faith in a radicalism that has dominated the traditional political theatre of the left, whereby alternative realities are evoked to disrupt the hegemonic reality of the dominant discourse. Miller, however, avoids the charge, often levelled at such an approach by a sceptical poststructuralism, that he is merely replacing one ideological totality with another, through his emphasis on the pluralism of the personal account as discussed in relation to verbatim performance in Chapter 4 of this book. By combining the potentially radical model of the performance walk with testimonial theatre's ethos of enabling disempowered communities to speak for their own histories, Miller's work foregrounds the political potential of re-membered realities that have to be imagined and actively brought into being by the spectating/performing walker, in the absence of theatre's traditional representational and mediating frameworks.

After Dubrovka (2007) was not a performance walk, but it had

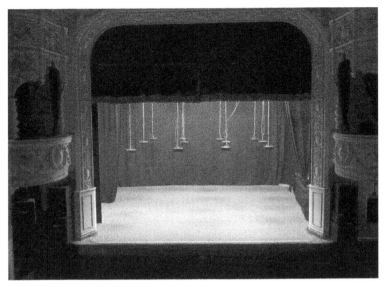

11   Opening state of *After Dubrovka.*
Photographer: Neil Mackenzie

many features in common with the work I have examined so far. Most significantly, it eschewed theatre's visual representational apparatus in favour of audioscapes that were designed to conjure up an experiential real for the participant in the absence of theatrical representation. Unlike *Linked,* however, the reality that the participants were asked to re-member, was not offered by those who had directly experienced it but by artists with no connection to the event itself, raising crucial questions regarding the ideological implications of the work. Produced by Neil Mackenzie, Mole Wetherell and Spencer Marsden, *After Dubrovka* was defined by its creators as a 'theatre installation', introduced on the artists' website as follows:

> In October 2002 Chechen rebels took over the Dubrovka theatre in Moscow during a performance of the musical Nord Ost, taking the audience and performers hostage. The siege lasted for nearly two and a half days and ended when the Russian military pumped in a sedative gas and stormed the building. 129 of the hostages died, almost all as a result of the gas. Five years on, After Dubrovka marks an opportunity to reflect on the significance of this event, and on other acts of performance and audience in the world today, both in theatres and beyond […] This is theatre and it is not theatre. This is an event in a theatre, remembering an event in a theatre – an act of remembrance. (*www.reckless-sleepers.co.uk,* 2007)

If the collation of the real event of the Moscow siege with 'other acts of performance and audience in the world today' resulted in a proposed equivalence between the two strands of the project, then there would be a real danger that the independent authority of the real event as experienced by others might be written over by a series of performative representations. In such an instance, the piece would risk reflecting the culture of cynicism identified earlier in this chapter by refusing to acknowledge that the real event, which had been experienced by others, was of a different order from the mediated realities that were to be presented to the audience by the artists. Speaking on a panel after one of the performances, Karen Jürs-Munby confessed her reservations, and posed some pertinent questions to which my own analysis will seek to respond:

> I have a nagging unease about After Dubrovka which I would like to try to articulate thus: my question is: can this kind of piece live up to or testify or even make us aware of the horrendous events in the Dubrovka theatre in 2002? Or will it remain an exercise in theatre reflecting on itself? (Jürs-Munby, 2007)

The two performances I attended took place at the Dancehouse in Manchester on 23 October 2007.[3] The performances were running in forty-minute slots throughout the afternoon and evening, and I attended one at 6.30 pm and a second at 8 pm. The maximum number of audience members was eight, and on my first showing, I was one of an audience of three. We were led by an usher from a small waiting area, down a backstage corridor and into the wings of the Dancehouse stage, accompanied by a brief summary of the events of the Moscow siege. We were then instructed to walk to the centre of the empty stage and stand together under a lit speaker that was hanging from the lighting grid.

There were three or four people sitting at some distance from each other in the faded red velvet seats of the old-fashioned auditorium, dimly lit, who were watching us. There were nine speakers hung over our heads equally spaced out on the lighting grid. We were welcomed by a voice emanating from the speaker above us:

> Hello, I'd like to introduce you to where you are. You are standing in the playing area. If you look to your left, that's stage left, or prompt side, the side where the prompt corner normally is. To your right is stage right, or opposite prompt, and our lighting operator. If there were a bastard prompt, that is a prompt corner stage right, everything would be different [...] Please don't cross the plaster line, please don't touch the bounce [...] It's easy to get lost on stage, It's easy to lose a sense of where you really are, Where in the world this is, and you are, right now.

At some point during this text other speakers began to light up, three or four at a time, as voices speaking different texts emerged from them. The three of us on the stage moved around freely to stand where we chose, sometimes under one particular speaker, sometimes between speakers where more than one text could be heard overlapping. Some texts, like the first, spoke to our immediate present position, asking, by implication, that we occupy the roles of actors, and, by imaginative extension, the actors who were on stage prior to the siege. Others placed us in the roles of the Chechen rebels who took their place as actors on the theatrical-turned-political stage during the performance of *Nord Ost*: 'You are wearing the uniform, I assume you share the belief in what you are doing'. Most provocative, however, were the texts that offered the ambiguity of feeling simultaneously drawn to the present/real and past/imagined scenarios that were being evoked:

> This is not your space. You should not be here. They should not be look-ing at people like you. They were not expecting to see people like you. You are not welcome here. This is a theatre. You are where the entertainment should be. You are where the performers should be performing. You are standing where there should be a show, a play, a musical, for the audience. This should not be happening. This is not what this place is for.

To experience the overlapping juxtaposition of these texts, on stage, in front of an audience, moved us imperceptibly and simultaneously between our own experienced reality in the present – that of a spectator who is inappropriately positioned on the stage, without script, direction or intent – and our imagined and subjective embodiment of another's experienced reality in the past – that of an actor in a fictional musical who is about to become a hostage in a real event, or that of a Chechen rebel standing where the actor should be. In the second half of the installation we were invited to occupy one of the eight designated seats that were scattered throughout the auditorium. Small speakers were installed on the backs of the seats in front of us, and these began to address us as six people entered onto the stage from the side. In parallel with the first half of the installation, the voice addressing us from our individual speakers positioned us sometimes as spectators in the here and now, watching others go through the process we were now familiar with, sometimes as generic spectators who were expecting to watch a piece of theatre but were being given something very different, sometimes as embodiments of the spectators at Dubrovka who watched as a Russian musical turned into a political siege, and sometimes blurring the boundaries that distinguished the roles from each other: 'it shouldn't happen in a theatre

… this is a place for pretence, where people are pretending to do things, be things, where people go home'. This fluctuation – between the piece's meta-theatrical concerns with 'other acts of performance and audience in the world today' and its obligation to the real event of the siege – is potentially where the charge of equivalence might be levelled at the work, but I will now propose that this may be precisely where its greatest potential for ethical engagement with the real might be located.

What was very clear from all aspects of this production was that its objective was not to provide an alternative mediation of the real event in order to subvert the mass-media simulations available. Speaking on the panel, Karen Jürs-Munby outlined the oppositional narratives of the event that had not been explored by the piece: the cover-up operation by the Russian government over the deaths, the conspiracy theories regarding Russian involvement in the hostage-taking, and the subsequent assassinations of the Russians who voiced such suspicions. Yet, I will now suggest that, through a particular philosophical framework, this very refusal to offer alternative representations of the real event to those that dominated the media can be read as being central to the political potential of the installation.

The traumatic real

The influence of Baudrillard's simulacrum on performance frameworks over this period is accompanied by a growing interest in the psycho-analytical theories of Jacques Lacan, and there are cautious points of connection between the two. Where Baudrillard understands our everyday reality as integral reality, composed of simulations of the hyper-real designed to obscure the fact that the Real itself is 'radical illusion', Lacan designates everyday reality as the 'Symbolic Realm', or the world of representations we construct to compensate ourselves for the traumatic loss of the 'Real' itself (which, for Lacan, is not illusion, but is nevertheless forever inaccessible to us). In Peggy Phelan's seminal text, *Unmarked,* she draws on Lacan's psychoanalytic reading of the Real which has proved increasingly influential to performance theorists across the historical period of this study (Phelan, 1993). In Lacanian terms, the 'Real' can be understood as the 'full Being' that we inhabit as very young infants before we are taught to understand ourselves through language. At what Lacan calls the 'mirror stage' of development, a consciousness of the 'I' (subject) who can now perceive and contemplate the 'myself' (object) renders a split in the 'whole' and undivided self that is never recoverable. From this point on, the human subject inhabits the 'symbolic realm', where the once whole and true 'real' of the body is now overwritten by signifiers which, through language, now constitute our social, and inherently subjective, reality. Because we can only understand the world in the terms of the symbolic, and the 'Real' is that which exists beyond the symbolic realm, the Lacanian Real is, as Phelan describes, 'forever impossible to realize (to make real) within the frame of the Symbolic' (1993:3). For Phelan, more precisely, it is representation that becomes the means, within the Symbolic realm, by which we all attempt to produce and access a constructed reality that can stand in for the true 'Real' that is forever inaccessible to us.

The Lacanian Real, then, is that which is excluded from language and representation. It is an element, therefore, that disrupts our attempts to construct a symbolic and conceptually coherent reality. Lacan identifies this disruption as a stain on the screens of reality we erect, a trace of what must be kept absent from the field of reality for it to achieve its appearance of completion. For this reason, the Real is seen to suffer a traumatic relationship with symbolic reality; the Real cannot be articulated or brought forth in representation, but its very absence in our construction of a coherent reality is always already marked by a symptom of its inaccessible presence. The symptom points to the 'remainder', or excess, of the Symbolic, the absent Real, that, like the repressed trauma, belies the Symbolic's appearance of completion. In this way, as Lacan proposes in *Four Fundamental Concepts of Psycho-Analysis* (1978), trauma is inherently 'part of the structure of the subject's "missed encounter" with the Real' (Rothberg, 2000: 22).

Michael Rothberg draws on this relationship between the Lacanian Real and the traumatic event in *Traumatic Realism*, where he seeks to interrogate 'the constraints, demands, and possibilities of representations of the extreme' (2000: 12). Rothberg's study posits that the Holocaust was the central traumatic event of the twentieth century, and that Adorno's famous assertion that to 'write poetry after Auschwitz is barbaric' (Adorno, 1981: 34 in Rothberg 2000: 25) expressed the conviction that, like the Lacanian Real, the traumatic event might be beyond representation. Adorno further argues that

> by turning suffering into images, harsh and uncompromising though they are, it wounds the shame we feel in the presence of the victims. For these victims are used to create something, works of art, that are thrown to the consumption of a world which destroyed them ... The aesthetic principle of stylization, and even the solemn prayer of the chorus, make an unthinkable fate appear to have had some meaning; it is transfigured, something of its horror is removed. (1977: 189)

Adorno's analysis of the Holocaust as the epitome of the unrepresentable locates one source of the modernist suspicion of representational practice that remains central to later poststructuralist theory. Hayden White further claims that 'it is the anomalous nature of modernist events ... that undermine [*sic*] not only the status of facts in relation to events but also the status of the event in general' (White, 1999: 70 in Ackerman and Puchner, 2006: 11), leading Ackerman and Puchner to conclude that '[t]he historical consciousness that White describes explodes conventional forms of representation and, thus, ways of knowing' (2006: 11).

However, the logical conclusion that the difficulties of realist representation must condemn traumatic events to a negative aesthetic of silence would risk erasing such events from history. As Rothberg confirms, 'the fact that nothing has been left intact does not mean that nothing has been left. The comfort of oblivion is not an option, even if the traumatic kernel of the catastrophe cannot be represented' (2000: 81). What is left, in Lacanian terms, is the symptom of the traumatic event. This points to the real, rather than representing the real, and Rothberg suggests that this likens it to the semiotic concept of the index, except that, 'instead of [...] making the referent present, the traumatic index points to a necessary absence' (104). He concludes that 'traumatic realism is counter-ideological precisely because it does not produce an imaginary resolution, but rather programs readers to recognize the absence of the real' (104). Herbert Blau concurs, suggesting that '[a]nything can be cheapened by performance, but what's not there, and should be, preys upon the brain' (2006: 235).

This absence of the real was explicit in *After Dubrovka* and gestured insistently to the event that was not, in any way, represented in the installation, but re-membered uniquely and subjectively in the present space and time, by the imaginative complicity of the participants. David Savran distinguishes Memory from History, drawing on the work of Pierre Nora:

> Memory [....] connect[s] us with the past, it fills us out. It gives us an identity. It is alive, immediate, and concrete [...] History, on the other hand, is assumed always to be second-hand, to come to us from outside. It is reconstructed through cultural narratives we read or watch or listen to.
> (Savran, 2000: 586–7)

It is precisely within such cultural narratives, as Hayden White argues, that the threat of 'aestheticization' of the historical event lies. He warns that 'making it into the subject matter of a narrative, a story that, by its possible "humanization" of the perpetrators, might enfable the event', makes the event itself vulnerable to 'investment by fantasies of intactness, wholeness, and health which the very occurrence of the event denies' (1999: 81).

In its refusal to present either a second-hand narrative or a visual representation of the real event, *After Dubrovka* was attempting to avoid both 'narrative fetishism', in the terminology of Eric Santner, and repetition of the spectacle (Santner, 1992: 147, in White, 1999: 81). The production instead chose to reject the ideological risks of the historical in favour of the remembered, given that Savran's observations are equally pertinent when applied to remembering pasts with which we may never have had a personal connection. In such instances – a minute's silence on Remembrance Sunday or pilgrimages to Auschwitz or to Ground Zero – we reflect in order to find a deeper connection to events that we have only received, in the main, through the cultural and mediatised narratives of history, through others' (mis)representation; that have been made 'unreal' to us; that have been made commensurate with film footage and mythology. The memorial enables us to commit our personal imaginative and empathetic engagement to these events in order to elevate them from such commensurability; to make them 'real' for ourselves, in recognition of their undeniable reality to others.

Refusing to offer an alternative truth to the simulations of the mass media, *After Dubrovka* chose instead to offer its audience an alternative perception of the real event, rejecting both the narrative form of history and the spectacular emphasis of our mediatised culture. The installation consequently counteracts the model of the televised memorial tribute where the real event gets obscured behind the televised footage, effaced by the representations of itself, as Baudrillard's critique of mediatisation suggests. Richard Kilborn explains how television's obsession with 'hyping the real' has made reality 'into a commodity like any other, in the sense that it is shaped and offered for sale like any other consumer product' (Kilborn, 2003: 65). Citing Beard, he concludes that, 'reality as it appears on TV is a produced or invented discourse ... no longer representation, but the simulation of reality' (Beard, 1993: 35, in Kilborn, 2003: 94). Conversely, as we sat in the theatre auditorium, the text of *After Dubrovka* explicitly informed us that we would not see any set tonight, nor any guns tonight; the representational apparatus was conspicuously absent, there was nothing here to displace the real historical event, nothing here to obscure it behind a narrative version of itself. James Thompson commented from the panel that such an approach corresponded with the advice of Yugoslavian director and Professor of Theatre Dragan Klaic who, in the wake of the country's civil wars, had concluded that:

> we shouldn't be working with the absolute spectacle, the pain of the spec-
> tacle, the horror, because in many ways, that is terrain that certain peo-
> ple who use the spectacle of violence in certain events have dominated.
> (Thompson, 2007)[4]

Linda Taylor, also speaking on the panel, suggested that the politics of
the spectacle were correspondingly pervasive at a micro level, and she
observed how *After Dubrovka* had consciously worked against the images
that can be found on YouTube, featuring the corpses of Chechen rebels
dying in the theatre, thus rejecting 'a spectacle of violence ... a titillation
of violence and the way the media is using that' (Taylor, 2007). Taylor
concludes, apropos Susan Sontag's *Regarding the Pain of Others* (2003),
that, in such instances, 'we don't have the right to look at a piece of
violence ... simply for the spectacle ... we don't have the right to look
unless we are committed to actually processing what we see' (Taylor,
2007). *After Dubrovka* committed us to processing what we could only
imagine; refusing to offer us a mediation of the real event that we could
merely spectate and consume, offering us, instead, a space to rethink
the real event for ourselves, to conceive of an imagined real that might
'stand in' for the experience of others, but never assume to replace it or
to be commensurate with it. As the text that follows the minute's silence
reminds us:

> You are standing in my place. You are standing in for me. And for all the
> people who are not where you are now. Thank you. On behalf of all of us,
> thank you for standing there. Thank you for your performance. For being
> those different people, for playing those different parts.

This acknowledgement was more than a conceit. Our presence, our
'standing in', our imaginative complicity was vital for the memorial
to function, for the event of remembrance to happen. When some
participants did not comply, but rather performed for their audience in
spite of the request to remember, embody, imagine, the spell was broken,
and all that was left was the meta-theatrical structure of the present time.
When participants did comply with the conventions of the memorial,
moving in silent response to the speaker lights going on and off, or to
the texts coming in and fading away, they gave the impression of actors
moving to cues, or with some kind of pattern or intention, providing
a ghosting of all the actors who had ever moved on this stage and, by
imaginative implication, on any stage throughout history, and, by textual
prompting, on the stage in Dubrovka, that night.

Such ghostings could be said to validate the meta-theatrical enquiry of *After Dubrovka* as the perfect vehicle for the memorial form. In his article 'Modernity's Haunted Houses', David Savran observes the long tradition of theatre's haunting 'by that which it believes it has displaced' (2000: 584) and argues that 'ghosts are so important on contemporary stages because they function as a point of intersection between memory and history' (586). In *The Haunted Stage: The Theatre as Memory Machine,* Marvin Carlson elucidates precisely how the theatre 'remembers' through its tendency to 'recycle past perceptions and experience in imaginary configurations that, although different, are powerfully haunted by a sense of repetition' (2001: 3). In this way, *After Dubrovka* invites us to perceive what we have not seen, through imaginary configurations provoked by ghosted disembodied texts. Beliz Güçbilmez describes how the 'dematerialised sound / voice [...] create[s] an auditory visuality on stage', and 'indicate[s] the violation of the stage by the offstage' (2007: 155). He goes on to identify the 'offstage' as the locus of the 'uncanny':

> The 'then' is the imaginary time of the off-stage. If the 'then' as represented by the offstage has been a 'now' sometime, which is to say, when that past was present, it was onstage. [...] Thus, there is a close affinity between memory, the unconscious, and the offstage. (2007: 155–6)

This concept of 'offstage' can be usefully applied to *After Dubrovka*, which, in common with *Linked* and, of course, ancient Greek tragedy, refrains from putting 'onstage' the representations of the real event as if in the present. It locates, instead, the ghostings of the real event, in the past or remembered or imagined time of the 'offstage', the 'forbidden area for real visitors and onlookers, where we have reached the boundary of seeing' (Güçbilmez, 2007: 154). If stagelessness, as Güçbilmez suggests, 'constitutes an obstacle for the gaze' (154), then the participants of *After Dubrovka* were asked instead to turn that gaze inwards, to imagine the real event of others for themselves; standing in for, at different times, the actor, or spectator, whom they replaced in the meta-theatrical framework of the piece; generic actors, actors from *Nord Ost*, generic terrorists, Chechan terrorists, generic spectators and spectators of *Nord Ost*. In this way, the meta-theatrical framework of the piece enabled us to segue from 'standing in for' the usual actors and audience who were not there, to the greater political significance of 'standing in' for others on the world stage. Just as we, in our theatre seats on that night in Manchester, were, in some small aesthetic way, standing in for the audience of that night in Moscow; so they too, on a political level, were 'standing in' for others. They were not targeted as individuals, but as stand-ins for 'Russia'; or, under the American version of events, as stand-ins for the West, for Imperialism, for the *Kuffar*. They were standing in for bigger narratives than themselves, just as we were. Were we then also standing in for, not only as the voice told us, 'all the people who are not where you are now', but also, perhaps, for all the people who were not where the Moscow audience was then; for all the theatre audiences who could have just as easily 'stood in for' Russia, or the West, or Imperialism, but who, on this occasion, were spared the reality of these particular consequences? Is it not also part of a memorial, particularly one where, in some small way, it could have been you, to pay homage to those who unwittingly 'stood in' your place? Conversely, when, on stage, I am placed in the role which lies somewhere between an actor and a terrorist, am I then being asked to 'stand in for' all of those people who did not stand on the stage in Dubrovka that night; for all of those people who do not take political action, do not put themselves on the line and 'act' for a cause they believe in; but merely 'act' within the parameters of a theatrical fiction?

This is the alternative mode of perception *After Dubrovka* offers; a mode which rejects the 'deceptively comforting duality of here and there, inside and outside', as Lehman describes, but instead 'can move the *mutual implication of actors and spectators in the theatrical production of images* into the centre and thus make visible the broken thread between personal experience and perception' (Lehmann, 2006: 185–6, original emphasis). In the absence of representation, narrative, mediatised spectacle and historical context, the radical engagement with the real event lies, perhaps, in the very space that is left; space that neither consumes nor threatens the distinction of the experienced real but eradicates all possible mediations of it. Our commitment to the distinction of the real event, its singularity, its independent authority, may best be shown by our complicity in re-membering the absent real for ourselves, through an evocation of its ghosts. For, as Derrida advised:

> the 'intellectual' of tomorrow should learn [...] from the ghost. He should learn to live by learning not how to make conversation with the ghost but how [...] to let them speak or how to give them back speech, even if it is in oneself, in the other, in the other in oneself. (Derrida, 1994: 176)

In Chapter 6, I will broaden my investigation into models of performance that seek to uphold a distinction between experiential and mediated understandings of the real. Whether revisiting the potential of characterisation and fictional narratives, or developing actions within the time and space of the event itself, all share a repositioning of the spectator as active participant and co-creator of the performance. In the work to be examined, the represented real of the traditional theatrical framework, or the 'staging of meaning' (Baudrillard, 2007: 101), is compromised, to varying degrees, in favour of offering the spectator the potential to act and author the events which ensue.

Notes

1   This analysis is based on my participation in the Edinburgh run of *En Route* on 10 August 2010. All quotations are transcribed from the audio sound-track by courtesy of One Step At a Time Like This.

2   This analysis is based on the performance of *Nights in this City* which took place in Sheffield in May 1995. All quotations are taken from the unpublished performance text courtesy of Forced Entertainment.

3   All quotations are taken from the unpublished performance text courtesy of Neil Mackenzie.

4   This was paraphrased by Thompson from Klaic (2002).

6

From spect-actor to corporate player: reconfigurations of twenty-first-century audiences

In *Theatre and Audience*, Helen Freshwater notes the 'extraordinary increase' in the use of participation in new British (and I would add European) performance practices in recent years (2009: 4). In this chapter, I will examine the different ways in which certain recurring models are seeking to enable the spectator to co-author the event, and become an active participant in the performance text, in order to offer an experiential real in place of the representations formerly contained in the conventional theatrical framework. This move towards participation is an integral part of the wider ideological narrative discussed throughout the book, which seeks to categorise as radical those practices that look to evade the representational bind and logocentric authorship of the conventions of dramatic theatre, as discussed in Chapter 2. This chapter will trace the discursive construction of the 'active' spectator or participant, in opposition to the pervasive myth of the 'passive' spectator that is tied, in particular, to the dramatic model, and will interrogate the claims to radicalism, democracy and empowerment that underpin the orthodox ideological framing of contemporary participatory, immersive or interactive practice.

In *Theatre Audiences*, Susan Bennett traces the history of the modern audience, defining the wide-ranging developments that occurred between the seventeenth and the mid-nineteenth centuries as 'a steady progression' towards the separation of fictional stage world and audience. As a consequence, she remarks, 'audiences became increasingly passive' (1997: 3). Bennett notes that in the early twentieth century the emerging form of naturalism was held responsible for suppressing the participation and imaginative capacity of the audience. In *Theatre and Audience*, Helen

Freshwater highlights Bertolt Brecht's well-known condemnation of the perceived passivity of audiences, arguing that Brecht's theories were 'fuelled by a deep frustration with the passive audiences of the bourgeois theatre, which he called "culinary theatre" because its audiences were like diners sating themselves with pleasure' (2009: 47).

In 'The emancipated spectator', Jacques Rancière moves beyond the more familiar historical narrative outlined by Freshwater and Bennett to trace the charge of audience passivity all the way back to Plato, arguing that Plato's anti-theatrical prejudice was underpinned by his vilification of the spectator. Rancière summarises Plato's objections as follows:

> Being a spectator means looking at a spectacle. And looking is a bad thing, for two reasons. First, looking is deemed the opposite of knowing. It means standing before an appearance without knowing the conditions which produced that appearance or the reality that lies behind it. Second, looking is the opposite of acting. He who looks at the spectacle remains motionless in his seat, lacking any power of intervention. Being a spectator means being passive. The spectator is separated from the capacity of knowing just as he is separated from the possibility of acting. (2007: 272)

Rancière argues that Plato's objections to the theatre have paradoxically been accepted and taken up by theatre practitioners and theorists such as Brecht and Antonin Artaud, who have attempted to answer Plato's objections, not by dismissing theatre as Plato did, but by attempting to address the perceived passivity of the spectator through the creation of new forms of theatre in which the spectator is reconfigured as active. Brecht's conception of an active spectator, unlike most of those to be discussed in this chapter, was more cerebral than physical, as his following definition of a passive audience confirms:

> their eyes are open, but they stare rather than see, just as they listen rather than hear … Seeing and hearing are activities, and can be pleasant ones, but these people seem relieved of activity and like men to whom something is being done. (1964: 187)

Brecht's ideological commitment to Marxism, which was the impulse behind his impatience with the passivity of bourgeois audiences, may no longer be common amongst artists at the turn of the millennium, but the active critical response he required continues to underpin many configurations of the ideal spectator within a poststructuralist discourse. As discussed in Chapter 2, the theories of Roland Barthes and Jacques Derrida seek to transfer the authority of a text from the author to the reader/spectator, thus requiring the latter to be an active producer, rather than a passive recipient, of meaning. In his analysis of the work of Forced Entertainment, Florian Malzacher distinguishes between the active spectator required by Brecht 'to apply what was shown on stage as a concrete model to society' and the contemporary audience who are 'asked to relate texts and images to themselves [...] to make their own stories, rather than follow a closed, linear narrative' (2004: 123).

In this sense, it can be seen that the active spectator at the beginning of the twenty-first century is still positioned in opposition to the (implicitly passive) spectator of predominantly naturalistic drama. In both historical contexts, however, the audience is asked 'not so much to act, but rather to see and to think actively' (Malzacher, 2004: 123). In *Modes of Spectating*, Alison Oddey and Christine White also agree that the twenty-first century spectator 'is no longer content simply to view the work. More is required. The spectator wants to engage in a more active way, to play a significant part or role in the reception of the work' (2009: 8–9). Consequently, Malzacher argues, for Tim Etchells, artistic director of Forced Entertainment, 'the spectator thus becomes a witness – the counter model to the idea of a passive being in Guy Debord's *The Society of the Spectacle*' (2004: 124). The necessity for a politically progressive theatre practice to configure its audience in radical opposition to the passive consumer of the advanced spectacular society of late global capitalism is one that this chapter will return to. However, Malzacher's distinction between the spectator who is asked 'not so much to act, but rather to see and to think actively' draws a pertinent distinction between the witness required by the work of Forced Entertainment and the participant required by the new wave of interactive performance. If the first is a direct descendent of Brecht, then the second can be traced more pertinently back to the influence of Antonin Artaud.

Rather than Brecht's desire for a certain distancing of the spectator that might enable critical reflection on what was observed, Artaud demanded that the spectator become physically at one with the performance, 'seated in the centre of the action ... encircled and furrowed by it' (1970a: 74). For Artaud, this would return theatre to its ritual origins and enable the spectator to become immersed in the unfolding event, no longer a part of the seated public of spectators or consumers who were required to merely observe from a distance the repetition of the 'false' reality that was dramatic representation. As Kimberly Jannarone (2009) persuasively argues, it is important to note that the kind of audience immersion Artaud was seeking can be seen to reflect a distinctly different ideological influence from the Marxism which underpinned Brecht's response to the problem of the bourgeois spectator. Indeed, the fascist implications of Artaud's vision, Jannarone argues, suggest that, contrary to received notions of Artaud's work, the spectator is far from empowered by their release from a specifically bourgeois passivity. Rather, the immersion desired by Artaud would envelop them in an even greater level of passivity as they would become entirely subject to the artistic environment that had been imposed upon them: 'the Theatre of Cruelty does not encourage the creative input of the spectators: it requires that it alone establish the rules and flow of communication' (Jannarone, 2009: 198).

Nevertheless, as Jannarone confirms, the ways in which Artaud's thinking was taken up by the neo-avant-garde established the myth of Artaud as a visionary who was calling for a politically radical practice that would place the physical engagement of the spectator at the heart of the action. The Living Theatre and The Performance Group were just two of the many companies to demonstrate the influence of his radical, if mythical, legacy, during the wave of interactive performance that dominated the 1960s and 1970s (Jannarone, 2009; Sell, 2006). David Callaghan articulates the mission of the Living Theatre as one committed to forging 'a theatrical playing space where the spectator can abandon a passive role, become empowered, and take "significant action"' (2003: 33), most pertinently through a participatory role 'that could theoretically offer them potential status as co-creators of the artistic event' (2003: 25). Likewise, Erika Fischer-Lichte highlights the democratic principles that underpinned the infamous audience involvement in The Performance Group's *Dionysus in 69* (2008: 41). In her introduction to *Participation,* published in 2006, Claire Bishop argues that such ideological claims persist and notes that 'activation; authorship; community – are the most frequently cited motivations for almost all artistic attempts to encourage participation in art since the 1960s' (2006: 12). Despite the ideological distinctions, which I will later detail, between the participatory work in the 1960s and 1970s and the resurgence of such experiments in the 1990s and 2000s, this narrative of empowerment has remained intact. So, too, has its flip side, which implicitly, or at times explicitly, proposes that an absence of audience participation, that is a seated and silent audience, reflects a passivity which is politically disempowering by comparison. Bishop writes that the conviction of the earlier artists and theorists that 'physical involvement is considered an essential precursor to social change' is 'no less persistent' today, although she does add, and more on this later, that 'its terms are perhaps less convincing' (2006: 11).

Often evoked to support this connection is the work of theatre director Augusto Boal (1979). Boal's influential forum theatre was designed to enable economically and politically oppressed communities to address specific social and political issues that impacted on their lives. Orchestrated by a Joker character, performers would enact scenarios that revealed a particular problem or dilemma in relation to their audience's wider context of oppression. Spectators who wished to participate were then invited to join the performers in order to propose and act out possible solutions to the scenario being played out, which might, in turn, offer the community as a whole the possibility of real social change. Susan Haedicke explains that '[p]articipation becomes empowerment … as the audiences begin to understand how the power structure actually works and to recognize how they unconsciously cooperate in their own oppression' (2003: 79). To define these spectators Boal coined the term 'spect-actor', a term that is now often appropriated to describe participating spectators across a wide range of interactive performance (see Paris, 2006: 191; Lancaster, 1997: 82). In this way, the radical implications of Boal's original terminology of empowerment are carried over to work that rarely shares the ideological context or political aims of his theatre, as I will demonstrate later in this chapter.

Unsurprisingly, the Marxist politics that informed, in very different ways, the applied practice of Boal and the participatory practice of the Living Theatre, is rarely found in performance models at the turn of the century. In the 1960s and 1970s, the raising of individual consciousness through active participation was designed to lead to wider political change. In the 1990s and 2000s, I will now argue, the importance of co-authorship might still be read as a means by which participants are expected to model and restructure new and politically resistant subjectivities in the face of global capitalism, but this is in the absence of any corresponding or subsequent objective for radical social change.

Inventing ways of being together

Nicolas Bourriaud's discourse on relational aesthetics is one of the most influential theoretical studies of audience participation in the arts at the turn of the twenty-first century, and he claims that the key distinction between historical and more recent practice is that artists are now:

> *learning to inhabit the world in a better way*, instead of trying to construct it based on a preconceived idea of historical evolution … the role of art- works is no longer to form imaginary and utopian realities, but to actually be ways of living and models of action within the existing real' (2002: 13, original emphasis)

Although Bourriaud's analysis is directed at developments in the field of visual and live art practice, his insights offer an ideological analysis of participatory work that can be as pertinently applied to the trends in performance practice under discussion. He is clear that the radical potential of such work does not lie in the 'social utopias and revolutionary hopes' (2002: 31) of the 1960s but in the artists' capacity to create new models of human interaction through their work. These are to be produced in the interstices of the world as it currently exists, 'where human relations are no longer "directly experienced" but start to become blurred in their "spectacular" representation' (2002: 9). Bourriaud argues that work that seeks to involve its audience in the creation of an event, which then itself constitutes the artwork, holds political efficacy in its ability to forge new models of human relationships and interactions:

> Contemporary culture … means inventing ways of being together, forms of interaction that go beyond the inevitability of the families, ghettos of technological user-friendliness, and collective institutions on offer … The most pressing thing is no longer the emancipation of individuals, but the freeing-up of inter-human communications, the dimensional emancipation of existence. (2002: 60)

This positioning of contemporary culture's 'inventing ways of being together' as an ideological and radical intervention is apparent throughout the discourses and polemics accompanying recent explorations of audience involvement in theatre and performance practice. In this field, of course, unlike the historical conventions of visual art addressed by Bourriaud, a direct and present-time relationship between the artist/actor and the audience has always existed. Experiments in theatre practice consequently seek not to introduce the artist/audience relationship into the equation *per se*, as in the live art experimentation that is the focus of Bourriaud's study, but to invent new ways for the actor/audience to be together. If the conventional relationship between the actor and the audience has been understood, since at least the mid-nineteenth century, as one of distance and separation, then it is not surprising that the emphasis in work that seeks to renegotiate this relationship is consistently on the importance of establishing intimacy and involvement. The *Guardian's* influential theatre critic, Lyn Gardner, argues that audiences:

> hunger for cultural experiences which not only are different but which have an authenticity. They crave the intimacy and emotional connectedness that live art can deliver, but which is mostly absent from the traditional well made play produced in a Victorian playhouse where from the back row of the stalls everyone on stage looks Lilliputian. How can such an

experience compete with the intimacy of Kira O'Reilly's encounters ... in which she invited audience members to either cut her or hold her? (2007: 14)

It is not only the proxemics, of course, that are so often claimed to distance the historical spectator from the action but also the representational nature of the fiction from which they are excluded. As explored in depth in Chapter 2, the representational foundation of dramatic theatre, according to Artaud, eclipses the reality of the present moment for the spectator, obscuring it with a fictional reality that is merely repetition. I argued in Chapter 2 that this analysis applies not only to dramatic theatre but also to any theatre practice that relies on rehearsal to maintain an illusion of present-time spontaneity. Work discussed in this chapter, as in Chapter 5, seeks to escape the bind of theatrical representation by offering its audience an experience that, to a greater or lesser degree, can only exist in that way in that moment due to its significant reliance on the present-time contribution of each spectator to the performance text itself. In this way, the intimacy proposed by the work under discussion here carries with it a claim to a greater authenticity, offering its audience an experiential reality that is unique to them, as opposed to the communal viewing of a mediated representation of the real that is repeated as if for the first time.

In 2010 the British Council sent a showcase of new work to Singapore that was entitled *Connected* and defined as

a series of directions or challenges to the conventional relationship bet- ween audience, artists and the world around them. One of those potential directions is undoubtedly a move towards a more intimate relationship between performer and audience. (British Council, 2010)

Adrian Howells, one of the artists featured in *Connected,* was performing his latest piece, *Foot Washing for the Sole,* which was a one-to-one performance where he would wash, dry and massage the feet of the single participant whilst engaging them in conversation. Speaking on YouTube, Howells talked about the project as a 'nurturing experience' that often led to a 'special connection' between himself and the participant, due to the intimate nature of the task and the exposure of the feet which were often perceived as a vulnerable part of the body (Howells, 2010). Howells' previous piece, *Salon Adrienne,* was likewise designed for a single participant who, on this occasion, was treated to a shampoo, blow dry and head massage whilst being asked to answer the question 'what comes up for you when you take a long hard look at yourself in

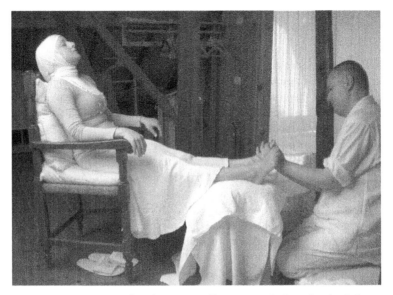

12   Participant with Adrian Howells in *Foot Washing for the Sole*,
Nazareth, 2008.

Photographer: Hamish Barton

the mirror?' (Howells, 2007). Howells talks about this piece as giving
him the opportunity to 'have a meaningful interaction … with another
person' (Howells, 2007), and the confessional exchanges that dominate
both pieces are positioned by the artist as having the potential to model
new ways of being together in the wider world.

Howells explains how the phrase Jesus used to address his disciples
when washing their feet – 'what I do for you now go and do for others'
– was central to his *Foot Washing* project, and with tongue slightly, but
not entirely, in cheek, he confesses that 'global catharsis' is what he was
ultimately after (Howells, 2010). Bourriaud's theories also suggest that the
new kinds of performance relationships that are facilitated by Howells,
and artists working with similar models, have a significant role to play in
the wider political landscape:

> Through little services rendered, the artists fill in the cracks in the social
> bond […;] through little gestures art is like an angelic programme, a set
> of tasks carried out beside or beneath the real economic system, so as to
> patiently re-stitch the relational fabric. (2002: 36)

Bourriaud contrasts these relationship models with those currently existing in society, reconfiguring Debord's society of the spectacle into a 'society of extras, where everyone finds the illusion of an interactive democracy in more or less truncated channels of communication' (Bourriaud, 2002: 26). Drawing directly on Debord (1995: 12), he goes on to explicitly correlate resistance to the spectacle with the relational aesthetics of the work under discussion:

> If the spectacle deals first and foremost with forms of human relations (it is '*a social relationship between people, with imagery as the go-between*'), it can only be analysed and fought through the production of new types of relationships between people. (Bourriaud, 2002: 85, original emphasis)

Building on the theories of Felix Guattari, Bourriaud clarifies that what is at stake in the existing human relations engendered by the spectacle is a threat to the nature of contemporary subjectivity itself. 'We must ... *seize, enhance and re-invent* subjectivity', he declares, 'for otherwise we shall see it transformed into a rigid collective apparatus at the exclusive service of the powers that be' (2002: 89, original emphasis). Bourriaud argues that the only way contemporary subjectivity can be freed from the ideological shackles that threaten to subsume it is by a re-invention of the relationships through which it is formed: 'subjectivity ... cannot exist in an independent way, and in no case can it ground the existence of the subject. It only exists in the pairing mode.' (2002: 91)

Consequently, it is only through the invention of new 'ways of being together', Bourriaud argues, that contemporary subjectivity itself can be remodelled. For progressive models to be fashioned, he suggests, it is vital that the subject themselves, that is the spectator/participant, is empowered to take on an active role in the negotiation of the new 'ways of being together', and the models of subjectivity which might ensue. This is where we see most clearly the continuing narrative of empowerment that I identified as being so critical to the participatory work of the 1960s and 1970s. With this later work too, as Bourriaud insists, it is the '*democratic* concern that informs it' (2002: 57, original emphasis) that is critical to the radical nature of the enterprise. This enterprise can be seen to be

> [g]overned by a concern to 'give everyone their chance', through forms which do not establish any precedence, a priori, of the producer over the beholder (let us put it another way: no divine right authority), but rather negotiate open relationships with it, which are not resolved beforehand. (2002: 58)

In this way, the participant/spectator, through active co-creation of the performance text, is empowered to play a key authoring role in the construction of their own subjectivity through the exploration of new ways of being together with others. The one-to-one work of Adrian Howells is explicitly designed to offer each participant 'the opportunity [...] to take a really qualitative half an hour out of their lives, and to be very present and engage with themselves' (Howells, 2010). This provides a space that is not simply 'time out' in a prosaic sense but, it might be argued, a space that is resistant both to the spectacular society of representations, through its emphasis on touch and presence, and to the economic domination of mass communications and virtual relationships, through its emphasis on physical intimacy.

The 'social utopias' and 'revolutionary hopes' of the 1960s and 1970s might have given way to the micro-level personal relations that dominate radical politics at the turn of the millennium, but Bourriaud's discourse of relational aesthetics shares with its Marxist predecessor the key motivation of a wider political emancipation that is achieved primarily through resistance to the false consciousness induced by the capitalist spectacle. For Bourriaud also, this is a communal enterprise, as empowered individual subjectivities can only be won through the re-invention of new ways of being together. Bourriaud's theoretical framework begs a number of critical questions to which I will return in the course of this chapter, but he does, nevertheless, offer a convincing starting-point for an ideological analysis of participatory practice that we will now take up. If, as Bourriaud's work would suggest, the principal claim to progressive radicalism lies in the democratic nature of the relationships that the work establishes, then the ideological analysis of any individual model of performance practice must begin by questioning to what degree it can be seen to truly empower the participant/spectator to co-create the performance text from which a sense of their own re-invented subjectivity may emerge.

Democratic co-authorship and audience misrecognition

The one-to-one work of Adrian Howells, and that of other artists working in what Howells calls confessional performance, potentially offers the greatest capacity for the individual participant to take an equal responsibility for the creation of the resulting performance text. As with therapeutic practice or the religious confessional – in that both share the same formal structure – the participant is placed at the centre of the discourse and holds significant authorial control. A more limited capacity to artistically contribute is offered to audiences through models such as Forced Entertainment's *Instructions for Forgetting*

(2001), Stan's Cafe's *Radio Z* (2010), and Uninvited Guests' *Love Letters Straight from Your Heart* (2009), where networking devices, phones and digital communication are commonly used to solicit substantial artistic contributions from the audience in advance of, or during, the event itself. Uninvited Guests' publicity for *Love Letters Straight from Your Heart* declares:

> If you want to join us on this happy occasion, send a dedication to some-one you love to info@uninvited-guests.net. Tell us what they mean to you and why you've chosen this piece of music. Your letters of love may become part of the show, romantic gestures or signs of friendship, shared publicly between us. Be our witnesses and we'll be yours. (Uninvited Guests, 2009)

Here we see, rather than the one-to-one confessional of *Foot Washing for the Sole,* the framework for a communal sharing of autobiographical material. As with any form of verbatim theatre, as discussed in Chapter 4, the company will necessarily maintain overall artistic control through the process of selecting, editing, arranging and performing the submitted dedications. But, nevertheless, the emphasis here is clearly on the democratic co-creation of a communal piece of work, the dedications and selected songs constituting the core framework for the rehearsed elements of the performance text that were interspersed by the two performers throughout the series of dedications. However, there were some notable tensions between the democratic framework of the piece and the nature of the audience's required participation in the performance itself. As Erika Fischer-Lichte cautions, in certain contexts, audience participation 'requires a prior empowerment of the actors and disempowerment of the audience: the artists force new behavior patterns onto the audience, often plunge them into crisis, thus denying the spectators the position of distanced, uninvolved observers' (2008: 50).

On entering the space,[1] the audience were invited to sit around a long table with glasses of champagne, while the selected dedications were read out by the performers and the requested tracks were played. Despite the intentions to place the audience, as the *Guardian* review acknowledges, 'at the very heart of this show' (Gardner, 2009), we were, nevertheless, required to participate, once present, in ways which might be construed as less than empowering. After the first couple of dedications, an instruction came from the performers for us all to stare into the eyes of the person opposite us at the table for the duration of the song, 'The first time ever I saw your face'. Unlike the company's open invitation to contribute text, here there was no option that empowered the individual to refuse this request without imposing the consequences of their decision on the spectator opposite them, by removing their opportunity to gaze. My less than enthusiastic compliance, however, may have provided a better experience for my partner than the one reported by Dominic Cavendish, who describes how 'within about a minute the poor woman holding my gaze had started crying, scooped up her bags and fled' (Cavendish, 2009). Either way, I felt that the performative moment of us all holding a gaze with a stranger was offering much more to the production than it was offering to me. My over-riding feeling was that I had been coerced to conspire in a performance text that had imposed on me new 'ways of being together' with strangers that had reconfigured my own role and identity in ways I found less than empowering or desirable.

Contemporary audiences are often reconfigured within the world of the performance to operate as an integral element of the pre-structured performance text. Tim Etchells refers to this process as a 'misrecognition' of the audience that Forced Entertainment achieve by 'putting the audience in a fictional place by addressing them wrongly' (Heathfield, 2004: 83). Conversely, in *Love Letters,* my discomfort had arisen from the absence of any fictional framework and the sense, given the (auto) biographical foundation of the piece, that I was being asked to perform a public action 'as myself' that was at odds with my own sense of self-authorship or rights to self-presentation. The request at the close of the piece to 'take one last look in your partner's eyes, are you sure there isn't something there?' further consolidated a role and relationship that I had neither desired nor consented to. It was my 'self', in this instance, that was being appropriated to serve the designs of the performance text, and objectified for the benefits of the piece.

Drawing on the theories of Erving Goffman and Pierre Bourdieu, Gareth White describes this strategy as a 'process of putting participants on display' (2009: 224), which calls upon the audience to 'take part in extra-everyday performance, for which they fear they do not have the resources' (225). Discussing the immersive theatre of Punchdrunk, where all spectators are masked as they enter the environment of the performance, White defines this particular innovation as an interruption of the potential display of the participant, as 'the individual is placed in the performance, and yet remains absent from it to those watching' (224). On attending the company's production *The Duchess of Malfi* (2010), the impact of wearing the mask did indeed imbue a sense of invisibility that enabled meetings with other spectators and performers to take place without the usual self-consciousness. To others, we were masked figures who became part of the overall performance environment, reconfigured and incorporated into each individual's subjective narrative, but, crucially,

13 Opening state of *Iris Brunette*.
Photographer: Gemma Riggs

we were no longer 'on display' as ourselves, being obscured by the masks
we were wearing.

In Melanie Wilson's *Iris Brunette* (2009),[2] the audience was offered a
comparative opportunity to take refuge behind the guise of character.
Set in a darkened square space with a limited audience of twenty people
seated around the edge of the playing area, *Iris Brunette* told the story of a
woman searching for a man in a future world on the brink of annihilation.
The narrative switched between the third person relayed through
the narrated soundtrack (given in italics below), and the first person as
narrated by Wilson herself (given in standard typeface below) and points
where the two overlapped (given in bold typeface below). As the piece
opened, the audience was immediately 'misrecognised' and, as each one
of us was introduced into the story, a single light came on over the head
of the individual spectator to position them, for that moment, in the
role in question; the light would fade out as the story moved on. The
framework of the dramatic fiction is maintained throughout the piece,
but with numerous knowing overlaps into the reality of the performance
situation:

It was hazy in the room. There was a clinging vapour in the city outside and it penetrated even in here. The figures were silent and still, watchful.

A bureaucratic clearing house.

One of many that thronged that particular pre-war city, punctuating each street corner.

Never inside.

Until now.

An expectant silence lines the walls.

Citizens from all sectors wait for

for…

Their turn.

A facility civil servant

A walker from the Upper Finsbury Skyway

Two engineers from the aqueduct authority

A lone yachtsman [3]

In this way, Wilson disarmingly draws her spectators into the fiction. We are offered fictional roles, but the performance reality of our presence is held in a pleasurable and comfortable tension, to enable us to move, at will, between the two, or choose our preferred position. Thus, we can author our own meanings, even whilst we are playing a fictional role in another spectator's narrative. This mutual 'misrecognition' is a familiar feature of performance in this period and, as Małgorzata Sugiera observes, is 'a means of inducing the audience to watch themselves as subjects which perceive, acquire knowledge, and partly create the objects of their cognition' (2004: 26).

When Wilson first begins to relate directly to individual members of the audience, the text is constructed to ensure that they are clear that nothing is expected of them; their own simultaneously real and fictional presence is all that is required:

Sitting on the opposite side of the room. Something about the face. The way of holding the hands. It's very familiar. I feel some connection, but I can't place it.

She stares

I stare

14   Melanie Wilson in *Iris Brunette.*
Photographer: Gemma Riggs

She knows she is staring, but…

I cannot help it

He notices.

He looks back.

Other people notice. They look at her too.

Just as the audience members are offered the opportunity to shift from the fictional to the present space and time and back again, so Wilson, as Iris Brunette, makes minute shifts in her performance persona, to move, almost imperceptibly, from the character of Iris to the performer in the space.

Although the shifts are subtle, the nature of her knowing eye contact, when she does begin to request participation from the spectator, shares the 'game' with them, which enables them to respond either in character or as themselves. In this sense, the spectator does not feel coerced into a responsibility to give the appropriate response to maintain their role within the fictional text, as both the text and the performance persona have been carefully crafted to work simultaneously across both real and fictional levels of presence. Having warmed her audience up to trust her to take care of their participation, Wilson then adopts a more clearly defined role as narrator in the present time and asks a spectator, 'Shall we play a little game? Very easy. Very calm.' The trust is not broken as she begins to outline a narrative, at first merely giving the spectator options to choose from, and then gradually requesting more creative contributions:

> Ok, now picture this ... you are standing on the edge of a crossroads in a large metropolis. The sun is just beginning to rise and for the first time in nine hours you are warm. The streets are deserted, but debris from a ticker tape parade blankets the roads as far as the eye can see.
>
> Do you cross the road or do you turn left?
>
> (*audience response*)
>
> As you are walking, you put your hand in your pocket. You feel a piece of paper. You take it out. What is written on the piece of paper?
>
> (*audience response*)

Wilson, in her dual role as Iris/Performer, was able to establish quick rapport; supporting the answers she received by artistically framing them without undermining the spectator in question. At the performance I attended, the spectator responded to the last question with the answer 'buy milk', to which Wilson replied, 'buy milk? Very cryptic'. Later in the dialogue they shared the following exchange:

> WILSON: Do you follow the crowd back, or go on alone
>
> MAN: Go on alone.
>
> WILSON: Go on alone? Are you sure?
>
> MAN: We can follow the crowd back.
>
> WILSON: No, no, you want to go alone, you should go on alone.

In this way Wilson plays with her audience, suggesting that there is a 'right' answer before confirming that she will take the narrative whichever way the spectator chooses. At a certain point in this co-authored narrative, she segues seamlessly from narrator in the present to Iris in the fiction and concludes by involving the audience as a whole in the narrative choices that follow, through a re-introduction of the characters identified at the beginning of the piece, the relevant lights appearing over the identified members of the audience. What Wilson achieves in *Iris Brunette* is the communication of an offer for us to participate in the piece under different rules from those we would more conventionally assume. The possible rules are introduced to us as an integral part of the performance framework and are carefully and precisely established in a way that gives the spectator clear choices to participate, either as representations of the fiction or as themselves in the reality of the performance event, or to abstain from either. Whilst the given fiction remains the context of the piece and provides the boundaries and limitations of participation, Wilson is nevertheless seeking to invent new 'ways of being together', whilst maintaining the capacity for each spectator to occupy a position that is, to some degree at least, self-determined.

Through diverse and distinctive performance frameworks with varying degrees of authorship, and drawing on both fictional and auto-biographical texts, the work of Adrian Howells, Punchdrunk and Melanie Wilson can all be seen to offer the capacity for self-transformation, and the renegotiation of subjectivity and identity, that underpins Bourriaud's ideological analysis of participatory practice. Unfortunately, not all work that casts its spectators as active participants can necessarily achieve the same capacity for democratic participation, and there are countless examples of performances that have failed to meet Bourriaud's challenge, of which *Love Letters,* in my own view, is only one relatively harmless example. Badac Theatre's now infamous Edinburgh Festival production, *The Factory,* came under heavy criticism for its misrecognition of the audience as Jewish prisoners in the death camps; 'yelling in our faces, deafening us with metal-bashing and general psychological bullying' (Shuttleworth, 2008). When theatre critic Ian Shuttleworth attempted to assert his own authorial capacity within the production and to politely refuse the command to 'fucking move', the performer offered no other response than to continue shouting until Shuttleworth eventually left and the framework of the piece had been irrevocably broken. In this instance, the new 'ways of being together' were clearly not conducive to co-authorship or audience empowerment but rather, as Ian Shuttleworth himself commented, merely replicated their intended 'indictment of a complacently abusive system which took no account of others as autonomous beings' (Shuttleworth, 2008).

It may appear obvious to conclude that artists instigating participation are well able to abuse their authority, which they have in no sense given up, to objectify and disempower their audience through an enforced incorporation into the performance event. Yet, critical ideological distinctions between such work and participatory practice which rather seeks to empower its spectators through their contributions are obscured by an increasingly indiscriminate eagerness to situate all audience 'activity' as radical. In an over-simplistic opposition to the myth of the 'passive' spectator who must sit still in their seat in the stalls, *Guardian* critic Lyn Gardner draws on historically revolutionary metaphors when she states of the rise in participatory practice that

> [i]t is clear that such encounters are addictive. The scripted play seems tame once the audience has tasted this power and the possibility of inter-action. We are no longer content to sit quietly in our seats when we can storm the stages. (Gardner, 2007: 14)

Whilst I accept, as Helen Freshwater cautions, that Gardner is a journalist rather than an academic, and her use of language has a particular aim and purpose – in this instance to offer her influential support for the rise in new forms of contemporary practice – her voice is, nevertheless, instrumental in informing artists, venue promoters and funding bodies of what is perceived as in/radical and out/regressive trends in contemporary practice. In this particular article, she implicitly suggests that an inherent radicalism underpins all new work that requires its audience to leave their seats and participate in the action on the stage, without consideration for the ideological disparities demonstrated in the examples given above. The multiple frameworks and contexts through which interactive performance can take place necessitate detailed analysis, not only to assess on which occasions the participatory offer is fulfilling its implicit commitment to co-authorship and audience empowerment but also, more fundamentally, to ask the bigger question as to whether such authorship and empowerment, even when present, can continue to underpin a narrative of radicalism in this particular historical context of production.

The politics of compensation

The premise that maps the notion of empowered subjectivities directly onto increased potential for social resistance can be seen in Bourriaud's application of Guattari's theories, as detailed earlier in this chapter. This is a quite different understanding of individual empowerment, however, from that which underpinned the work of Boal, which was designed specifically to empower those individuals whose subjectivities were oppressed and whose potential for authorship was suppressed by the economic power structures of capitalism. Whilst there is certainly an argument to be made in support of Bourriaud's claim that the self-determining potential of every individual subject is under threat from the spectacular power of globalised capital, the claim of radicalism becomes less convincing in contexts where participants and artists alike can be seen to be those already holding significant cultural power themselves, and so, to some degree, inescapably complicit with the suppression and oppression of those who do not. Whilst it is beyond the scope of this chapter to undertake a detailed audience survey of interactive performance, it is not overly contentious to claim that new contemporary practice is not known for its capacity to generate significant paying audiences beyond the university educated who, in general, can be said to hold comparatively greater cultural capital. The more challenging in form the work is, the more likely the above is to apply, and consequently there is often much less distinction than might be imagined between those who make up the artists and those who make up the spectators. That many of the participants already hold some degree of cultural capital on arrival at the event diminishes the claims that work which enables their physical participation as spectators is somehow a devolvement of the artists' cultural authority. It is, more accurately, a pooling of existing cultural power already shared between audience and artists. Claire Bishop's observation that gallery-based events which principally result in productive 'networking among a group of art dealers and like-minded arts lovers' are not 'emblematic of democracy' (2004: 67) seems to go to the heart of the problem. This is not to say that work produced in galleries and art centres, and so drawing on their regular audiences, should necessarily be held to account for this, nor is it to say that work in these contexts cannot be characterised, on other grounds, as politically progressive or radical. However, claims of radicalism based merely on the fact of bringing people together and enabling them to participate as co-creators of an artistic event cannot be upheld when those who are being 'empowered' are already 'empowered', and the highlighting of this fact is not addressed self-reflectively within the piece itself. This is the key fallacy of parallels made between professional contemporary practice and the traditions of Boal, whose theatre was specifically designed to empower communities that were living under social or political oppression.

There are further important aspects of Boal's work, however, that could be transposed into the very different context of professional contemporary practice, such as his aim to provoke his participants to look critically at the workings of power and, crucially, how they themselves might be contributing to their own oppression or that of others. This imperative of self-realisation that was also central to Brecht's work, and present in the intentions of companies such as the Living Theatre, could then drive the spectator to seek political change beyond the theatre. Whilst the shift in the global political landscape over the last fifty years would make it unlikely, as Bourriaud points out, that the Marxist conception of radical social change would remain the ultimate goal of contemporary artists, if the claims to radicalism made on behalf of their work are to be sustained then the work must surely still ignite the critical capacity of the spectator to think beyond the personal pleasure of the immediate experience.

In the work of both Adrian Howells and Uninvited Guests there is evidence that they desire the impact of their practice to extend beyond the performance framework itself. Adrian Howells was clear how he hoped his piece *Foot Washing for the Sole* might provoke a chain reaction of such new 'ways of being together' when he talked of how he wanted to use Christ's action of washing his disciples' feet, and his instructions to them to 'now go and do for others 'as a 'humanitarian challenge [...], to do for somebody that might be a stranger, a neighbour, or a perceived enemy even' (Howells, 2010). Uninvited Guests' *Love Letters Straight from Your Heart* requested comparable action from their audience at the close of the piece, stipulating, 'when we leave this room in the future [...] if one person in this room cries, we all cry, if one person in this room laughs, we all laugh,' and to 'love everyone in this room just a little'. What distinguishes this kind of work from the practice of the 1960s and 1970s is that the politics of the desired interventions appear to be compensatory, not confrontational. Rather than seeking a deconstruction or destruction of the existing power structures, they offer a palliative model of how we might better survive them. This is not at all to suggest that such work is without value, but merely to begin to offer a more refined ideological analysis of different models of participatory practice. A Brechtian critique of such practice would, for example, observe that the politics of compensation hold the very real danger, not only that the power structures of global capitalism are reconfigured as inevitable but also that our very consciousness of existing ideological structures is weakened whilst, crucially, our own complicity within them is consolidated. Work that then seeks to challenge the oppressions of the contemporary world by offering pockets of compensation that might constitute some level of resistance can also risk inadvertently supporting the status quo of global capitalism which requires compensatory elements to counteract its more brutal consequences. Whilst the potential for co-authorship in contemporary interactive performance might be individually empowering, there is little basis for claims of radicalism without the presence of a corresponding commitment to inspire the spectator's critical reflection on the ideological power structures operating within the piece itself and in the world beyond.

The necessity for critical reflection on the ideological structures within which one is permitted to participate is particularly vital in an age when, despite the overwhelming influence of the globalised spectacle of late capitalism, the political gestures towards more active citizenship and democratic participation have never been greater. Helen Freshwater introduces her study of theatre audiences in the United Kingdom in the context of the emphasis on public participation under Tony Blair's New Labour government (1997–2007), 'reflected in public policies which aim to increase the electorate's engagement with the democratic system' (2009: 4). Yet, many would argue that the more emphasis democratic governments across Europe and America place on the importance of public participation, the more the limits of such participation, always restricted within the parameters of an unquestionable capitalist discourse, become clear. A suspension of awareness of the ideological predicates of the debate, it seems, inevitably enables them to go uncontested. A similar criticism can be levelled at the democratic participation aspired to by much of the interactive performance under discussion in this chapter; in particular, in those instances when the intended impact of the work is reliant upon detracting the participant's attention from the production's own ideological predicates. The overwhelmingly enthusiastic media endorsement of *Love Letters* is summed up in the following review extract:

> There is something so sincere and so utterly simple about Uninvited Guests' piece that you can't help but fall in love with it, not least because it makes you fall in love with everybody else in the room. Resistance is futile because, with its glitter balls, soppy songs, toasts to absent lovers and slow dances, it wears its cheese quite shamelessly all over its sleeve. I have never seen an audience weep so openly. This show should come with a flood warning. (Gardner, 2009)

The appreciation of significant numbers of spectators for the opportunity to indulge in this collective cathartic experience is not, if reviews are to be believed, in question, and may well support Lyn Gardner's suggestion, as quoted earlier in the chapter, that this kind of intimacy is what audiences are now demanding. However, this intimacy is not necessarily the radical alternative to the alienated viewing of representational spectacle that the orthodox analysis might suggest. Brecht, for one, would argue that it is precisely the space of distance, occupied by witness rather than participant, which tempers emotional engagement with intellectual critique. Where any potential for critical reflection is subsumed, as in *Love Letters*, by a willing abandonment of oneself into mutually perpetuating sentimentality, then the ideological implications of the piece itself, which I will now address, will too often go unnoticed.

Whilst *Love Letters* does indeed seek to reinvent 'ways of being together' in relation to the audience/actor conventions of theatre, it does so through very familiar ways of being together in a society that appears insatiable in its demands for the authenticity of true stories based on interpersonal, rather than social or political, relationships, as Jon Dovey suggests in his examination of first-person media and factual television. Dovey observes the 'enormous growth in our appetite for the personal, the intimate detail which has come to signify authenticity' (2000: 23), and draws on Nicci Gerrard to argue that public life is in danger of becoming 'a revolution of sentiment; a revolution for the therapy age, where subjectivity is our only certainty and sorrow our greatest claim to heroism' (Gerrard, 1997, in Dovey, 2000: 23). It is here that the most significant challenge to Bourriaud's theories becomes clear. If an obsession with subjectivity, with interpersonal relationships, with the construction(s) of self, lies at the very heart of the current ideological climate of neo-liberalism, as Dovey claims, then artistic practice which simply mirrors such imperatives might not be as automatically radical as Bourriaud would suggest. The review of *Love Letters* in the *Independent* demonstrates clearly the issues at stake:

> the dedications are manifestly authentic and heartbreakingly sincere. At the performance I attended, there were testimonies of love for an adored girlfriend; for a disabled child; for a paternally abused and suicidal sister. I don't think I have ever wept so much in a show, just seeing others quietly trying not to cry when it came to their contribution. (Bassett, 2009)

This craving for the authenticity of the real and the thrill of the confessional underpins not only the dramatic rise in reality television over the last decade, but also the popularity of much contemporary performance work that seeks to democratise artistic practice and challenge the authority of the playwright by its inclusion of autobiographical contributions provided by its audience. In this context, a piece such as *Love Letters* is enabling its spectators, through their dedications, to perform, in Dovey's words, 'the ordinariness of their own extraordinary subjectivity', whereby their lives and experiences can be transformed into art and are thus authorised as being worthy of public attention. Dovey argues that this trend for the authentic story of the ordinary individual is far from being radical, but is, in fact, 'part and parcel of neo liberal economics' (2000: 4).

Drawing on Gareth Palmer's research, Dovey further observes 'how far the concept of empowerment has travelled ideologically – once associated with an oppositional critique concerned with personal liberation it has become part of the language of neo-liberalism' (2000: 87). For when individual empowerment is detached from its original goal of collective empowerment it remains in service only to itself, to its own advancement and exclusivity.

The argument that translates the personal into the political is well known, but, increasingly, critical commentators are noting the distinction between the personal as used to political effect in the 1970s, and the personal as it is celebrated at the beginning of the twenty-first century. Dovey argues that the media obsession with the narratives of 'real' ordinary people is central to the discourse of neo-liberalism that celebrates 'a world in which the grand narratives are exhausted and we're left with the politics of the self to keep us ideologically warm' (2000: 26). The personal narrative, as Dee Heddon warns, can also function 'as a useful marketing tool in today's culture where the personal is a popular and cheaply manufactured commodity' (2008: 7). Heddon notes the distinction between this use of the personal and those contexts in which the personal can constitute a force of resistance:

> The radical feminist act was not only the publicising of the personal but also the insistence that the personal was never only personal since it was always structural and relational ... The politics of the personal is that the personal is not singularly about me [...] The personal is not implicitly political, and remains simply personal when it is removed from its cultural and historical location. (161–2)

Jon Dovey makes a vital and related distinction between personal 'confession' and personal 'testimony', claiming that, unlike the act of confession, 'to testify ... is to assert the ontology of self in a way that is implicitly linked to a collective identity' (2000: 113). Conversely, both the personal dedications of *Love Letters* and the confessions that Adrian Howells hopes to elicit from his one-to-one work are located purely in the valorising of individual experience, in line with the therapeutic model. Howells explicitly defines his work as confessional and suggests that its popularity lies in the fact that 'it reflects the culture we're now living in [...] wherever you turn people are confessing' (Howells, 2010). He clearly envisages his role as a therapeutic one, articulating that his interest lies in 'giving people an opportunity to alleviate shame and guilt, to release it and to lift it as a load from themselves' (Howells, 2010). *Love Letters,* on the other hand, did offer a communal framework for the autobiographical exchanges to take place, a fact which is reflected in the language of the reviews which highlighted 'the sense of collective sympathy' (Bassett, 2009) or the feeling of being 'part of a huge community' (Gardner, 2009). Yet, this was more of a shared appreciation of the valorisation of the individual experience than an individual experience which spoke on behalf of a wider collective. In contrast with the testimonial theatre discussed in Chapter 4, these kinds of personal or autobiographical contributions to performance texts are not situated by the artists within a cultural or historical location; nor are they specifically empowering the voices of the culturally marginal, but rather are written by and offered to, in the main, a relatively exclusive, and already culturally privileged, community of interest.

Thus, Boal's situating of the personal experience in particular and specific social and political contexts, in order to empower the narrative choices of the oppressed individual to impact on the wider political or social environment, cannot be ideologically aligned with participatory practice that celebrates the personal as the aggrandisement of the individual experience that lies at the heart of the neo-liberalist discourse. The authenticity that is accorded to the personal, and that provoked the collective catharsis induced by *Love Letters*, effaces utterly the spectator's critical perspective that Brecht, and many since him, have advocated as imperative for a radical theatre practice. As Darlene M. Hantzis warns, personal experiences are becoming, not 'texts to be interrogated and theorized, but texts to be understood as simple evidence, to be simply affirmed or to be "honored"' (1998: 203). Thus, when the spectators in *Love Letters* are invited to stand for any track or dedication that means something to them, we see the celebration of the contribution of the 'real'-life individual whose story is now authorised to take centre stage, and whose subjectivity is publically re-invented, as Bourriaud would wish. Yet, such an individual is simultaneously protected by their claim to authenticity, from a critical analysis of their text that might position their subjectivity as divorced from any structural or relational obligations, and firmly situated within the historical and cultural location of twenty-first century neo-liberalism.

The experience economy

That the participation of the individual spectator in the creation of artistic practice can no longer be assumed to be, in Claire Bishop's words, 'automatically political in implication and emancipatory in effect' (2004: 62) becomes particularly evident when we examine the emerging parallels between the turn to participation within performance and the turn to participation within the capitalist market place. In *The Death of Character,* published in 1996, Elinor Fuchs declares her interest in the spectator as 'market follower, the late capitalist consumer trained like an athlete to the hectic pace of product turnover and market strategies' (138). Moreover, Fuchs positions the emerging spectator-participant as one who 'abolishes the pedestal of the artistic event' but, unlike the witness demanded by Brecht, does so 'not to gain the distance of dialectical inquiry, but to close the distance in what could be called *simulacrity*' (1996: 138, original emphasis). Fuchs defines the commercial hits *Tamara* and *Tony 'n Tina* as 'shopping theater' and highlights the parallels between the 'trying on' experiences of the retail consumers on the mall, actively moving amongst the options on offer to make their choice, and the 'trying on' experiences of the audiences who participated in these shows. In both instances, Fuchs argues, participants were purchasing a new experience that might enable different identities to be performed. Fuchs significantly makes no distinction between 'the frankly commercial enterprises and their poor but intellectual avant-garde cousins' (139), and observes that:

> This revision of the spectator's relationship to theater matches well with research in market studies concluding that consumers regard objects, experiences, and even places as possessions that can be claimed as part of their 'extended selves'. (139)

In her critique of Bourriaud, Claire Bishop also observes how participatory arts practice might sometimes be seen to 'dovetail with an "experience economy", the marketing strategy that seeks to replace goods and services with scripted and staged personal experiences' (2004: 52). Consequently, as Philip Auslander argues, far from offering a radical alternative to the commodification of the art object, such experiences 'can be merchandised as events that must be purchased over and over again' (2008: 65); or, conversely, as one-off and non-repeatable experiences which then offer symbolic capital to those who were there (67). Bishop argues that, in this way, the shift from consumer to participant within performance reflects, rather than challenges, the latest strategies of multi-national corporations.

Maurya Wickstrom offers a detailed analysis of such strategies in *Performing Consumers: Global Capital and its Theatrical Seductions,* suggesting that the flagship store designers of brandscapes such as Nike, Coke and Disney have now 'deemphasized the consumption of specific commodities and instead create experiential environments through which the consumer comes to embody the resonances of the brand as feelings, sensations, and even memories' (2006: 2). Wickstrom's central thesis is that the consumer's physical participation in the experiential environment provided by these flagship stores can be seen as 'immaterial labor' (4), or 'corporate performance' (5), undertaken not only on behalf of that particular corporation but also as an essential supporting mechanism of capitalism as a whole. She argues that the immersive and embodied nature of the consumer's participatory experience translates into an imagined escape from everyday life that the brand associated with the experience then begins to subliminally represent:

> Brandscapes offer us a chance to manufacture, in our mimetic and affectual labor, in the palpable medium of our flesh-full bodies, in our faculty of pleasure, a feeling of being free […] we're creating the feeling that we need the brand because it slips us off the grid. (26–7)

She continues that 'given the corporate context … we can assume that with each play at moving outside constriction we are being further embedded into a logic of containment' (39). Whilst I am not suggesting that participation in this corporate context equates to participation in the artistic performances under discussion here, there are some interesting parallels that merit further exploration. In the Coke store in Las Vegas, Wickstrom reports, 'there's an in-store theatre where ordinary people's experiences with Coke, their "Coke Stories", are presented on film. We are invited to write down and submit our own.' (4) Whilst the appropriation of avant-garde strategies by big business is hardly new, I would argue that an alternative reading of what is happening here is that both *Love Letters* and the *Coke* design team are drawing on the same cultural mainstream that fetishes the authenticity of the 'real life stories' of 'ordinary' people who are then empowered to star in their own show; a process which represents an implicit confirmation of their unspoken ideological containment within the prevailing climate of neo-liberalism.

Wickstrom also highlights the growing awareness amongst the designers of the flagship stores of the importance of total sensory immersion (18), a strategy that is replicated by much contemporary performance practice and often evoked in support of its challenge to the 'passivity' of the conventional spectator. 'If we are encouraged to use the full range of our sense perception, we become active participants rather than passive, isolated viewers detached from the artistic experience' (Di Benedetto, 2007: 133). Yet, if immersion is such a key tool of the multinational corporations, then it is clearly a strategy for involvement that can be utilized for diverse ideological ends. The participant who is 'active' by nature of her increased physical involvement can, as a direct result, have her potential for cerebral and critical activity effaced, as Wickstrom makes clear in her description of her own experience in the Nike flagship store:

> The big brands are investing a great deal in making me productive in a very different way. I, we, want to, and do, go back to the stores, over and over. It's there we get our best shot at our potential for change and movement. The swoosh pumps my blood and so I'm ready to go, I'm moving on, I'm feeling life's vivacious charge. And so, I'm a fully corporate player. I'm off the grid. In breaking free I'm failing to notice how my capacity to imagine real political and economic change atrophies with every swoosh, every red pear, and waiting slipper. (42)

It is no surprise that the corporate world has latched onto the marketing potential of immersive performance as demonstrated by Louis Vuitton's engagement of Punchdrunk Theatre to host a performance for VIP guests in celebration of the opening of their new store in Bond Street, London (Garrett, 2010). Whilst immersive or interactive performance may not always share the economic agenda of the multi-nationals, or their manipulation of the pleasure principle of the consumer to serve their own ideological purpose, there is still the possibility that performance that seeks to immerse the spectator in order to enable them to feel 'off the grid', might simultaneously be effacing the spectator's capacity for radical action. I would not personally argue that this renders immersive theatre without value; my own enjoyment of the Punchdrunk experience would testify to my belief in its significant artistic worth. But any rigorous ideological analysis should seek to distinguish such examples of participatory practice from those that attempt, in the very different traditions of Brecht and Boal, to utilize participation in order to enable the participant to better embody positions of active and critical resistance to cultural forms of oppression. Without such distinctions, the claim of empowerment to underpin the radical credentials of participatory experiences *per se* can extend almost indefinitely. The dangers are fully demonstrated in Kurt Lancaster's article 'When spectators become performers', which conflates experiences as ideologically diverse as movie theme parks, karaoke performances, participatory theatre productions such as *Tony n' Tina's Wedding*, role-playing games, televised talk shows, murder mystery dinners and Boal's theatre of the oppressed (Lancaster, 1997).

If the rise of participatory performance in the 1960s and 1970s has been read as part of a wider movement of political emancipation *in opposition to* the capitalist narrative, then there is clearly work within the latest wave that might conversely be seen as *reflective of* the wider cultural and economic shift 'from a goods to a service-based economy' (Bishop, 2004: 54). It is ironic that Bourriaud positions his theory of relational aesthetics as a mode of resistance against 'the spread of the supplier/client relations to every level of human life' (Bourriaud, 2002: 83), as this same relation can also be seen to underpin much of the practice that might be defined as radical within the frames of his reference. If Lewis, Inthorn and Wahl-Jorgensen argue that the market ideal of the consumer is now subsuming the democratic ideal of the active citizen, no longer 'actively engaged in the shaping of society and the making of history' but rather consigned to 'simply choose between the products on display' (Lewis *et al.*, 2005: 5–6), then I would argue that the ideal concept of the 'critically active spectator' of the 1960s and 1970s is likewise in danger of being reduced to the 'passive consumer' of the latest experiments in audience/actor relationships, content to enjoy playing the game without the game itself being subjected to critical question.

This slippage, I would argue, has come about by a misleading conflation of Brecht's emphasis on active, critical spectatorship that continues to be highlighted by companies such as Forced Entertainment, and a physically active involvement by the spectator in the creation of the performance text itself. Participatory work in the 1960s and 1970s tended to combine these two notions of activity, seeing the physical participation of their spectators as a means to the end. In such work, it was envisaged that embodiment would lead to a phenomenological modelling of behaviour and decision-making that could then be a catalyst for the critical reflection that would follow. This critical reflection would then be expected to lead, in turn, to political action beyond the performance itself. In more recent practice, however, there is a much wider ideological spectrum at play. Some work can be seen to merely reflect the dominant cultural trends of a neo-liberalist discourse, by offering a mode of participation that dulls any critical analysis in its focus on compensating the individual for the brutalities of global capitalism. Some work, on the other hand, continues to use participation to empower the individual to critique and challenge dominant ideological frameworks. Thus, it can no longer be taken for granted that the degree of physical immersion afforded to the spectator can, in and of itself, define interactive performance as politically progressive or radical. In the same way as Brecht sought a theatre practice that demanded a demystification of naturalism in order that the ideological workings in society might also be exposed and challenged, so today's radical challenge for the work under discussion might be to

15   Private booths in *Internal.*
Photographer: Aaron De Keyzer

demystify the power structures that are too often concealed under the narratives of democratic participation in all spheres. In this way, we might begin to look more critically at the nature of the empowerment we are being offered through participation in the allegedly democratic workings of government, and the compensatory, and allegedly liberating, experiential offerings of the multi-nationals.

In its 2008 production, *Internal,* Belgian theatre company, Ontroerend Goed, invites five audience members to meet five actors with whom they will share a twenty-five-minute long blind date. On 28 August 2009, I was one of the five audience members who were led into the space in the Mercure Point Hotel, Edinburgh, and asked to line up in front of a black curtain. The curtain went up and we found ourselves face to face with the five actors. After staring at each other for a few moments the actors began to change places with each other, negotiating silently which spectator they would partner, before holding out their hands to introduce themselves. Immediately, they initiated physical contact, placing one arm around the spectator's shoulder as they led them off to a small private booth where they sat facing each other, to engage in intimate conversation over a glass of whisky.

An analysis of the piece up to this point would demonstrate clear parallels with the aims of Adrian Howell's work; to offer each spectator a personal one-to-one experience that would give them time out from the routine of their lives, nurture them and make them feel special; a therapeutic escape, perhaps, but with no wider political impact underlying it. However, in the next section of the piece, such assumptions were overturned.

16   Group session in *Internal.*

Photographer: Aaron De Keyzer

We were led from the booths to sit in a circle of chairs in the middle of the space to join the other actors and participants. Each actor then began to tell the circle what his or her partner had revealed. Whilst the blind dating element was clear on the publicity, spectators had not been warned that the information they had chosen to offer up in what they believed to be an intimate and private one-to-one performance was now to be shared, along with the actor's sometimes brutal analysis of their personality, amongst a group of strangers whilst they sat and listened.

Such interchanges confirmed that the piece had set up its illusory confessional/therapeutic model specifically to pull the rug from under our feet by public, and potentially humiliating, betrayals of our confidence, in order to awaken a critical reflection on the game that was being played, and the roles we were being asked to play within it. This critical response not only highlighted the naivety of the assumptions I had made – that the booths, glasses of whisky, and seductive and conspiratorial performance were an unspoken contract of intimacy and trust – but also raised questions about the claims to intimacy in other one-to-one pieces, however genuine the aspirations of such performances might be. Could 'real' intimacy and trust ever be the result of a shared moment between a paid performer and paying audience member, or is the alleged intimacy merely a strategy in an economic encounter much closer to the contractual relationship between call girl and customer, or therapist and client?

In a discussion of her own one-to-one work, Helen Paris proposes that each performance is designed to 'explore how intimacy, proximity, language and the placing and displacing of performer and audience' (2006: 179–80) conspire to ask 'how close can you get?' and 'how close is too close?' (179). Whilst there is clearly critical questioning underpinning the work, the nature of the 'intimacy' reported by certain spectators is never fully interrogated, but is assumed to be the successful result of a series of strategies such as the proxemic placement of performer/spectator facing one another from either side of a glass/mirror, or the use of the telephone to create an 'intimate acoustic distance' (181) between spectator and performer. Paris gives examples of a number of audience responses to *Vena Amoris* that appeared to confirm that intimacy had been achieved and that encouraged her to continue to pursue her 'quest of closeness' (183). One such response read:

> I felt so connected, so guided, so cherished and so much as if I belonged in each moment of, I would say journey, but I feel as if I have been immersed in the same moment wherever you led me. And now I feel bereft, now you have sent me away. (183)

For the purposes of this article, a more critical question than the one Paris poses is the question as to whether the 'intimacy' that is experienced by the spectator is a reality or a fiction. Clearly the spectator referenced above experienced it as a reality and engaged, consciously or subconsciously, in a state of false consciousness that the experience was, as with 'real-life' intimacy, both emotionally 'authentic' and unique to them. From the audience feedback on video at the end of *On the Scent*, Paris reports how it became clear that 'there was a desire on the part of the audience to be reassured that the experience in the house, the closeness they had felt to the performers and the stories they had shared with them had been unique and special, just for them' (187). Whilst there is no denying that each interchange in Ontroerend Goed's *Internal* would have been unique, the very fact that it was clearly advertised as a theatre show, running throughout the day on the half hour every half hour over a three-week run, with tickets purchased from the Traverse Theatre box office, should have been enough contextual framing to suggest that the back-to-back marathon blind dating undertaken by the actors was unlikely to be special – to them at least – in any conceivable way. Yet, the performances of the performers suggested otherwise, as was, of course, an integral part of the piece. Yet, sure as I was that my own critical awareness of the game that had been played on us would have been shared by the other spectators, this proved not universally the case. In the feedback book that was displayed in the hotel foyer, amongst simple thank-you messages and congratulations for the show, I read responses such as the following: 'I feel a bit sad and vulnerable. I wanted you to like me'; 'I was confused as to what was real and what wasn't, but nice to hold hands.' These spectators appeared to have invested in, and believed, the illusion of intimacy that had been offered to them, despite the betrayal that had followed.

For some spectators, it seemed, the piece had gone no further than offering them a nurturing experience as they chose to invest in the fiction that was created. For others, however, the piece had not even offered the solace of a fiction of intimacy such as that more ethically honoured by Adrian Howells, but had broken the contract and induced, not the critical reflection that comes with the realisation that the intimacy was never real in the first place, but personal distress caused by a continuing belief in the reality of both intimacy and betrayal. *Internal* was a powerful piece of performance, and the charm and skilled seduction techniques of my partner ensured that I left the piece with a smile on my face, despite all my rational and critical defence mechanisms being firmly in place. It was easy to imagine, therefore, that a spectator whose guard was down might have willingly suspended their disbelief for the pleasure that enabled them to feel 'off the grid', and that such a suspension might weaken the potential for the kind of critical analysis that I felt *Internal* was clearly setting itself up for. The framework of the piece itself, regardless of individual response, was designed to offer the kind of embodied 'experiential high' that Wickstrom describes undergoing in the Nike flagship store, as a means to an end, the end being the critical awareness that became activated by the betrayal of our naïve belief in the illusion of intimacy and specialness that we had been seduced into believing was real. This critical awareness ensured, for me at least, critical reflection after the event on a range of allegedly intimate relationships, from internet dating to one-to-one performances, or from customer services to therapeutic practice. Rather than replicating the commercial trend for 'real' encounters with 'real' people, and the resulting exoticisation of face-to-face contact in a world of technically mediated communications, *Internal* asked its spectators to interrogate all such experiences, artistic and commercial, with a vital scepticism.

An ethics of relation

I would like to conclude this examination of the role of the contemporary spectator by returning to the premises on which the 'active' spectator of recent participatory performance and much related criticism has been constructed. As I have discussed, the initial premise of the 'passive' spectator, as identified by Brecht and Meyerhold, was defined in relation to a lack of critical, rather than physical, activity. Potentially radical work in the 1960s and 1970s that utilised physical participation in order to increase the spectator's engagement with the performance situation nevertheless relied on the endgame of critical activity to ensure that self-reflexive analysis of the engagement could take place. Conversely, the more recent characterisation of the 'active' spectator, which is still opposed to a nominally 'passive' one, signifies physical, rather than critical, involvement. The radical mantle is thus detached from the requirement of critical activity and harnessed to the notion of physical participation, regardless of the varying ideological implications of each particular piece of practice. In turn, this repositions the notion of 'passivity' as pertaining to lack of *physical* participation – a passivity to which the regressive implications, first identified in the lack of *critical* activity, are now aligned.

Rancière confronts the myth of audience passivity in his seminal article, 'The emancipated spectator' (2007). He suggests that both the Brechtian advocation of critical distance to induce political action and the Artaudian insistence that the audience must abandon their role as spectators altogether, are both based on 'allegories of inequality'; that is, the problematic oppositions that have been created such as 'looking/knowing, looking/acting, appearance/reality, activity/passivity' (2007: 277). Rancière rather advocates the principle of equality that

> begins when we dismiss the opposition between looking and acting and understand that the distribution of the visible itself is part of the configuration of domination and subjection. It starts when we realize that looking is also an action that confirms or modifies that distribution, and that 'interpreting the world' is already a means of transforming it, of reconfiguring it. (277)

Rancière's argument posits that this act of interpretation, in and of itself, is the spectator's unique *participation* in each performance, thus challenging the more common use of the term to define physical co-creation of the performance text that I have outlined in this chapter. The idiom of theatre, he proposes, 'calls for spectators who are active interpreters, who render their own translation, who appropriate the story for themselves, and who ultimately make their own story out of it' (280). This would align the emancipated spectator of Rancière to the poststructuralist spectator, or witness, required by Tim Etchells, whose task, as defined by Malzacher, would be 'to relate texts and images to themselves [...] to make their own stories' (Malzacher, 2004: 123).

Although, in her study of the audience, Alice Rayner highlights the act of listening as the pivotal obligation of the spectator, such an act is not limited to the aural, but extends metaphorically to encompass 'the ability and willingness to hear meaning (or hear its deconstruction) as opposed to noise or empty silence' (1993: 17). In this sense, Rayner also identifies the making of meaning, or interpretation, as the primary act of the spectator and, moreover, asserts that such an act is 'fundamentally ethical' (1993: 6) in its obligation to negotiate meaning in relation to the text of the other. 'It is perhaps a borderland more than a boundary between the capacity to hear and the obligation to listen to what one cannot immediately understand or comprehend' (1993: 18).

Rayner does suggest that the collaborative positioning of the audience in direct relationship to the performers offers potentially high ethical impact, thus substantiating the political validity of certain experiments in ways of being together, as Bourriaud proposes. However, Rayner warns against the oversimplification of conflating form with ideological effect, which lies behind the efforts of Brecht and Artaud 'to change their audiences by changing the forms of representation' (16). Rayner cautions that this position, whilst holding significant validity, is in danger of denying 'the sources of opposition in the individual's capacity to oppose and criticize even the forms, culture and historical moment in which it is implicated' (16). Rayner's caution against the absolute conflating of theatre form and presumed ideological reception upholds the thesis of this study and supports the poststructuralist imperative that would seek to enable audiences to 'make their own stories', regardless of authorial intent. Whilst I would argue that *Internal* was designed to induce a critical response, there were clearly those who were overwhelmed by its strategies of seduction and were unable, or unwilling, to read the structure of the piece once it was exposed. For those who had a pleasurable experience this would position the piece as compensational in my terms. For those who had a distressing experience this would position the piece as politically disempowering. Likewise, it was also clearly possible for me to 'oppose and criticize [...] the forms, culture and historical moment' in which *Love Letters* was implicated, despite the strategies that I have argued were in place to engineer the effacement of its own ideological positioning.

Rayner's caution evokes the philosophical thesis of Michel de Certeau, who argues that an ideological analysis of any given model of production requires that we take into account the potential for the consumer to subvert its intentions by using 'innumerable and infinitesimal transformations of and within the dominant cultural economy in order to adapt it to their own interests and their own rules' (de Certeau, 1984: xiv). De Certeau's position, which was explored more fully in Chapter 5 is, however, challenged by Maura Wickstrom, who draws on Hardt and Negri to argue that 'power in global capitalism depends on its ability to spread laterally, across geographical boundaries, through virtual space, and in the bodies and affective responses of human beings' (2006: 105). Thus de Certeau's consumer, Wickstrom would contend, is always already primed to respond in the ways in which the models of production intend.

Rayner seeks a balance between these two positions, but the evident complexity of any analysis of audience makes the oversimplified equation of form and ideological impact a risky undertaking, as I hope this study has demonstrated. The actor–audience relationships that are being re-invented in this new wave of participatory performance practice in the first decade of the new millennium cannot simply be banded together as radical or revolutionary on the basis of a mistaken conflation of critical and physical activity. My ideological analysis of the particular interactive performances offered above is necessarily subjective and has been undertaken to propose alternative readings of influential trends and models in order to offer certain means of ideological distinction. None of these analyses are conclusive, but I hope to have at least demonstrated the fallacy of the orthodox equation between participation and empowerment that has been constructed in opposition to the myth of the passive and politically unengaged spectator.

Both Rancière and Rayner demonstrate that the activity of the spectator is an obligation in any theatrical configuration and that this obligation, if accepted, 'legitimates' the performance ... through the ability to donate to the performer both presence and judgment: this donation is an ethics of relation not simply of power over, for it returns the speaker to itself with a difference' (Rayner, 1993: 21). Whilst Rayner accepts that passive audiences exist, who can 'undoubtedly function only as consumers' (21), these are audiences who are shirking their ethical obligation. Content to be confirmed in their ideological stasis they are refusing to take up the challenge to actively negotiate their own terms of reference:

> The difficulty in dialectic, then, is to recognize the coercive force of ques-
> tions and to remain open to an 'impossible' answer that would constitute

not-yet-determined possibilities, rather than only to reconstruct an already completed meaning. The obligation is to allow that the frames – or frequencies, in acoustical terms – of one's own questions may need adjustment in order to hear. Such adjustment allows for the possibility of learning something genuinely new, not just what one already knows. (19)

It follows that if the seated, silent and still spectator undertakes this obligation for action, then participation is already inherent in any act of theatre. For this reason, the new wave of physical participation and co-creation of the performance text cannot construct its radical credentials merely in opposition to the narrative of the 'passive' spectator, who only, in truth, exists as a 'failed spectator' who has shirked their obligation to participate. If the key to a radical and ethical theatre practice is the audience's obligation to offer 'presence' and 'judgment', then this must surely apply also to physically participatory practice which, when at its best, can use its increased potential for co-presence and intersubjective relations to enhance, rather than subsume, the spectator's potential for ethical and critical judgment. If this judgment is absent, then the participation, not unlike participation in the theme parks, role playing and performance-entertainments described by Kurt Lancaster (1997), merely facilitates a means of escapism, a fantasy playground that is contained by the system that makes it necessary, and which therefore cannot lay claim to the political lineage of radical participation practice that dominated the last century. Without critical reflection on the ideological predicates that are framing the act of participation, the 'active' spectator of interactive performance is merely the latest incarnation of the consumer/spectator of global capitalism, which has now traded in its domination of the market through the packaging of representations, for a domination of the market through the packaging of authentic and embodied experience.

Notes

1   This analysis is based on the performance of *Love Letters* at McEwan Hall, Edinburgh, on 27 August 2009.
2   This analysis is based on the performance of *Iris Brunette* at Axis Arts Centre, Crewe, on 9 October 2009.
3   All extracts are taken from an unpublished script of *Iris Brunette,* written by Melanie Wilson, and made available to me courtesy of Melanie Wilson.

Afterword

If Derrida's deconstructive imperative demonstrates the 'counterviolence of *solicitation*'; that 'every totality can be *totally shaken* ... can be shown to be founded on that which it excludes' (Bass, 2001: xviii), then this study has committed itself, above all, to shaking the potentially totalising narrative of radicalism that has long been applied to performance practices that seek to challenge the dramatic model of theatre. The poststructuralist imperative, I have argued, rather demands a radical practice that is not based on the reification of its own conclusions, but on a self-reflexivity that can serve to always and already destabilise its own manifestations of authority, wherever these might lie.

If the initial performed responses to the deconstructive project fore-grounded a critique of dramatic representation through citational performance strategies, emphasis on the real time and space of the performance event, and a shift from spectator to participant, it is imperative, by the project's own premises, for these conclusions to be subjected, by the next wave of work, to the same 'shaking' process they themselves initiated, in order to prevent a new totalising narrative from emerging. Once critical questioning is permitted to settle into conclusion, such conclusions quickly become repeatable conventions in their own right. At this point they can be too easily appropriated and commodified by market structures, thus stripping them of their potential for any radical impact in a repetition of capitalism's incorporation of the historical avant-gardes.

It is thus the self-reflexive *movement* of Derrida's deconstructive project that must be sustained, as such an imperative is essential to counteract the stasis preferred by the status quo, most succinctly displayed in

Fukuyama's *The End of History and The Last Man* (1992), which offers global capitalism as the best bet for humanity's ultimate endgame. This stasis, as exposed in Adam Curtis's 2011 documentary *Watched Over by Machines of Loving Grace*, will find, against its publicly expressed wishes, any number of ingenious ways to maintain the current global crisis, inequality, injustice and entrenched privilege which have sustained, and will continue to sustain, the economically powerful who now control governments and the futures of entire populations across the developed and developing worlds.

The forms and methods of resistance need to be constantly in transition, in performance as in all other aspects of cultural and political life, to maintain their potential to counteract the influence of the spectacle of global capital. To get stuck in previously radical conclusions is to risk unwitting collusion through adherence to a would-be oppositional narrative that has long since been absorbed and manipulated by those in power for their own benefit and continued control. Only with this level of vigilance will performance be able to maintain any semblance of radical potential in the century to come. Only by subjecting the conclusions of previous narratives of radicalism to Derrida's 'counterviolence of *solicitation*' can new and productive performance strategies be adopted and developed, to stay one step ahead of the increasingly versatile and devious movements of containment and appropriation, which are always seeking to re-appropriate the would-be radical and subversive back into the service of global capital.

This study hopes to have begun such a process, and fully expects – and requires – that its own conclusions will be interrogated in turn by future practice and theoretical enquiry. For those who share my commitment to developing radical models of performance that can persist in 'digging down' to excavate the ever-changing manifestations of ideological authority as and where they emerge, this theoretical study is intended to inspire future self-reflexive innovations in practice. For those who have previously dismissed either the notion of radical poststructuralism or the notion of radical dramatic practice, this study has suggested where the possibilities of both might lie. For those who believe that the postmodern condition has effaced the very notion of radical performance, I would refer them back to Žižek's exhortations to persist 'in this impossible position: although no clear line of demarcation separates ideology from reality, although ideology is already at work in everything we experience as 'reality', we must none the less maintain the tension that keeps the *critique* of ideology alive' (1994: 17, original emphasis).

For, well-versed as we now are in the discourses of the always ideological real, it appears that we may choose whichever narrative we wish. We can choose to uphold the Marxist narrative of Emancipation; we can choose to uphold the narrative of neo-liberalism; we can choose to uphold the narrative that claims there is a 'beyond ideology' where questions of power and authority are no longer relevant and everything is equitably relative. But let us be very clear that our choice of which narrative to uphold, through our artistic practice and analysis, will have real political consequences. In a world where we are increasingly asked to construct our own reality, let us assess with some care what the implications of the reality we choose to construct might be. In an age of scepticism where there is no longer any originary authority to turn to, it becomes more, not less, important to subject our choices to self-reflexive scrutiny and our conclusions to the 'counterviolence of *solicitation*'. In this way, we can interrogate where the contradictions at the heart of our own narrative might lie, and evade unwitting collusion with the ever-shape-shifting structures of ideologies we might prefer to think that we are challenging.

References

Ackerman, A., and M. Puchner (2006), 'Introduction: modernism and anti-theatricality', in A. Ackerman and M. Puchner (eds), *Against Theatre: Creative Destructions on the Modernist Stage* (Basingstoke: Palgrave Macmillan) 1–17.

Adorno, T. (1977), 'Commitment', trans. F. McDonagh, in E. Bloch (ed.), *Aesthetics and Politics* (London: NLB) 177–95.

Adorno, T. (1981), *Prisms*, trans. S. Weber and S. Weber (Cambridge, Mass.: MIT Press).

Alcoff, L. (1991–92), 'The problem of speaking for others', *Cultural Critique* 20, 5–32.

Amin, S. (1998), *Spectres of Capitalism: A Critique of Current Intellectual Fashions* (New York: Monthly Review Press).

Ansell-Pearson, K. (1994), *An Introduction to Nietzsche as Political Thinker* (Cambridge: Cambridge University Press).

Artaud, A. (1970a), *The Theatre and its Double*, trans. V. Corti (London: Calder & Boyars).

Artaud, A. (1970b), *Œuvres complètes*, vol. 4 (Paris: Gallimard).

Aston, E. (1999), *Feminist Theatre Practice: A Handbook* (London and New York: Routledge).

Auslander, P. (1997), *From Acting to Performance: Essays in Modernism and Postmodernism* (London and New York: Routledge).

Auslander, P. (2006), 'The performativity of performance art documentation', *Performing Arts Journal* 28:3, 1–10.

Auslander, P. (2008), *Liveness: Performance in a Mediatized Culture* (London and New York: Routledge).

Auster, P. (1988), *The Invention of Solitude* (New York: Penguin).

Bailes, S. J. (2011), *Performance Theatre and the Poetics of Failure* (London and New York: Routledge).

Barish, J. (1981), *The Anti-theatrical Prejudice* (Berkeley and Los Angeles, Calif: University of California Press).

Barker, H. (1990), *The Europeans / Judith* (London: John Calder).

Barker, H. (1993a), *Arguments for a Theatre*, 2nd edn (Manchester: Manchester University Press).

Barker, H. (1993b), *Collected Plays Volume 2* (London: Calder Publications).

Barnett, D. (2008), 'When is a play not a drama? Two examples of postdramatic theatre texts', *New Theatre Quarterly* 24:1, 14–23.

Barthes, R. (1977), *Image-Music-Text*, trans. S. Heath (London: Fontana).

Bass, A. (2001, reprinted 2009), 'Translator's introduction', in J. Derrida, *Writing and Difference*, trans. A. Bass (Abingdon: Routledge).

Bassett, K. (2009), 'Love letters straight from your heart', *Independent* (30 August 2009) http://goo.gl/5DWUt [accessed 7 April 2010].

Baudrillard, J. (2003), *The Spirit of Terrorism*, trans. C. Turner (London and New York: Verso).

Baudrillard, J. (2005), *The Intelligence of Evil or the Lucidity Pact*, trans. C. Turner (Oxford and New York: Berg).

Baudrillard, J. (2007), *In the Shadow of the Silent Majorities*, trans. P. Foss, P. Patton and J. Johnston (New York: Semiotext(e)).

Baudrillard, J. (2008), *The Perfect Crime*, trans. C. Turner (London and New York: Verso).

Beard, S. (1993), 'The artful fly on the wall', *New Statesman & Society* (15 October 1993), 34–5.

Behrndt, S., and C. Turner (2008), *Dramaturgy and Performance* (Basingstoke: Palgrave Macmillan).

Bell, P. (2005), 'Fixing the TV: televisual geography in the Wooster Group's *Brace Up!*', *Modern Drama* 48:3, 565–84.

Bennett, S. (1997), *Theatre Audiences: A Theory of Production and Reception*, 2nd edn (London: Routledge).

Bennett, T., L. Grossberg and M. Morris, eds (2005), *New Keywords: A Revised Vocabulary of Culture and Society* (Malden: Blackwell Publishing Ltd).

Ben-Zvi, L. (2006), 'Staging the other Israel: the documentary theatre of Nola Chilton', *The Drama Review* 50:3, 42–55.

Beverly, J., 'Real thing', in G.Gugelberger, ed. (1996), *The Real Thing: Testimonial Discourse and Latin America* (Durham: Duke University Press), 266–86.

Billington, M. (2008), 'The girlfriend experience', *Guardian* (25 September 2008) www.guardian.co.uk/stage/2008/sep/25/theatre [accessed 26 March 2011].

Bishop, C. (2004), 'Antagonism and relational aesthetics', *October* 110, 51–79.

Bishop, C. (2006), 'Introduction: viewers as producers', in C. Bishop (ed.), *Participation* (London: Whitechapel, and Cambridge, Mass: MIT Press) 10–17.

Blau, H. (2006), 'Seeming, seeming: the illusion of enough', in A. Ackerman and M. Puchner (eds), *Against Theatre: Creative Destructions on the Modernist Stage* (Basingstoke: Palgrave Macmillan), 231–47.

Blythe, A. (2008), *The Girlfriend Experience* (London: Nick Herne Books).

Boal, A. (1979), *Theatre of the Oppressed*, trans. C. McBride and M. Leal McBride

(London: Pluto Press).

Bottoms, S. (2006), 'Putting the document into documentary', *The Drama Review* 50:3, 56–68.

Bottoms, S. (2009), 'Authorizing the audience: the conceptual drama of Tim Crouch', *Performance Research* 14:1, 65–76.

Bottoms, S. (2011), 'In defense of the string quartet: an open letter to Richard Schechner', in J. M. Harding and C. Rosenthal (eds), *The Rise of Performance Studies: Re-thinking Schechner's Broad Spectrum* (Basingstoke: Palgrave Macmillan), 23–38.

Bourriaud, N. (2002), *Relational Aesthetics,* trans. S. Pleasance and F. Woods (Dijon: Les Presses du Réel).

Brecht, B. (1964), *Brecht on Theatre*, trans. J. Willett (London: Shenval Press).

British Council, www.connected-uk.org (18 February 2010) [accessed February–March 2010].

Bull, J. (1984), *New British Political Dramatists* (London: Macmillan).

Callaghan, D. (2003), 'Still signalling through the flames: the Living Theatre's use of audience participation in the 1990s', in S. Kattwinkel (ed.), *Audience Participation: Essays on Inclusion in Performance* (London: Greenwood) 23–36.

Carlson, M. (1996), *Performance: A Critical Introduction* (London and New York: Routledge).

Carlson, M. (2001), *The Haunted Stage: The Theatre as Memory Machine* (Ann Arbor, Mich.: University of Michigan Press).

Carlson, M. (2002), 'The resistance to theatricality', *SubStance* 31:2–3, 238–50.

Casey, E. (1997), *The Fate of Place: A Philosophical History* (Berkeley, Calif: University of California Press).

Casey, M. (2009), '*Ngapartji Ngapartji*: telling Aboriginal Australian stories', in A. Forsyth and C. Megson (eds), *Get Real: Documentary Theatre Past and Present* (Basingstoke: Palgrave Macmillan), 122–39.

Cavendish, D. (2009) 'Edinburgh Fringe 2009: Is increased intimacy the future of theatre?', *Telegraph* (28 Aug 2009) http://goo.gl/bnMeh [accessed March–April 2010].

Craig, S., ed. (1980), *Dreams and Deconstructions: Alternative Theatre in Britain* (Ambergate: Amber Lane Press).

Crimp, M. (2008), *The City* (London: Faber and Faber).

Debord, G. (1990), *Comments on the Society of the Spectacle*, trans. M. Imrie (London and New York: Verso).

Debord, G. (1995), *The Society of the Spectacle,* trans. D. Nicholson-Smith (New York: Zone Books).

De Certeau, M. (1984), *The Practice of Everyday Life*, trans. S. F. Renall (Berkeley and Los Angeles, Calif.: University of California Press).

Derrida, J. (1973), *Speech and Phenomena,* trans. D. A. Allison (Evanston, Ill.: Northwestern University Press).

Derrida, J. (1974), *Of Grammatology,* trans. G. Spivak (Baltimore, Md., and

London: Johns Hopkins University Press).

Derrida, J. (1981), *Dissemination*, trans. B. Johnson (London: Athlone Press).

Derrida, J. (1982), *Margins of Philosophy*, trans. A. Bass (Brighton: Harvester Press).

Derrida, J. (1994), *Spectres of Marx: The State of the Debt, the Work of Mourning, and the New International*, trans. P. Kamuf (London: Routledge).

Derrida, J. (2001, reprinted 2009), 'The theatre of cruelty and the closure of representation', in J. Derrida, *Writing and Difference*, trans. A. Bass (Abingdon: Routledge), 292–316.

Diamond, E. (1997), *Unmaking Mimesis: Essays on Feminism and Theatre* (London: Routledge).

Di Benedetto, S. (2007), 'Guiding somatic responses within performative structures: contemporary live art and sensorial perception', in A. Lepecki and S. Banes (eds), *The Senses in Performance* (New York and London: Routledge), 124–34.

Dolan, J. (2002), 'Finding our feet in the shoes of (one an) other: multiple character solo performers and utopian performatives', *Modern Drama* 45:4, 495–518.

Dolan, J. (2005), *Utopia in Performance: Finding Hope at the Theater* (Ann Arbor, Mich.: University of Michigan Press).

Dovey, J. (2000), *Freakshow: First Person Media and Factual Television* (London: Pluto Press).

Erickson, J. (2003), 'Defining political performance with Foucault and Habermas: strategic and communicative action', in T. C. Davis and T. Postlewaite (eds), *Theatricality* (Cambridge: Cambridge University Press), 156–85.

Etchells, T. (1999), *Certain Fragments: Contemporary Performance and Forced Entertainment* (London: Routledge).

Etchells, T. (2006), 'Instructions for forgetting', *The Drama Review* 50:3, 108–30.

Feral, J. (1982), 'Performance and theatricality: the subject demystified', trans. T. Lyons, *Modern Drama* 25:1, 170–81.

Fischer-Lichte, E. (2008), *The Transformative Power of Performance*, trans. S. I. Jain (London and New York: Routledge).

Fisher, M. (2007), 'Aalst', *Variety* (26 March 2007) http://goo.gl/qAdgJ [accessed 26 March 2011].

Foster, H. (1985), *Recodings: Art, Spectacle, Cultural Politics* (Port Townsend, W.A.: Bay Press).

Foucault, M. (1984), 'What is an author?' trans. J. V. Harari, in P. Rabinow (ed.), *The Foucault Reader* (Harmondsworth: Penguin Books) 101–20.

Freeman, S. (2006), 'Towards a genealogy and taxonomy of British alternative theatre', *New Theatre Quarterly* 22:4, 364–78.

Freshwater, H. (2009), *Theatre and Audience* (Basingstoke: Palgrave Macmillan).

Frieze, J. (2009), *Naming Theatre: Demonstrative Diagnosis in Performance* (Basingstoke: Palgrave Macmillan).

Fuchs, E. (1985), 'Presence and the revenge of writing: re-thinking theatre after

Derrida', *Performing Arts Journal* 9:2/3, 163–73.

Fuchs, E. (1996), *The Death of Character: Perspectives on Theater after Modernism* (Bloomington and Indianapolis, Ind.: University of Indianapolis Press).

Fuchs, E. (2001), 'Clown shows: anti-theatricalist theatricalism in four twentieth century plays', *Modern Drama* 44:3, 337–54.

Fukuyama, F. (1992), *The End of History and the Last Man* (London: Hamish Hamilton).

Gardner, L. (2007), 'There is something stirring', in D. Brine and L. Keidan (eds), *Programme Notes: Case Studies for Locating Experimental Theatre* (London: Live Art Development Agency), 10–16.

Gardner, L. (2009), 'Love letters straight from your heart', *Guardian* (26 August 2009) http://goo.gl/8rEE3 [accessed March–April 2010].

Garner, S. B. (1994), *Bodied Spaces: Phenomenology and Performance in Contemporary Drama* (Ithaca, N.Y.: Cornell University Press).

Garrett, S. (2010), 'Punchdrunk theatre company opens Louis Vuitton's new Bond Street store', *Telegraph* (24 June 2010) http://goo.gl/UX96t [accessed June 2011].

Gergen, K. J. (1991), *The Saturated Self: Dilemmas of Identity in Contemporary Life* (New York: Basic Books).

Gerrard, N. (1997), *Observer Life* (28 December 1997).

Goffman, E. (1959), *The Presentation of Self in Everyday Life* (Garden City, New York: Doubleday).

Gorman, S. (2010), 'Wandering and wondering: following Janet Cardiff's missing voice', in N. Whybrow (ed.), *Performance and the Contemporary City* (Basingstoke: Palgrave MacMillan), 167–78.

Grehan, H. (2010), '*Aalst*: acts of evil, ambivalence and responsibility', *Theatre Research International* 35:1, 4–16.

Gubrium, J. F., and J. A. Holstein (2000), *The Self We Live By: Narrative Identity in a Postmodern World* (New York and Oxford: Oxford University Press).

Güçbilmez, B. (2007), 'An uncanny theatricality: the representation of the offstage', *New Theatre Quarterly* 23:2, 152–60.

Haedicke, S. (2003), 'The challenge of participation: audiences at Living Stage theatre company', in S. Kattwinkel (ed.), *Audience Participation: Essays on Inclusion in Performance* (London: Greenwood), 71–88.

Hammond, W. and D. Steward, eds (2008), *Verbatim Verbatim: Contemporary Documentary Theatre* (London: Oberon).

Hantzis, D. M. (1998), 'Reflections on "A dialogue with friends: 'performing' the 'Other'/'Self'" OJA 1995"', in S. J. Dailey (ed.), *The Future of Performance Studies: Visions and Revisions* (Annandale, Va.: National Communication Association), 203–6.

Hare, D. (2003), *The Permanent Way* (London: Faber and Faber).

Hare, D. (2004), *Stuff Happens* (London: Faber and Faber).

Heathfield, A. (2004), 'As if things got more real: a conversation with Tim Etchells', in J. Helmer and F. Malzacher (eds), *Not Even a Game Anymore* (Berlin:

Alexander Verlag), 77–99.

Heddon, D. (2008), *Autobiography and Performance* (Basingstoke: Palgrave Macmillan).

Heddon, D. and J. Milling (2006), *Devising Performance: A Critical History* (Basingstoke: Palgrave Macmillan).

Helmer, J., and F. Malzacher (2004), 'Plenty of leads to follow: Foreword', in J. Helmer and F. Malzacher (eds), *Not Even a Game Anymore* (Berlin: Alexander Verlag), 11–23.

Hesford, W. S. (2006), 'Staging Terror', *The Drama Review* 50:3, 29–41.

Heyvaert, P. (2007), 'Aalst: interview with the director', http://goo.gl/lKqkA [accessed 26 March 2011].

Highberg, N. P. (2009), 'When heroes fall: Doug Wright's *I Am my Own Wife* and the challenge to truth', in A. Forsyth and C. Megson (eds), *Get Real: Documentary Theatre Past and Present* (Basingstoke: Palgrave Macmillan) 167–78.

Highfield, J. (1995), 'Coach tour to dark side', *Sheffield Star* (17 May 1995) 26.

Hilliaert, W. (2005), 'Victoria Theatre Company reacts to lawsuit', De Morgan (8 February 2005) trans. N. den Hertog, cited on http://goo.gl/Kfwg9 [accessed 26 March 2011].

Hoffmann, B. (2009), 'Radicalism and the theatre in genealogies of live art', *Performance Research* 14:1, 95–05.

Holmes, J. (2007), *Fallujah: Eyewitness Testimony from Iraq's Besieged City* (London: Constable).

Howells, A. (2007), 'Salon Adrienne: homotopia festival' (19 November 2007) www.youtube.com [accessed April 2010].

Howells, A. (2010), 'Adrian Howells: British Council Arts Sg' (22 April 2010) www.youtube.com [accessed April 2010].

Hutcheon, L. (2006), *A Theory of Adaptation* (Abingdon and New York: Routledge).

Irmer, T. (2006), 'A search for new realities: documentary theatre in Germany', *The Drama Review* 50:3, 16–28.

Itzin, C. (1980), *Stages in the Revolution: Political Theatre in Britain Since 1968* (London: Eyre Methuen).

Jackson, S. (2004), *Professing Performance: Theatre in the Academy from Philology to Performativity* (Cambridge: Cambridge University Press).

Jameson, F. (1991), *Postmodernism: or the Cultural Logic of Late Capitalism* (London and New York: Verso).

Jannarone, K. (2009), 'Audience, mass, crowd: theatres of cruelty in interwar Europe', *Theatre Journal* 61:2, 191–211.

Jones, A. (2008), 'The girlfriend experience', *Independent* (25 September 2008).

Jones, S. (2009), 'The courage of complementarity: practice-as-research as a paradigm shift in performance studies', in L. Allegue, S. Jones, B. Kershaw, A. Piccini (eds), *Practice-as-Research in Performance and Screen* (Basingstoke: Palgrave Macmillan), 18–32.

Jürs-Munby, K. (2006), 'Introduction', in H. T. Lehmann *Postdramatic Theatre*, trans. K. Jürs-Munby (London and New York: Routledge).

Jürs-Munby, K. (2007), Unpublished transcript of panel discussion in Manchester, UK (24 October 2007).

Jürs-Munby, K. (2009), 'The resistant text in postdramatic theatre: performing Elfriede Jelinek's *Sprachflachen*', *Performance Research* 14:1, 46–56.

Kaye, N. (1994), *Postmodernism and Performance* (Basingstoke: Macmillan).

Keiller, P. (2001), 'Popular science', in A. Gallagher (ed.), *Landscape* (London: British Council), 61–7.

Kelly, D. (2007), *Taking Care of Baby* (London: Oberon).

Kershaw, B. (1999), *The Radical in Performance: Between Brecht and Baudrillard* (London and New York: Routledge).

Kershaw, B. (2009), 'Practice-as-research: an introduction', in L. Allegue, S. Jones, B. Kershaw and A. Piccini (eds), *Practice-as-Research in Performance and Screen* (Basingstoke: Palgrave Macmillan), 1–16.

Kilborn, R. (2003), *Staging the Real: Factual TV programming in the Age of Big Brother* (Manchester: Manchester University Press).

Kirshenblatt-Gimblett, B. (1991), 'Objects of ethnography', in I. Karp and S. D. Levine (eds), *Exhibiting cultures: The Poetics and Politics of Museum Display* (Washington, D.C.: Smithsonian Institution Press), 11–24.

Klaic, D. (2002), 'The crisis of theatre? The theatre of crisis!', in M. Delgardo and C. Svitch (eds), *Theatres in Crisis? Performance Manifestos for a New Century* (Manchester: Manchester University Press), 144–59.

Kritzer, A. H. (2008), *Political Theatre in Post-Thatcher Britain: New Writing: 1995-2005* (Basingstoke: Palgrave Macmillan).

Kron, L. (2001), *2.5 Minute Ride and 101 Humiliating Stories* (New York: Theatre Communications Group).

Kwon, M. (1997), 'One place after another: notes on site specificity', *October Magazine* 80, 85–110.

Lacan, J. (1978), *Four Fundamental Concepts of Psycho-Analysis*, trans. A. Sheridan (New York: Norton).

Lancaster, K. (1997), 'When spectators become performers: contemporary performance-entertainments meet the needs of an "unsettled" audience', *Journal of Popular Culture* 30:4, 75–88.

Lavery, C. (2005), 'The Pepys of London E11: Graeme Miller and the politics of *Linked*', *New Theatre Quarterly* 21:2, 148–60.

Lavery, C. (2009), '*Mourning Walk* and pedestrian performance: history, aesthetics and ethics', in R. Mock (ed.), *Walking, Writing and Performance* (Bristol: Intellect), 41–56.

Lavery, C. (2010), 'Situationism', in N. Whybrow (ed.), *Performance and the Contemporary City* (Basingstoke: Palgrave Macmillan), 92–4.

Lehmann, H. T. (1999), *Postdramatisches Theater* (Frankfurt: Verlag der Autoren).

Lehmann, H. T. (2002), 'Wie Politisch ist Postdramatisches Theater', in *Das Politische Schreiben: Essays zu Theatertexten* (Berlin: Theater der Zeit),

11–21.

Lehmann, H. T. (2006), *Postdramatic Theatre,* trans. K. Jürs-Munby (London and New York: Routledge).

Lewis, J., S. Inthorn and K. Wahl-Jorgensen (2005), *Citizens or Consumers? What the Media Tell us about Political Participation* (Maidenhead: Open University Press).

Limon, J. (2011), 'Performativity of the Court: Stuart Masque as Postdramatic Theater', in P.Cefalu and B. Reynolds (eds), *The Return of Theory in Early Modern English Studies: Tarrying with the Subjunctive* (Basingstoke: Palgrave Macmillan), 258–77.

Lyotard, J. (1984), *The Postmodern Condition: A Report on Knowledge* trans. G. Bennington and B. Massumi (Manchester: Manchester University Press).

Malzacher, F. (2004), 'There is a word for people like you: audience: the spectator as bad witness and bad voyeur', in J. Helmer and F. Malzacher (eds), *Not Even a Game Anymore* (Berlin: Alexander Verlag), 121–38.

Mann, P. (1991), *The Theory-Death of the Avant-Garde* (Bloomington and Indianapolis, Ind.: Indiana University Press).

Martin, C. (2006), 'Bodies of Evidence', *The Drama Review* 50:3, 9–15.

Martin C. (2009), 'Living simulations: the use of media in documentary in the UK, Lebanon and Israel', in A. Forsyth and C. Megson (eds), *Get Real: Documentary Theatre Past and Present* (Basingstoke: Palgrave Macmillan), 74–90.

Marx, K., and F. Engels (1988), *Economic and Philosophic Manuscripts of 1844 and the Communist Manifesto,* trans. M. Milligan (New York: Prometheus Books).

Massey, D. (2005), *For Space* (London: Sage Publications).

McDonough, T., ed. (2002), *Guy Debord and the Situationist International: Texts and Documents* (Cambridge, Mass., and London: MIT Press).

McGrath, J. (1978), Unpublished lecture given by John McGrath at King's College, Cambridge (Conference on Political Theatre, April 1978).

McKenzie, J. (2001), *Perform or Else: From Discipline to Performance* (London: Routledge).

McKenzie, J., H. Roms and C. J. W.- L. Wee, eds (2010), *Contesting Performance: Global Sites of Research* (Basingstoke: Palgrave Macmillan).

McLean, D. (2007), *Aalst* (London: Methuen Drama).

Merkimedes, A. (2010), 'Forced Entertainment – *The Travels* (2002) – the anti-theatrical director', in J. Harvey and A. Lavender (eds), *Making Contemporary Theatre: International Rehearsal Processes* (Manchester and New York: Manchester University Press), 101–20.

Merleau-Ponty, M. (1968), *The Visible and the Invisible,* trans. A. Lingis (Evanston, Ill.: Northwestern University Press).

Miller, G. (2005), 'Walking the walk, talking the talk: re-imagining the urban landscape', *New Theatre Quarterly* 21:2, 161–5.

Mitchell, K. (2009), *The Director's Craft: A Handbook for the Theatre* (London and

New York: Routledge).

Müller-Schöll, N. (2004), 'Theatre of potentiality: communicability and the political in contemporary performance practice', *Theatre Research International* 9:1, 42–56.

Nicholson, H. (2005), *Applied Drama: The Gift of Theatre* (Basingstoke: Palgrave Macmillan).

Nietzsche, F. (1913), *The Will to Power* (vol. 2), trans. A. M. Ludovici (London: T. N. Foulis).

Nietzsche, F. (1969, reprinted 1975), *Thus Spoke Zarathustra*, trans. R. J. Hollingdale (London: Penguin Books).

Nietzsche, F. (1974), *The Gay Science*, trans. Walter Kaufmann (New York: Vintage Books).

Nietzsche, F. (1990), *Beyond Good and Evil*, 2nd edn, trans. R. J. Hollingdale (London: Penguin Books).

Norris, C. (2000), *Deconstruction and the 'Unfinished Project of Modernity'* (London: Athlone Press).

Oddey, A., and C. White (2009), 'Introduction', in A. Oddey and C. White (eds), *Modes of Spectating* (Bristol and Chicago, Ill.: Intellect), 7–14.

Paget, D. (1987), 'Verbatim theatre: oral history and documentary techniques', *Theatre Quarterly* 3:12, 317–36.

Paget, D. (1990), *True Stories? Documentary Drama on Radio, Screen and Stage* (Manchester: Manchester University Press).

Paget, D. (2009), 'The broken tradition of documentary theatre and its continued powers of endurance', in A. Forsyth and C. Megson (eds), *Get Real: Documentary Theatre Past and Present* (Basingstoke: Palgrave Macmillan), 224–38.

Paget, D. (2010), 'Acts of commitment: activist arts, the rehearsed reading, and documentary theatre', *New Theatre Quarterly* 26:2, 173–93.

Paris, H. (2006), 'Too close for comfort: one-to-one performance', in L. Hill and H. Paris (eds), *Performance and Place* (Basingstoke: Palgrave Macmillan), 179–91.

Pearson M., and M. Shanks (2001), *Theatre / Archaeology* (London and New York: Routledge).

Phelan, P. (1993), *Unmarked: The Politics of Performance* (London and New York: Routledge).

Poggioli, R. (1968), *The Theory of the Avant-Garde*, trans. G. Fitzgerald (Cambridge, Mass.: Harvard University Press).

Power, C. (2008), *Presence in Play: A Critique of Theories of Presence in the Theatre* (Amsterdam and New York: Rodopi).

Price, A. (1993), 'Introduction to the second edition', in H. Barker, *Arguments for a Theatre*, 2nd edn (Manchester and New York: Manchester University Press), 3–13.

Puchner, M. (2006), *Poetry of the Revolution: Marx, Manifestos, and the Avant-Gardes* (Princeton, N.J., and Oxford: Princeton University Press).

Quick, A. (1996), 'Approaching the real: reality effects and the play of fiction', *Performance Research* 1:3, 12–22.

Quick, A. (2004), 'Bloody play: games of childhood and death', in J. Helmer and F. Malzacher (eds), *Not Even a Game Anymore: The Theatre of Forced Entertainment* (Berlin: Alexander Verlag), 139–65.

Quick, A. (2007), *The Wooster Group Work Book* (London and New York: Routledge).

Quick, A. (2009), 'The stay of illusion', *Performance Research* 14:1, 29–36.

Radhakrishnan, R. (1989), 'Poststructuralist politics: towards a theory of coalition', in D. Kellner (ed.), *Postmodernism Jameson Critique* (Washington, D.C.: Maisonneuve Press), 301–32.

Ranciere, J. (2007), 'The emancipated spectator', *Artforum International* 44:7, 271–80.

Rayner, A. (1993), 'The audience: subjectivity, community and the ethics of listening', *Journal of Dramatic Theory and Criticism* 7:2, 3–24.

Read, A. (1993), *Theatre and Everyday Life: An Ethics of Performance* (London and New York: Routledge).

Reckless Sleepers (2007), www.reckless-sleepers.co.uk *[accessed 10 October 2007]*.

Reinelt, J. (2009), 'The promise of documentary', in A. Forsyth and C. Megson (eds), *Get Real: Documentary Theatre Past and Present* (Basingstoke: Palgrave Macmillan), 6–23.

Rilke, R. M. (1997), 'Letter 10th March, 1899', in *Diaries of a Young Poet* trans. S. and M. Winkler (Norton).

Roms, H. (2010), 'The practice turn: performance and the British Academy', in J. McKenzie, H. Roms and C. J. W.-L. Wee (eds), *Contesting Performance: Global Sites of Research* (Basingstoke: Palgrave Macmillan), 51–70.

Rothberg, M. (2000), *Traumatic Realism: The Demands of Holocaust Representation* (Minneapolis, Minn.: University of Minnesota Press).

Santner, E. L. (1992), 'History beyond the pleasure principle: some thoughts on the representation of trauma', in S. Friedlander (ed.), *Probing the Limits of Representation: Nazism and the 'Final Solution'* (Cambridge, Mass., and London: Harvard University Press), 143–54.

Sarrazac, J. (1998), *L'Avenir du Drame,* 2nd edn (Belfort: Circe).

Savran, D. (2000), 'The haunted houses of modernity', *Modern Drama* 43:4, 583–94.

Savran, D. (2005), 'The death of the Avantgarde', *The Drama Review* 49:3, 10–42.

Schechner, R. (1981), 'The decline and fall of the (American) Avant-Garde', *Performing Arts Journal* 5:2, 48–63.

Schechner, R. (1992), 'TDR Comment: A new paradigm for theatre in the academy', *The Drama Review* 36:4, 7–10.

Schechner, R. (2006), *Performance Studies: An Introduction,* 2nd edn (New York: Routledge).

Schimmelpfennig, R. (2002), *Arabian Night,* trans. D. Tushingham (London: Oberon Books Ltd).

Sell, M. (2006), *Avant-Garde Performance and the Limits of Criticism: Approaching the Living Theatre, Happenings/Fluxus, and the Black Arts Movement* (Ann Arbor, Mich.: University of Michigan Press).

Shaw, H. (2011), 'Extra! Extra! The Wooster Group's version of Tennessee Williams' *Vieux Carré*', *Time Out New York* (8 March 2011).

Shuttleworth, I. (2008), 'Possessed by a past that shouts back', *Financial Times* (13 August 2008) http://goo.gl/BwrMx [accessed March–April 2010].

Smith, A. D. (1993), *Fires in the Mirror* (New York: Random House).

Solomon, R. C. (1988), *Continental Philosophy Since 1750: The Rise and Fall of the Self* (Oxford: Oxford University Press).

Sontag, S. (2003), *Regarding the Pain of Others* (New York: Farrar, Straus and Giroux).

Sugiera, M. (2004), 'Beyond drama: writing for postdramatic theatre', *Theatre Research International* 9:1, 16–28.

Szondi, P. (1987), *Theory of the Modern Drama*, trans. M. Hays (Cambridge: Polity Press).

Taylor, L. (2007), Unpublished transcript of Panel Discussion, in Manchester, UK (24 October 2007).

Thompson, J. (2007), Unpublished transcript of Panel Discussion, in Manchester, UK (24 October 2007).

Tigner, A. L. (2002), 'The Laramie Project: western pastoral', *Modern Drama* 45:1, 138–56.

Tomlin, L. (1999), 'Transgressing boundaries: postmodern performance and the tourist trap', *The Drama Review* 43:2, 136–49.

Tomlin, L. (2004), 'English theatre in the 1990s and beyond', in B. Kershaw (ed.), *The Cambridge History of British Theatre, Volume 3: Since 1895* (Cambridge: Cambridge University Press), 498–512.

Tomlin, L. (2006), 'A new tremendous aristocracy: tragedy and the meta-tragic in Barker's theatre of catastrophe', in K. Gritzner and D. I. Rabey (eds), *Theatre of Catastrophe: New Essays on Howard Barker* (London: Oberon books), 109–23.

Tomlin, L. (2008), 'Beyond cynicism: the sceptical imperative and (future) contemporary performance', *Contemporary Theatre Review* 18:3, 356–69.

Tomlin, L. (2009), '"And their stories fell apart even as I was telling them": poststructuralist performance and the no-longer-dramatic playtext', *Performance Research* 14:1, 57–64.

Tomlin, L. (2010), 'A "political suspension of the ethical": *To Be Straight With You* (2007) and *An Evening with Psychosis* (2009)', *Performing Ethos* 1:2, 167–80.

Turner, C. (2009), 'Getting the "Now" into the written text (and vice versa): developing dramaturgies of process', *Performance Research* 14:1, 106–14.

Uninvited Guests (2009), 'Love letters straight from your heart', www.uninvited-guests.net [accessed March–April 2010].

Van der Speeten, G. (2005), 'Theatre faces charges', *De Standaard* (2 February 2005) trans. N. den Hertog, cited on http://goo.gl/HDlU7 [accessed 26

March 2011].

Weiss, P. (1971), 'The material and the models: notes towards a definition of documentary theatre', *Theatre Quarterly* 1:1, 41–5.

White, G. (2009), 'Odd anonymized needs: Punchdrunk's masked spectator', in A. Oddey and C. White (eds), *Modes of Spectating* (Bristol and Chicago, Ill.: Intellect), 219–30.

White, H. (1999), *Figural Realism: Studies in the Mimesis Effect* (Baltimore, Md.: Johns Hopkins University Press).

Wickstrom, M. (2006), *Performing Consumers: Global Capital and its Theatrical Seductions* (New York and London: Routledge).

Williams, K. (2006), 'Anti-theatricality and the limits of naturalism', in A. Ackerman and M. Puchner (eds), *Against Theatre: Creative Destructions on the Modernist Stage* (Basingstoke: Palgrave Macmillan), 95–111.

Williams, T. (1977), *Vieux Carré* (New York: New Directions Books).

Wirth, A. (1980), 'Vom Dialog zum Diskurs: Versuch einer Synthese der nach-brechtschen Theaterkonzepte', *Theater Heute* 1, 16–19.

Wright, E. (1989), *Postmodern Brecht: A Re-presentation* (London: Routledge).

Young, S. (2009), 'Playing with documentary theatre: *Aalst* and *Taking Care of Baby*', *New Theatre Quarterly* 25:1, 72–87.

Žižek, S. (1994), 'The spectre of ideology', in S. Žižek (ed.), *Mapping Ideology* (London and New York: Verso).

Index

Lightning Source UK Ltd.
Milton Keynes UK
UKOW06f0238290916

284048UK00024BA/585/P